1902

GRAND OPENING

GLEN PARK

SUNDAY, APRIL 29TH.

season of 1900.

Direction of C. F. M

EXECUTIVE

Morosco's Burbank Theatre Program.

OLIVER MOROSCO · · · · · LESSEE & MANAGER

J. E. SPRIGHTLY, Printer and Publisher,

125 Temple St.   Telephone James 751

ALCAZAR THEATRE

FRED. BELASCO
MARK THALL

CINEOGRAPH PARLORS.

747 MARKET ST.

Admission 10c

LIFE SIZE Moving Pictures

luxuriously equipped "The Angelus,"
Special arrange-
large Cafe or
cially for
Will
den or
4th

CORDRAY'S THEATRE PROGRAM

JNO. F. CORDRAY
MANA

EXCEL

COULD NOT

B. E. WRIGHT

342½ WASHI

CENTRAL Theatre

Belasco & Mayer
Sole Proprietors
Chas. E. Cook
Business Manager

ORWINSKI BROS.

MY FIRST LOVE WEARS TWO MASKS

Dora Barrett

Rose Cordeiro Miller

Seaview Press

Library of Congress CATALOG CARD NO. 80-54266
Barrett, Dora, & Rose Cordeiro Miller
My First Love Wears Two Masks.

ISBN 0-9606048-0-4

Published by: Seaview Press
               P.O. Box 32
               El Cerrito, California 94530 

CONTENTS

Baby Dody
CHILD ACTRESS

Baby Dody

List of Photographs

Preliminary Pages

Chapter I

Chapter II

Chapter III

Chapter IV

Chapter V

Chapter VI

Chapter VII

Chapter VIII

Epilogue

FOREWORD

Through a sequence of events I have, at last, achieved the desire of a lifetime—to consign to print my unusual and still poignant memories of a childhood spent in the "fairyland" world of the theaters of, mainly, San Francisco. It has always distressed me deeply when I have mentioned the names of the fine artists—the lovely ladies and gentlemen of that day, with whom I played before the footlights as a child—only to discover that they are unknown. I have a great desire to preserve my colleagues from oblivion. It was through my association with, and the unbelievable diligence and tenacity of my collaborator, Rose Cordeiro Miller, who has become my beloved friend, that I have been able to produce this volume. Her dogged research has verified my memories.

"Let my hearth with splendor glow—
Until the last twig's burned
And let me read my book full through
Before the closing cover's turned.
Dora Barrett

El Cerrito, California
June 2, 1976

FOREWORD

From the start of our partnership—Dora Barrett's and mine—there was a tacit understanding that my husband and family would take precedence over all. Research and writing have sometimes suffered while I pursued these priorities. Both family and Dora Barrett, in turn, have endured my preoccupations, with forbearance and love.

And how did the partnership come about? Unexpectedly! While our lives had, until then, taken quite divergent paths, these were to converge six years ago under unpredictable circumstances. An anniversary, the sixty-fourth, of San Francisco's disastrous earthquake and fire of 1906 was approaching.

Russ Coughlan, "communicaster" of Radio Station KGO at that time (now General Manager of KGO-TV, San Francisco), announced several days ahead that on April 18, anniversary day, there would be an interview with a Mrs. Dora Barrett who had been an eyewitness to the event. My interest in historical events and a desire to tape the program for a dear friend in a convalescent hospital impelled me to make a mental note of the coming presentation. But in spite of my good intentions, I failed to catch the first half of the interview. The question-and-answer portion I heard and taped, I found compelling. When Mrs. Barrett volunteered the information she lived in the same little city, El Cerrito, California, in which I reside, I made another mental note: to telephone the very articulate and fascinating lady. Though in her late seventies then, she spoke with clarity and authority, and her diction did justice to her anecdotes and recollections.

Almost two months elapsed before I looked up Mrs. Barrett's name in the telephone directory. I discovered that she lived on our hillside, only two blocks above me. When I telephoned her, I congratulated her on her radio appearance and allowed that I had taped the second portion of her broadcast. She was elated to hear that, for her grandson had had time to tape only the first half, and she desperately wanted a complete taping. I offered to make copies of our tapes, thereby completing a mutually happy exchange.

From our first encounter, a warm bond developed between us. I learned she had been in the theater during most of her active years, but that her life as "Baby Dody," the child dramatic actress, was most dear to her, and she was anxious "to tell the story while it still can be told." I was startled to hear her express the conviction that I was just the person to do it.

Her unquestioning faith in me was flattering, to say the least. And so, after a long period of doubts and vacillation, and with my husband's blessing, I finally undertook the captivating, albeit time consuming, assignment of chronicling Dora Barrett's memoirs as "Baby Dody."

It is a story that needs to be told, for there are few left who can articulate their memories of San Francisco theater history as Dora Barrett has done. Who remembers such names as Cineograph Parlors, Olympia, Columbia, Central, Chutes, and the first Alcazar? And who, besides Baby Dody, played in these San Francisco theaters of old? The numbers, to borrow a line, "have dwindled down to a precious few." In these times of nostalgia, I found irresistible the appeal of her recollections of San Francisco for the decade before and after the turn of the century, 1896–1906.

Like her make-believe world, Dora Barrett's real life as Baby Dody was filled with joy and sorrow, exhilaration and frustration, and comedy and pathos. As Dora Barrett the octogenarian, she still has all the wondrous and searching qualities of Baby Dody. Her quest for knowledge remains unsated, for the "Prison Walls" will never alter her spirit. That is as it should be.

Rose C. Miller

El Cerrito, California
June 2, 1976

ACKNOWLEDGMENTS

In order to join the links of Baby Dody's story, there was need of assistance and cooperation from various sources. Posthumously, to George W. Poultney, Northern California Representative of Actors' Equity Association, goes our gratitude for his encouragement and contributions. While still a very active nonagenarian, he not only exchanged personal recollections that corroborated Baby Dody's own, but made available some of his own material: *Long Run Plays in San Francisco, A History Of The Alcazar Theatre 1885–1956.*

To the following East Bay libraries, we wish to extend our deepest appreciation: the Bancroft Library of the University of California, whose material, supplied by a cordial and courteous staff, constituted the major source of our research; our home-town El Cerrito Library, whose librarians graciously sought "outside" help to obtain for us books not available at their branch; the Berkeley Library, where their research staff so cordially augmented our personal research material; the Oakland Main Library, whose Senior Librarian, Mrs. Frances H. Buxton and her successor, Mr. William W. Sturm, supplied us with much needed information by mail and telephone; and the Oakland Museum Library for its willingness to accommodate us during our research.

San Francisco libraries offering material, assistance, and counsel, included the following repositories of prodigious amounts and varieties of San Francisco lore: the California Historical Society Library (Mr. Jay Williar) and the Society of California Pioneers Library; and the San Francisco Library, whose Librarian, Mrs. Gladys Hansen, readily supplied us with answers to the many questions we posed.

When the need to rejoin the final links of our story necessitated travel to "out-of-town" libraries, the following were of incalculable assistance: the Los Angeles Library, the Santa Barbara Library, the Santa Barbara Historical Society Museum Library, and the Fresno County Free Library.

Finally, "out-of-state" sources that closed our chain of links included: the magnificent Seattle Library with its handsomely and efficiently equipped history and art departments and its very helpful staff; the Pinal County Historical Society Museum,

Florence, Arizona, whose curators supplied us with the background material used in the story of the Uncles, Fuller; and the Oregon Historical Society.

We are especially indebted to Marston Thall for so generously making available his two collections, inherited from his father, Charles M. Thall; and from which collections come much of the background for the story of his grandfather, Mark Thall, who played such a prominent part in the history of the first Alcazar Theatre of San Francisco. The Thall Collections have also provided a well of information on San Francisco theaters, extracted from the score of theater programs within its pages, and detailed accounts of the San Francisco Earthquake and Fire of 1906.

Our gratitude also extends to the following:

Hercules Incorporated, Hercules, California, for their leads to material on the Melrose Explosion of 1898.

Commandant, Twelfth Naval District, and Commander, Naval Base, San Francisco, for their communication on the National monuments to the U.S.S. Battleship MAINE.

Actors' Equity Association, Mr. Dan Hogan, Administrative Aide to the Executive Secretary, New York, for the copy of "About Equity" and the leads on the "White Rats Actors' Union of America."

Douglas Harding, Executor of the Alfred Harding Estate, for so graciously offering his permission to reprint any part of his father's THE REVOLT OF THE ACTORS.

Professor Emeritus J. William Ladd, Speech Communications, Humboldt State University, for generously granting his "full permission to use any of the material in A SURVEY OF THE LEGITIMATE THEATRE IN SEATTLE SINCE 1856, M.S. Thesis in Speech, The State College of Washington, 1935."

Walker A. Tompkins (SANTA BARBARA YESTERDAYS), for advising the authors on several fine points bearing on the history of the Potter Hotel of Santa Barbara and its famous and colorful founder, Milo M. Potter; and for sharing pictures of the Potter Hotel, from his personal collection.

Russell Hartley, Director: San Francisco Archives For the Performing Arts, for his generosity in supplying minute details to very vital information on the San Francisco theaters in which Baby Dody played. Mr. Hartley's Archives are a veritable treasure trove of San Francisco theater history.

DEDICATION

This book is lovingly dedicated to the memory of the many fine and cultured artists of the "Baby Dody Era." They shall always be remembered for their many kindnesses and courtesies, creating a backstage spirit beyond comparison.

INTRODUCTION

Dora Barrett and Rose C. Miller give us close views of performance conditions in variety shows at the Cineograph Parlors (as of 1897, San Francisco's first movie house), at the Chutes, and at the Olympia Music Hall. Every melodrama, it seems, had a child's role. Baby Dody played them—at the first Alcazar ("the Moorish Gem"), the Columbia, the Orpheum, and at the Central with its huge water tank. *East Lynne. The Adventures of Nell Gwynne. The First Born* (about San Francisco's Chinatown). *Buried At Sea.* Not only was she Little Eva indoors but also on the road, in Connors' Mammoth Pavilion Tent Show. Gifted with a prodigious memory—as well as a beautiful face—she even became for a time Little Lord Fauntleroy. Wide-eyed she watched her surroundings. And she remembered not only larger silhouettes but also many of those particulars that tend with time to fade: people, processes, objects.

Accompanying original photographs greatly enhance the story of Baby Dody.

Dunbar H. Ogden
Associate Professor
Department of Dramatic Art
University of California, Berkeley

Chapter One
Out of the Mists

Ode on Immortality
Our birth is but a sleep and a forgetting;
The soul that rises with us, our life's star
Hath had elsewhere its setting,
And cometh from afar;
Not in entire forgetfulness,
And not in utter nakedness,
But trailing clouds of glory, do we come
From God, who is our home;
Heaven lies about us in our infancy;
Shades of the prison-house begin to close
Upon the growing boy,
But he beholds the light,and whence it flows
He sees it in his joy;
The youth, who daily farther from east
Must travel, still is Nature's priest,
And by the vision splendid
Is on his way attended;
At length the man perceives it die away
And fade into the light of common day.
William Wordsworth

Looking back from a mountain of years, across the changing seas of life, I behold the sad-faced little child who gazes at me from the many photographs—photographs that have traveled far, at the bottom of a trunk, and that have survived flood, fire, earthquakes, and time, as though reluctant of destruction. They call to me, and they bid me to tell her story while it may yet be told.

She was beautiful, with large blue, questioning eyes and long flaxen curls, a tiny rounded body and delicate hands with wrists that arched. Her fairy-like appearance was enhanced by the wreaths of roses and the tinsel on her tarlton skirts. But she could also play a peasant child, or a page in the court of Richard III. Still, always the same sad mystery looks back at me from her eyes, a soul pleading with me for release. She is gone and I hold the only key to her memory, that Never-Never-Land where only children dwell, and strange to say, this key is a pet name, a sort of magic word—"Dody." With this sesame we shall pass through the looking glass into her world of sometimes reality, sometimes make-believe:

She had no grandma who kept a full cookie jar, no uncle's ranch to roam about on the hot vacation days. There *were* no vacations. There was no attic to explore when it rained. Often she would press her pale little nose against the window pane and watch other children play in the delightfully muddy gutter that sent little leaf-ships on the swift tide—perhaps to some fairyland where boisterous laughter is not forbidden, and one did not have always to keep one's white dress clean and be "lady-like." And when the clamorous children had romped away after their leafy argosies, when the restraining pane forbade even visual pursuit, she was alone again, for she was not allowed to play with other children. The good sun would turn her alabaster skin to bronze, and her careful manners might become rugged like the manners of the other healthy children.

How I should love to reach back through the years and take her hand, and lead her for a romp in my hillside garden, where the sun glows warm and the fresh breeze blows in from the sea; where she might make shapely mud pies on the bank of my brook under the willow; or, perhaps, caress my two loyal canine friends and listen to my pet canaries sing. How she would have loved to feed my tame pigeons and wild birds who flutter down among the hollyhocks at feeding time. I feel that she would have known all these friends even better than I, for her "clouds of glory" were still about her, and she "beheld the light and whence it flows," while for me, "the shades of the prison-house" have long since begun to close. Oh, that I may yet ward off "the

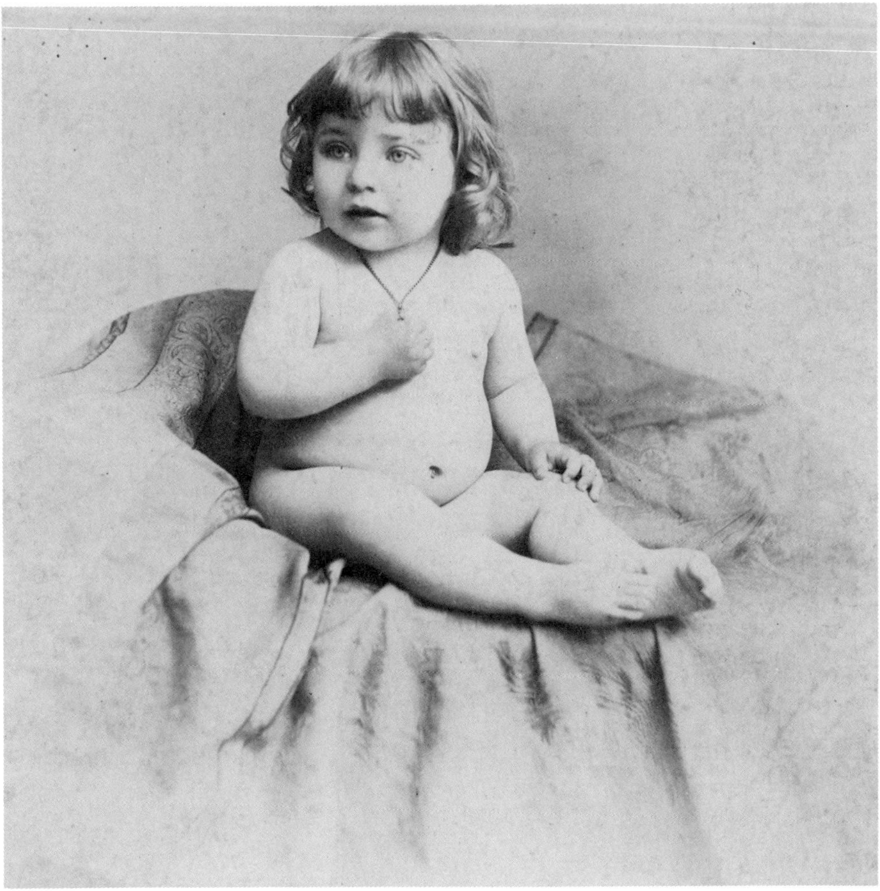

Baby Dody c. 1894

light of common day." But, I shall pronounce the magic word —"Dody"—and she shall speak for herself.

Yes, I am Dody, and I shall reach into the past for memories. When from out of the mists, memory came into focus, I was but a babe. For me, awareness had come uncommonly early, and this was to have a profound bearing on my childhood and on my career. Since this is to be a book of memories, enhanced by research, I will call up some of the earliest. Some are quaint—objects, places, people, and the customs that went with them. In my first recollection, I was held up in someone's arms to look over a vine-covered fence at a pretty lady in a lacy gown as she descended some steps. Beside her was a beautiful Collie dog. In her house on East 21st Street, Oakland, California, I saw pictures she had painted. Many years later, the name Treglone came to me, and I found her. I was able to recognize the pictures I had seen as a baby and distinguish them from those she had painted since. This unusual gift of memory has played a major part in my life.

When I was two years old, we moved from our East 21st Street address to San Francisco where we lived in a lovely house with frescoed ceilings, located at 138 Tremont Avenue, now known as Downey Street. I was so intrigued by the frescoed ceilings that I would lie on the floor to look up at the faint lattice with pastel-colored grapes and leaves, pictured on the ceiling of the dining room. When I was able to pry open the sliding doors into the parlor, I was enraptured with frescoed clouds and cherub faces looking down at me—such warm and twinkling eyes on those dear faces!

There was one object in this room, however, which I avoided. It was a cuspidor. I have learned since, that these receptacles had many personalities. There were plain ones and colored ones, and they were found in every household. There were big brass ones in public places. I never knew just why. We seem to get along so well without cuspidors now. But, this one that sat on the tile hearth in our parlor was different. It was of the most delicate china. Square, with rounded sides that came up to support the gracefully flared top, the cuspidor was hand painted in the most delicate pinks, lavenders, and blues, much like the clouds that supported the cherubs on the ceiling. But what sinister mind could have decorated such a lovely thing with a black web and spider?

It was in this very parlor that big sister practiced piano— grudgingly, it seemed to me. She was always very cross then, and she chased me beyond the sliding doors where I remained to listen. Bertha would come home from school with songs and poems to learn, and as she repeated them, I sat in my highchair; and, like a parrot, have them memorized before she did. This seemed to startle everyone, so I did my best because it was such fun to startle people.

From Bertha I learned a song that was very popular then, and whose words I still remember. Written by Charles K. Harris in 1897, it was called, *Break the News to Mother*. A real "tear-jerker," it went like this:

While the shot and shell were screaming upon
  the battle-field;
The boys in blue were fighting their noble
  flag to shield;
Came a cry from their brave captain, "Look,
  boys! Our flag is down;
Who'll volunteer to save it from disgrace?"
"I will," a young voice shouted, "I'll bring
  it back or die";
Then sprang into the thickest of the fray;
Saved the flag but gave his young life; all
  for his country's sake.
They brought him back and softly heard him say:

"Just break the news to Mother;
She knows how dear I love her
And tell her not to wait for me,
For I'm not coming home.
Just say there is no other
Can take the place of Mother;
Then kiss her dear sweet lips for me,
And break the news to her."

From afar a noted general had witnessed his
  brave deed,
"Who saved our flag? Speak up, lads; 'twas
  noble, brave indeed!"
"There he lies, sir," said the captain, "he's
  sinking very fast";
Then slowly turned away to hide a tear.
The gen'ral, in a moment, knelt down beside
  the boy,

> *Then gave a cry that touched all hearts that day,*
> *"It's my son, my brave young hero; I thought*
>   *you safe at home."*
> *"Forgive me Father, for I ran away."*
>   *"Just break the news to Mother"—etc.*

After the evening meal, when a colorful, fringed tapestry cover was spread over the dining room table, the little mama would sit with her sewing basket, while foster-sister Bertha got out her very elaborate paper dolls and set them all up in appropriate order. The papa sat with me on his lap and we watched. When all the pageant of paper dolls was arranged, he would prompt me to pull on the fringe of the cover and knock them all down. I did not want to do this, but he insisted. I knew how Bertha felt about her dolls, for I, too, had a paper doll—a Melen's Food baby sitting in a highchair, holding a paper doll of a Melen's Food baby sitting in a highchair, holding a paper doll of a Melen's Food baby—oh no!

When I had finally succumbed to the papa's proddings, with a tug of the fringe, the dolls would tumble in disarray. I don't think the big sister liked me then; but I liked her, and I thought she was the grandest thing in the world. This was especially so when she took me to the front window and called the mama to, "Come see the horseless carriage," as it chugged laboriously up the block.

The potpourri of early impressions encompasses disparate ones. There were the big sister's funny pictures of the "Yellow Kid" (like the popular Happy Face of our times). The Yellow Kid had a round face, a tin can for a hat which perched on a bald pate, save for one shaft of hair. He was clothed in a long, yellow robe with long, loose sleeves. His feet were bare. His origin remains a mystery to me. And there were: the "Gold Dust Twins" on the box of granulated soap powder; "Sapolio," the grayish-white scouring soap, before the advent of "Dutch Cleanser"; heavy sadirons and curling irons that had to be heated on the stove; and the "Wells-Bach Mantle," a little white bag the papa put over the gas jet nipple and set afire. How the little mantle glowed and shone with a very bright white light. It retained its shape as an ash, but fell apart with the slightest jar. Other impressions, too numerous to list, shall linger as reminders of my childhood.

An important memory in the passing parade of late Nineteenth Century San Francisco was the "Affiliated Colleges." From our windows in the lovely house on Tremont Avenue, I watched in fascination as, day by day, the genesis of the modern-day "Medical Center of the University of California" slowly arose, on Parnassus Avenue and Third Avenue.

Since Tremont Avenue was within walking distance of Golden Gate Park, the mama occasionally took me there to the Children's Playground to ride the merry-go-round, the two-wheeled goat cart, and the ponies. After a round on these, I played on the swings and the "jumping board."

The latter was an all-time favorite of the children's. The board proper was about ten feet long, a foot wide, and three inches thick. It rested at each end on four-inch-thick uprights,

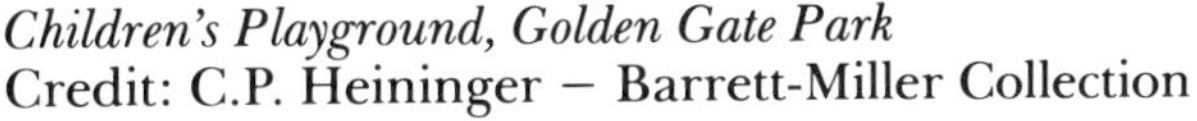

Children's Playground, Golden Gate Park
Credit: C.P. Heininger — Barrett-Miller Collection

also a foot wide, and to which it was secured by heavy iron bands. The midpoint of the board was the most sought after spot and, altogether, as many as eight children could bounce at a time. The aim was to create a rhythm by jumping; in turn, the momentum sent the children higher and higher. The exhilaration prompted squeals and shouts of joy, especially from the older, heavier, children. A small slight child, such as I was then, could scarcely cause a ripple. The older children, however, were considerate of the younger ones; they would take me by the hand onto the board and we jumped together. When the board reached the maximum of its springiness, or someone jumped out of rhythm, the jumping board began to "buck" and send shocking vibrations through feet and legs, and soon forced the children off. That seemed to be the ultimate thrill toward which we all worked anxiously. At that moment, the rollicking laughter of the jumpers rang out, as only children's laughter can.

Another favorite attraction of Golden Gate Park was its steam train, the Park, Beach and Cliff House Railway. From

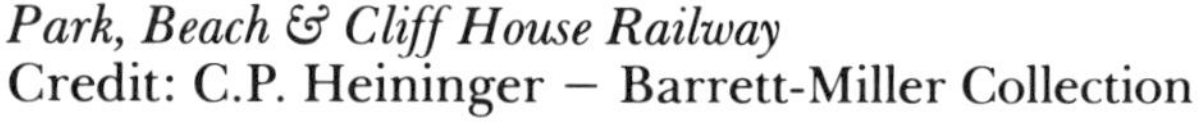

Park, Beach & Cliff House Railway
Credit: C.P. Heininger — Barrett-Miller Collection

Stanyon Street, opposite the terminus of the Haight Street Cable Car Line, it ran along the entire length of Golden Gate Park to the Ocean. I recall that the train's first section, with steam swirls billowing from the stack of its snub-nosed engine, was joined by an enclosed passenger cab. But most exciting of all was the third section—an open car with back-to-back benches, lengthwise its center. Riding this colorful, little, puffing steam train along Lincoln Way to the Great Highway, had a special reward as we approached the "Chain of Lakes," near the western terminus. As the mama announced we were nearing the "Chain of Lakes," it seemed, from the lilt of those words, that here, indeed, was the very special highlight of the entire trip. The "Chain of Lakes" was like an oasis among the sand dunes all about us. Gradually the city was to creep westward with its rows of joined houses that have all but obliterated the blinding white sand dunes, checkered with beach grass.

Later, we would ride a second steam train, the Sutro Heights-Cliff House Railroad, skirting the edge of the cliffs

Railroad To Sutro Heights, Showing Golden Gate
Credit: C.P. Heininger — Barrett-Miller Collection

The Cliff House From The Parapet
Credit: Courtesy Anita M. Bradley Collection

The Parapet—Sutro Heights
Credit: Courtesy Anita M. Bradley Collection

along Land's End, on a winding roadbed with two tracks. The outbound track ran close to the edge of the cliffs, while the return track hugged the relative safety of the high banks on its right. The mama usually begged off when the papa and I planned to ride this exciting train. She was always fearful it would fall over the steep cliffs into the great below. But the papa and I had no such qualms, and so each precipitous turn was a thrill to be savored until we reached the end of the line, near Sutro Heights.

Mr. Sutro had a magnificent estate perched high on the headland that overlooked: Sutro's Pleasure Grounds, Sutro Baths, his Cliff House, Seal Rocks, and the sandy beach of the Pacific Ocean. The high crenellated wall edging the cliff and enclosing the Sutro estate at that point, was especially impressive, with white marble statues and urns alternating on its merlons. The main house was nestled among the trees, and the entrance to the estate was marked by huge iron gates, flanked by recumbent stone lions on marble pedestals. The grounds proper, studded with statuary, were open to the general public during the daytime. How pleasurable it was, to walk about the resplendent gardens, with their panoramic view of the endless, blue Pacific.

Equally inviting, was the road below that wound down around the Heights. There was Sutro's Pleasure Grounds, on the left, with its ferris wheel riding high and commanding a breathtaking view for miles around.

Further along the bend, we came to the Sutro Baths, on the ocean side. This immense and well-known bathhouse had an imposing vestibule, facing southeast. Its seemingly endless, wide and steep stairway descending to the pool, counted some forty steps, interrupted by four landings. The entire stairway was bordered with palms and various tropical plants. For a small child like me, with short legs, it was formidable, indeed, managing such a steep stairway. This became a challenge I did not relish, and so I was always apprehensive about it.

On the rare occasions when the mama accompanied us, she enjoyed bathing at Sutro's. From the water level, rose several tiers where the spectators sat. I always waited anxiously for the

Sutro Baths, Looking West
Credit: C.P. Heininger — Barrett-Miller Collection

Interior, Sutro Baths
Credit: C.P. Heininger — Barrett-Miller Collection

moment the mama would swim over to the first tier, to the papa and me. There was something ominous about the echoes of splashing water and shouting voices bouncing off the glass dome above. And the eeriness cast by the colored-glass windows all about me, did nothing to allay my anxiety.

Leaving the baths, we continued our walk toward the Cliff House. I recall passing the man with the performing white cockatoos, and how his enchanting birds held an ever-growing, enchanted and captivated audience.

But no trip to the Beach was complete without the stop at the charming two-wheeled popcorn and peanut wagon. Half of this colorful wagon, with its glass enclosure, shielded mounds of warm popcorn, while the other, contained a whistling stove that kept warm little red-and-green striped bags of peanuts. I would watch attentively as the vendor pinched the top ends of the peanut bag, with thumb and forefinger of each hand, gave the bag a quick flip that sealed it securely, and then handed me the

The First Cliff House 1863-1896
Credit: C.P. Heininger — Barrett-Miller Collection

precious little package with its two little ears sticking up. I relished the peanuts, even though I was never allowed to eat the brown skin that encased the nutmeat itself. And now, fortified with my bag of peanuts, I would proceed in the direction of the Cliff House.

This Cliff House I remember so well was the second one, and had been built for Mayor Adolph Sutro in 1896. The first Cliff House, built in 1863 by Junius G. Foster, had been sold to Mr. Sutro in 1883. Mr. Sutro's second Cliff House, referred to as "Sutro's Gingerbread Palace" by some, I prefer to think of as a representation of French Chateau architecture. I have always considered it the most beautiful of the several Cliff Houses built on the same spot. This lovely six-storied chateau, overlooking Seal Rocks and the Pacific Ocean, had rounded turrets on each corner, starting on its fourth floor and ending at the sixth level with a peaked roof. Centrally located from the sixth floor, rose a prominent square tower with arched windows on its four sides and topped by a four-sided peaked roof. Smaller peaked turrets

The Second Cliff House 1896-1907
Credit: C.P. Heininger − Barrett-Miller Collection

adorned each corner of this central structure, while furbelows enhanced the entire building.

Dining at the lovely Cliff House was an experience I always looked forward to, for I never tired looking out on my friends, the seals, at play on the rocks below. Mr. Sutro's ornate palace survived the earthquake and fire of 1906, only to burn to the ground the following year.

Our day's excursion ended at the beach, where the daring braved the usually cold, windy day for a "dip" in the defying Pacific. I was not among them—but, no matter. It was rewarding enough just to stroll and observe the beach, with its backdrop of sparkling white sand dunes covered with the striking, vivid purple-blue lupin and bright golden California poppy.

A final recollection of life on Tremont Avenue, was being taken to my first play, probably at the Tivoli Opera House on Eddy Street, judging from the nature of the program. The name of the play was SORROWS OF SATAN. The protagonist wore a top hat, evening clothes, and a long cloak. Even to my young mind, the personality he presented was enigmatic. At the proper moment, he opened his cloak with a flourish, revealing the brilliant scarlet lining. Of course, the gesture was calculated to make an impact upon the audience, but it was wasted on me. The mama felt compelled to explain that he was the devil. As far as I was concerned, he was just another character, like Cinderella or Rumpelstiltskin.

From Tremont Avenue, we returned to Oakland for a brief but memorable stay in the Melrose District. Our family moved into a new house on Washington Street (now E. 12th Street), near Bassett (now 33rd Avenue). I am of the impression that the surrounding area was, at one time, part of the Bassett family holdings and had gradually been sold away. Very important in the business community, four of the Bassetts comprised the Bassett Brothers, Contractors and Builders. The back of our property, with its high board fence, adjoined that of one of the Bassetts'. Their lovely, large, gray two-storied house was nestled within a circle of tall, graceful trees. Included, too, were stables, a coach house, and a well, pumped by a squeaky windmill that was a continuing irritant to the mama. But I prefer to remember that their lovely pigeons flew over our house, and gracefully circled about, before returning to their dovecote.

Our home, still not completely finished when we moved in, was wooden throughout. It had a front porch supported by two round columns. A large bay window extended from the porch to the right corner. The house's high peaked roof marked off an attic that was to have been converted into bedrooms. When we first moved in, however, hanging curtains were used as makeshift partitions. The curtains afforded a quaint setting for the "Clara and John" drama in which sister Bertha and I participated after retiring. From her"bedroom," Bertha would introduce me to her two imaginary friends with, "Clara, meet Dody." From the other side of the curtains, I would acknowledge the introduction, leading to fanciful conversations between Bertha and Clara, Clara and me, and among the three of us. In due time, "John" was introduced into the script, and the four characters carried on a dialogue that terminated when I finally dozed off.

Bertha had named our imaginary playmate, "John," after a visit from the mama's Uncle John Fuller—a decision of questionable merit. Uncle John and his younger brother, Will, both bachelors, were pioneers in Arizona when it was still designated a "Territory." He was a tall, gaunt man with a mustache and short, trimmed beard. As a farmer, he found it hard to adjust to our "city-living." True to his ranch routine, he would arise early, fill the stove chuckfull of coal, a fuel to which he was not accustomed, and light the fire. Little did he know the heat potential of coal, but the papa did. Invariably, the stove would get red hot, and we had to throw windows and doors wide open. All the while Uncle John visited, the papa lived in mortal fear our house would burn to a crisp.

Another source of consternation to my father, was Uncle John's predilection for cream. Our milkman, who always came before dawn, filled the gray granite pot we put out on the front porch nightly. The pot, under which we left the money in lieu of "charga-plate," had a bail and, in the interest of sanitation, a very tight lid. Those were the days before milk bottles, when the milkman carried his supply of milk in large containers from which he dispensed his customers' needs. Since the milk was not homogenized, the cream soon rose to the top of the granite pot. Dear Uncle John, the first one up by hours, would skim the cream off the top of the milk for his coffee, leaving skimmed milk for the rest of us. This caper irritated the usually affable papa, beyond endurance.

But then, in all fairness, Uncle John found living with us a bit of a challenge, too. He thought we were "dirty" because we had inside plumbing.

He did not stay very long. The clincher that hastened his departure, came when, peering out of the living room window one day, he inadvertently rested both hands on the sheet of sticky flypaper on the ledge. A volley of oaths and epithets fractured the calm of that beautiful early morning. Like a running, panicky bear with entrapped paws, Uncle John vainly tried to lift first one hand and then the other, bellowing "damns" and the most graphic of four-letter words in his, hitherto, well-constrained vocabulary. From every direction of the house, the family converged on the enraged captive. The papa restrained John's flailing arms, as the mama calmly reassured her beleaguered uncle. Grabbing the smooth margins, she peeled the mucilaginous pungent flypaper off each of his hands, setting the livid Uncle John free. A solvent was used to dissolve the gummy substance from his hands and, in due time, Uncle John regained his composure. I thought I detected a twinkle in the papa's eye.

Not long after dear Uncle John's departure, we were startled out of our sleep, early one morning, by the tremendous, so-called "Melrose Explosion" eight blocks away. The papa snatched me out of my bed and carried me to the front window where we saw an enormous funnel of black smoke billowing from the Western Fuse and Explosives Company. There was a wide, vacant area between our house and the explosion, giving us an unobstructed view of what had taken place. Our house sustained no damage, but the papa's inspection, outdoors, soon revealed that all manner of debris, human and otherwise, had come to rest against one of the pillars of our front porch. Shouting admonitions, he forbade us to set foot outside until he had first cleared away the gruesome evidence, by burying it.

The sensitive little mama was so unnerved by this experience, that she determined, then and there, we would not remain at that house any longer than it took to find another residence.

Among the myriad accounts of the tragedy, the event is recorded in *History of the Explosives Industry in America* by Van Gelder and Schlatter. Two important corrections, however, are included parenthetically:

> *The WESTERN FUSE AND EXPLOSIVES COMPANY was started in 1888 by Edward G. Lukens, president of the Vigorite Powder Company. The factory was on Clark (Clarke) Street, near Hyde (High), in Oakland, California. In the next ten years, dwellings were erected in close proximity to the works, and it would probably have been necessary to move it before long, even if it had not been wrecked by an explosion on July 19, 1898. The explosion came about in a peculiar way. As in other California powder plants, Chinese help was employed almost exclusively. One of these Chinamen, Goon Ng Chung, who had been in the employ of the company for years, got into a quarrel with a countryman about a lottery ticket which he thought had won a prize of $100. In the course of the fight, Goon wounded the other man so severely that he died soon after midnight. When the deputy sheriff arrived he found that Goon had fled to the powder magazine and barricaded himself behind a wall of black powder kegs. When called on to come out and surrender, he threatened to blow up the magazine if the police came any closer. Neither Lukens, the president of the company, nor Quong Yong, a Chinese boss from San Francisco, had any better luck. The end of the siege came at dawn the next day. While the deputies crept closer to the door—some said that the criminal had offered to surrender—the Chinaman fired his revolver and immediately the powder in the magazine exploded, killing three of the deputies, two other men, and a woman who had re-*

mained in her house which was hardly more than the width of the street from the magazine. The factory and a number of houses in the neighborhood were wrecked.

The horrendous explosion, involving some five thousand pounds of dynamite, demolished a row of houses, and damaged two railroad cars and the barracks of Camp Barrett, where men were thrown clear of their cots to the floor. The military camp consisting of three battalions, four companies each, was located on the Bruguiere property, beyond Fruitvale Avenue.

Reports of the disquieting and demoralizing effect of the explosion on the residents of that area continued to distress the mama. She had only to look at the front porch pillar to be reminded, over and over again, of the ghastly event. The papa immediately set out on a search for another house. Very soon thereafter, we left the lovely new house on Washington Street, the home that held so much promise when we first moved in. From there, we moved to Brandon Street, near Lloyd. But, after a short stay there, we were irresistibly drawn to our beloved San Francisco.

Chapter Two
Thespian Perforce

Gradually, events began to change the course of my life. Because of my ability to memorize and to speak very plainly and fluently for a child my age, I attracted attention. I was between two and three years old when a Mrs. Lund who had a daughter, Pearly, "La Petite Lund," on the stage, came to the mama and said, "If that were my child, I would put her on the stage." She offered to take me along with Pearly to entertainments and theaters. The mama made me some pretty accordion-pleated dresses with lace, and rushed me off to Professor William W. Chapman's School of Dancing, at College Hall, 12th and Harrison Streets, Oakland.

This venture into the unknown, however, was to leave a dubious impression. The classroom was full of beautiful little girls with short dresses, and stars on their heads. They reminded me of the cherubs on the ceiling, and I loved them. While the mama talked with Professor Chapman, I tried to sit on one of the chairs along the wall. Alas, it was a folding chair; and when it collapsed on top of me, I found myself crouched on the floor, as though peering out of a chicken coop. All the pretty little girls laughed at me in my crushing humiliation. To add to the mortification, the Professor refused to teach me, saying to my mother, "Why Madam, the child is much too young." For the first time, I knew the sting of cruelty. The mama, in great indignation, dragged me from under the chair and out the door. I was very glad to get away from there.

I was then taken to an elocution teacher, Mrs. Carro True Boardman, at 478 12th Street, Oakland. She taught me to curtsy and recite, "See my pretty dress, see my dainty locket. 'Spects I most a lady 'cause I have a pocket." To my toy rubber cat, Mrs. Boardman had me recite, "Come here, you naughty kitten; what have you been about? There is cream upon your lips; now you know you need not pout." Mrs. Boardman was the mother of True Boardman, a noted actor with whom I later played on the stage. From her, I would learn the fundamentals of elocution and projection.

There were always others who felt a mission to teach me poems and songs, whether I liked them or not. A particular song, *Will I Find My Mama There*, was quite unsuitable for one as young as I, but apparently our next door neighbor, Mrs. Mc-Lean, did not think so. From her I learned the following sobering, sad words:

> *"Will I find my mama there, with her sweet*
> *face and golden hair?*
> *Will she kiss me once again; soothe all my*
> *sorrows and pain?*
> *Someday, papa, you'll come too; for I love*
> *you, indeed I do.*
> *Tell me, tell me ere I go, will I find my*
> *mama there?"*

Before long, I was taken to some entertainments, seen by some managers, and I was launched. It all happened very quickly. I was before hundreds of people, behind footlights, with orchestras playing at my feet, and billed as the youngest child on any stage.

The prelude to this more glamorous and exciting era, however, was my appearances at various benefits. In 1897, there were recitations before the Young Ladies Sodality of Mission Dolores Parish, at Mission Turner Hall, San Francisco, and at the Carmen Picnic in San Lorenzo.

The latter received a minimum of coverage: "Employees of the Oakland, San Leandro and Haywards Electric road, and their friends to the number of 500 attended their annual picnic. The road furnished free transportation and the Second Regiment Band." Although the event did not receive much attention from the press, for me it marked an unexpected, never to be forgotten incident. Before my presentation, I joined the children on the swings. Of the three swings available, I chose one of the end swings; but, because I was very tiny, my efforts to get up on it proved unsuccessful. I decided to try the other vacant end swing. Unfortunately, as I moved toward it, the middle swing, occupied by two standing girls pumping high and fast, struck me on the head. When I awoke, I found myself stretched out on a picnic bench. Someone was dousing my face with cold water that dripped over my beautiful lace dress. This ruination of my dress distressed me more than the ignominy of the accident. But I must have been a little trouper, even then, because, in spite of black eye and wet dress, I was determined "the show must go on," and it did.

That same year, I appeared at a fund-raising entertainment before the Catholic organization, The League of the Cross Cadets. It was Company D First Regiment that presented the affair at the Odd Fellows Hall in San Francisco, for the benefit of the uniform and armory fund. The League seemed to be a paramilitary-religious society that held encampments and wore uniforms. The "much-applauded address" delivered by Colonel William P. Sullivan Jr., described the cadets as, "soldiers ever ready to serve any just cause, and while it is to be hoped that the necessity of calling on them for military duty is far removed, yet they are always prepared and willing. The need of their services in behalf of an honest administration is, however, of such pressing necessity that their conduct of life should be directed to the accomplishment of such an honorable manhood that they will become all-important factors in the ruling of our great city." There was nothing sinister about the organization. They were religious, patriotic devotees of San Francisco, and they espoused high moral principles.

My contribution to the League of the Cross Cadets' show was a song and dance routine that, seemingly, was well received; for soon after, they sent me a solid gold bangle on a chain, with the inscription, "Baby Dody, from the League of the Cross Cadets."

A more impressive event that received much coverage, was "Columbia the Historical Pageant," January 3, 4, and 5, 1898. It was a benefit for the Hospital for Children and Training School for Nurses, held at the California Theatre, 444 Bush Street, San

California Theatre, 1869-1906
Credit: California Historical Society, San Francisco

Francisco. Although the program has the banner lead, "The Greatest Tragic Events Portrayed in the History of Our Nation," it really was not the dismal affair one would be led to believe. There were music, art, drama, singing, speaking, and dancing, with two hundred and fifty local artists participating. It was a "Grand, Beautiful and Patriotic" pageant in three parts:

  Act I Colonial Days
    Our Forefathers—Landing of the Pilgrims
    May Day on Boston Commons
    A Typical Courtship
    A Colonial Home
  Act II Revolutionary Period
    The Birth of the Nation
    The Peace Ball—Minuet
  Act III Civil War Times
    The Departure of the Volunteers
    The Hospital
    Emancipation

Music was provided by the California Theatre Orchestra, under the direction of Eugene E. Schmitz who, later, became San Francisco's twenty-fifth Mayor (1902–July 7, 1907).

When barely into his third two-year term, Schmitz (after a trial that had started November 15, 1906 when the Grand Jury voted five indictments on extortion against both him and San Francisco's notorious political boss, Abraham Reuf) was sentenced by Judge Frank H. Dunne on July 8, 1907 to five years in prison. "Handsome Gene," as he was known, served nine months of his term at the Ingleside County Jail, then gained his freedom after $400,000 bail was posted by two wealthy San Franciscans, William J. Dingee and Thomas H. Williams. A more capable violinist and showman than a politician, Schmitz had been elected Mayor through the aegis and machinations of the brilliant and slick manipulator, Abraham Reuf.

Reuf's own trial was marked by numerous delays and the sensational incident in which the chief prosecuting attorney, Assistant District Attorney Francis J. Heney, was shot in court by a disgruntled prospective juror, Morris Haas, who had been dismissed by Heney. Although seriously shot in the jaw, Heney survived the assassination attempt; Morris Haas, however, was later found dead in his cell, victim, it was decided, of a self-inflicted gunshot.

Though Heney, the dogged prosecutor, was now out of the picture, the trial went on relentlessly, until Abe Reuf was convicted of bribery on December 10, 1908 and sentenced to fourteen years in prison. Reuf's fight continued until March 7, 1911, when he was, finally, taken to San Quentin. On August 21, 1915, after he had completed four years and seven months of his term, Abraham Reuf was paroled.

Although the nefarious dealings of Abe Reuf and his political puppet, Eugene Schmitz, were widely discussed, I cannot blot my cherished memories of the tall, handsome, kind, and very popular "Professor" Eugene E. Schmitz—happy recollections when he and I were both on that same benefit program, The Columbia Pageant at the California Theatre, January 1898.

On that occasion, my contribution was a song act, during which my voluminous lace dress was caught in a chain that stretched in loops between the bars before the footlights. The audience registered dismay over my predicament, needlessly I might add. I simply signaled Conductor Schmitz to "vamp," or mark time, while I reached down and meticulously disengaged the lace from one of the chain links. With barely a moment of interruption, I resumed my song; the orchestra picked up the melody and, with the tumultuous approbation of the audience, we were on our way again. It was apparent from their initial reaction that they had expected the incident to completely "derail" me.

Proceeds from the Columbia Pageant went to the very deserving "helpless little humanity," as the program puts it. This "Save the Babies" project issued the compelling, "The Hospital Managers are calling upon the public often, not receiving State aid, and we trust the generous public of San Francisco will assist in making this a grand success, and replenish our depleted treasury. There are cared for monthly about 135 little children; 75 per cent are free." While the syntax was awkward, the appeal was genuine. The cause drew city-wide response, as witness the thirty prominent San Franciscans who served as members of the Board of Managers; the Active Patronesses; and the sixty-six Honorary Patronesses, among whom were the notables: Mrs. M.H. De Young, Mrs. W.E. Hopkins, Mrs. Ignatz Steinhart, and Mrs. Claus Spreckels. The honorary historians were Miss M.C. Craft and Mayor James D. Phelan.

In recognition of their participation in the pageant, theatrical children had one bed set aside for them, should they ever need it. Happily, I never had occasion to use it.

When the excitement of the Columbia Pageant died away, I played another benefit, before the Athens Lodge of the Modern Trojans. It was an "apron and necktie party," held at their hall on Grove and Twenty-second Streets, Oakland. I was only four-and-a-half years old. According to the write-up, "The little 'fairy' gave five recitations, each rendered as by a person of mature age and experience."

Of greater import was my participation in a special matinee at the Tivoli Opera House, Sunday, March 27, 1898 in aid of the Maine Memorial Fund. For the first time, I was working with professionals. The featured presentation was the musical comedy, THE WIDOW O'BRIEN, with Tommy Leary in the lead, and the entire Tivoli Company. During the second act, a "grand concert scene" was introduced, in which the following artists appeared:

> Stuart, the Male Patti (By kind permission of Manager Miller, "1492" Company)
> Josh Davis and Edwin Stevens, Comedians
> Tillie Salinger, singing "Young America" (She had made her first appearance in America at the Tivoli, December 8, 1890 as Josephine in "H.M.S. Pinafore")
> "Beau Brummels" Act—Sextet of Tivoli Girls
> Little Birdie Scholtz—The Cutest, Prettiest Tot, Who Will Show What a Three-Year Old Patriot Can Do To Help The Fund.

Once again, my name was misspelled, and they subtracted a year from my age, but I can forgive them because of kind reviews. Typical, was one that read, "Then there was Birdie Scholz, a tot of three years, who won every heart by her cunning ways (cute) and exceptional talents."

Newspaper coverage was extensive both before and after the fund-raising affair. It was still the era when the artist played a very important part, with his illustrations, in interpreting the news events. He rendered his subjects in line drawings, and when he was an accomplished artist, the results were quite representational. Photographs in San Francisco newspapers were used sparingly. The San Francisco Examiner's artist, Yardley, did line drawings of both Josh Davis and Miss Edith Hall, two featured artists on the bill. His drawings show Miss Hall swathed in a voluminous heavy woolen skirt, a matching bolero jacket with leg-of-mutton sleeves, a sailor straw hat, and a parasol—a dignified rendition of a dignified lady. Josh Davis, however, Yardley depicts as a character in a ministerial robe and high hat, holding in his hands an open book labeled, "Hymns" on one side and "Songs of Home" on the other. On a table beside Davis is a potted plant with a face peering from the foliage, simulating a bloom. The artist had captured well the humorous intent of Davis' role. Perhaps this was the "avant-garde" humor of the times.

Another artist, Flinn, did caricatures of some of the participants in the Tivoli's Maine Memorial Fund program. Miss Hall's he labels, "Clever Black Face Act"; Mr. Josh Davis', "Up to Date Songs"; Stuart's, "The Male Patti"; Tom Leary's, "The Widow Grows Sea-Sick"; and Miss Birdie Schultze's (sic), "The Coming Tragedienne."

That the Maine Memorial Fund-Raising Program was held on a Sunday, was touted as, "unusual in itself." The owner of the Tivoli Opera House, Mrs. Ernestine Kreling, made the exception in order that many of San Francisco's actors and actresses might participate in the worthwhile cause. The amount realized from this event, one of many held at various theaters throughout the city, does not seem impressive, by modern standards. But the $552 paid to James D. Phelan, Chairman Executive Committee, was generous, indeed, by 1897 standards. The check drawn on The Nevada National Bank of San Francisco stipulated, "Account Maine Memorial Benefit" and was signed, "Ernestine Kreling."

Besides direct donations from San Franciscans, other sources of money for the Monument Fund were: lodges, civic organizations, and business houses. The San Francisco Examiner published almost daily accounts of the grand totals of contributions from the latter, in its, "Merchants Roll of Honor." San Franciscans responded in their usual patriotic and generous way to the appeal for funds for the purpose of honoring the men who lost their lives on the battleship Maine, in Havana Harbor.

Although the United States has several National monuments to the U.S.S. Maine, there is none in San Francisco; still, she has two monuments to the Spanish-American War: the Commodore Dewey Memorial in Union Square, built in 1901, and one honoring the California Volunteers, situated at Dolores and Market Streets, erected in 1903.

Oakland, on the other hand, dedicated a Maine Memorial Monument in Lakeside Park on February 16, 1913. Reports show that, "A torpedo port taken from the Maine when she was raised from the floor of Havana Harbor was given to the city of Oakland in 1912. The city presented it to E.H. Liscum No. 7 U.S.W.V. and it was erected in Lakeside Park by members of Liscum Camp. Buried in the base of the Monument is a brass shell containing the roster of Liscum Camp members. Oakland is one of the very few cities in the United States to possess such a monument."

From the Commandant, Twelfth Naval District, comes further information on the subject:

> *"Monuments scattered around the country which contain parts of the ship* (Maine) *are her mainmast in Arlington National Cemetery, her foremast at the U.S. Naval Academy, Annapolis, one anchor is part of a memorial on Penn's Commons, Reading, Pa., a capstan is on display at Charleston, S.C., and a turret sight hood at Key West. Notable among other relics is a plaque cast from Maine metal and dedicated to the 'Americanism of Theodore Roosevelt' by his comrades in arms, on display at the Commissioned Officers' Mess at the Naval Station, Brooklyn, N.Y."*

But of all the places where honor has been accorded the Maine's martyrs, perhaps Key West, Florida, should be considered the most significant. It was to Key West the bodies of the victims were brought and interred. They rest in an especially fenced-off area in that city's cemetery. The enclosed turfed square is marked off by an attractive wrought iron fence, and just within its handsome gates, is an impressive marker with the names of the dead men. Beyond the marker, stands an imposing statue of a sailor with an oar in its right hand and its left, lifted to its forehead, as though keeping vigil over the rows of neat, white headstones. The statue rests on a pedestal with the inscription: "In Memory Of The Victims Of The Disaster Of

Burial Site Victims Battleship Maine Explosion (Key West, Florida)
Turret Sight Hood—Cor. Southard & Margaret Streets (Key West, Florida)
Inscription: "Preserved by Washington Camp No. 12 P.O.S. of A. In
Remembrance Of The Battleship Maine Blown Up In Havana Harbor
February 15, 1898."
Credit: Barrett-Miller Collection

U.S.S. Battleship Main In Havana Harbor Feb. 15, 1898.
Erected by Citizens of Key West, Florida."

Close by, at the corner of Southard and Margaret Streets,
within a school yard, a turret sight hood of the Main stands on
a pedestal bearing the plaque with the inscription: "This Relic Is
Preserved By Washington Camp No. 12 P.O.S. of A. In Remembrance of The BATTLESHIP MAINE Blown Up In
Havana Harbor February 15, 1898."

After all the excitement of the Tivoli Opera House, it was
somewhat of a letdown to find myself doing lodge benefits
again, but they, too, had their rewards. When I appeared before
the Live Oak Lodge, No. 17 of the Knights of Pythias, Castle
Hall, Oakland, my reward was the following prized letter:

> *"Our lodge fully appreciating your kind assistance on the*
> *occasion of their entertainment on the evening of April 30,*
> *1898 voted you an resolution of thanks. They realize you*

*was a 'little wonder'—May your pathway be strewn with
the flowers of love and the watchword 'Prosperity' be emblazoned in letters of gold upon your banner—Sincerely
yours."*

Who could ask for more?

A prize of a different nature was to come from my appearance at the S.P.C.A.'s Benefit, November, 1899. A children's
branch of the Society For The Prevention Of Cruelty To Animals, called "The Bands of Mercy," had been organized by the
ladies to further interest by the young people in the plight of the
animals. The ladies decided also that interest in these societies
would be enhanced by having identifying badges; but since
there were no funds available, a benefit was planned. To the
end of procuring 50,000 badges for the Bands of Mercy, a
city-wide performance, involving San Francisco's school children, was held in the Metropolitan Hall. Mayor Phelan introduced the program, Assistant Superintendent of Schools C.L.
Marks delivered a short address, after which there followed a
variety of musical renditions. My contribution was a song and
dance for which I received a letter of appreciation the following
day from C.B. Holbrook, their secretary.

In this letter, I take particular pride because my contact
with the Society For The Prevention of Cruelty To Animals, at
such an early age, initiated my unusual love and concern for all
animal life. This preoccupation has accompanied me all my life;
and I have derived much happiness from assisting in the estab-
lishing and aiding of the S.P.C.A., wherever I could. I feel this
awareness has been my real reward for the few minutes I added
to that benefit program so many years ago.

After the appearances in the "Columbia Pageant" at the
California Theatre and the Maine Memorial Fund Program at
the Tivoli Opera House in 1898, I began to receive offers from
several theaters. Before many months, I was playing, variously,
at the Chutes Theatre, Olympia Music Hall, California, Cineograph Parlors, and the Columbia, while still doing benefits
whenever called upon. This made for a very full and busy life
for so young a child. And yet, the excitement attendant to this
was nectar on which I existed.

Columbia Theatre, 1895-1906
Credit: Society of California Pioneers

Still another benefit appearance, though by now I was a "professional," was the Elks Annual Entertainment of the Golden Gate Lodge No. 6, held at the Columbia Theatre, November, 1899. It was a gala affair in which many artists volunteered their services.

Harry Connors, the stage director, delivered the address of welcome for Mr. Henry H. Davis, who was too ill to appear. He spoke of the "good and unostentatious work of the lodge in the cause of the sick and the distressed; its readiness to care for the families of brothers who had been gathered by the grim reaper." I am happy to add that his somber note did not affect the show, for the write-ups indicated it had been a big success, "with songs and specialties that pleased hundreds."

One "specialty" I particularly enjoyed was Dutch Walton. He was billed as "The Dutch Comedien with the Concertina," and was very popular with the San Francisco theater public. Walton always drew favorable reviews from the local press for his "exceptionally clever musical genius."

Of my humble offering, the same reviewer added, "Baby Dody Schultz (sic) as usual captivated the audience with her singing and dancing."

Save for an appearance before the Ladies of the Maccabees in April, 1900, the era of the benefits came to an end. So now, though still very young and very small, I had passed three years in which I had tried my wings and found the feat exhilarating. There was no turning back to the nest or cocoon. For some years to come, the stage was to be my real home of fantasy, to which I trailed the "clouds of glory" and where I found reflected the "vision splendid." The past three years had been the prelude that embarked me on a variety of appearances in several theatres; and these experiences constitute, in part, the sources of my early memories of life in the San Francisco theater world.

An event absorbing much interest in San Francisco, especially among the large Irish community, was the Irish Fair of August 20 to September 10, 1898. It was held at the sixth Mechanics Pavilion, a barn-like building of vast proportions, bounded by Grove and Hayes, and Polk and Larkin Streets, north of Market Street. That it was the sixth in a series of pavilions, is a historical fact worthy of note.

The first Mechanics Pavilion opened September 1857 on the site of the old Lick House, on the corner of Montgomery and Sutter Streets. It was there the Mechanics Institute's first annual fair was held. In 1864, another site, Union Square, was chosen. It covered the block bounded by Powell and Stockton,

SIXTH MECHANICS' INSTITUTE PAVILION
Larkin, Grove, Polk and Hayes Streets
Erected 1882; destroyed by fire April 18, 1906
Credit: The Archives For The Performing Arts, S.F.

and Geary and Post Streets. The following year, an annex of 6,000 feet was added. This building, in turn, was torn down in 1868 and another and much larger one, the fourth Mechanic's Pavilion, was erected on the same spot. In 1871, a third site, south of Market, was picked. It was the block bounded by Seventh and Eighth, and Market and Mission Streets. This fifth Mechanics Pavilion, larger than the previous ones, included a 3,000-foot-long conservatory garden on its west side, and was begun about mid-1874. In 1882, the sixth and final Mechanics Pavilion was built at a cost of $95,000, and was located on the site of San Francisco's present Civic Auditorium, north of Market Street. The Pavilion measured about 412 x 222 feet and the Annex on Hayes Street, 186 x 52 feet.

The Pavilions, especially the last one, served the purposes of San Francisco's present Brook's Hall and Cow Palace—arenas for all manner of fairs, dances, athletic tournaments, displays, horse shows, concerts, conventions, and miscellaneous gatherings. It was to this last Mechanics Pavilion that, in the early stages of the fire following the 1906 earthquake, the many injured were taken. The building served, temporarily, as a hospital until it was consumed by the holocaust.

Of the Irish Fair of 1898—could any ethnic group surpass the conviviality and joy of living of the Irish! Prodigious preparations were long in the making. For weeks before, newspapers and magazines carried detailed programs of what the public could expect during the three weeks of the great extravaganza. All manner of games, contests, dances, and shows were included to satisfy all manner of Irish; but all San Francisco joined in the festivities. Schools, lodges, clubs, and businesses were represented in the games and contests. Men, women, and the children—each had their specialty.

One notice urged, "Come and watch the grand Irish dance of the Irish Dancing School under the direction of Messrs. Kelleher and O'Connor." Although these two gentlemen were tailors, they seemed better known for their superb dancing; and they were in much demand at all festivals in the city. Memories of my involvement in the Irish Fair of 1898 consist of being taught an Irish jig and being given a silver medal for my performance. To this day, it is hard to believe I deserved it.

As early as the 1860's, San Francisco had amusement parks, such as the City Gardens, Hayes Park Pavilion, and Woodward's Gardens; but none were quite like the Chutes Amusement Park, a sort of prototype for others that followed. The Chutes opened November 2, 1895, on Haight Street, between Clayton and Cole Streets, with Charles L. Ackerman as president and Edward P. Levy, manager. It was to make two moves in its sixteen years of existence: In 1902, from its original site, east of Golden Gate Park, to the north side, on Fulton between Tenth and Eleventh Avenues; and in 1909, to its third site, the block bounded by Fillmore and Webster and Eddy and Turk Streets, where it remained until fire precipitated its closing in 1911. It is the first location, on Haight Street, however, that was to capture my fondest recollections. It was here that in 1897 the Chutes Free Theater I remember, was built—more of that, later.

1897-1902
Credit: The Archives For The Performing Arts, S.F.

Remembrances of the Chutes Amusement Park at Haight Street are childhood memories of animal acts, trapeze artists, balloon ascensions and parachute drops, side shows, souvenir counters, concessions, and all the other carnival-like delights that spellbind a child of four. Perhaps its most famous attraction was its "shoot the chutes." In the center of the park, was located a small artificial lake with a tower. Patrons paid ten cents to ascend to the top of the tower where an awaiting boat, hauled up on rollers, rested at the start of the chute. With water cascading down the chute, into the boat with the gondolier went the passengers; and so started the bumpy ride down the swift torrent and into the lake. The gondolier then ferried his passengers to the landing, where, disheveled but merry, they disembarked in front of the Pavilion. This very large structure with open sides, overlooked the lake. Once off the "shoot the chutes," the merrymakers could climb a few small shallow steps to the Pavilion where light lunches and beer were served. It was a popular pastime to while away the hours, seated at a table, watching the boats hurtle down the chute and plunge into the lake.

Equally as popular, if not more so with some, was the roller-coaster. Billed as the "greatest scenic railway on earth" when it opened July 4, 1896, it soon became an "in-thing" to do in that peaceable era. The roller-coaster outlined the perimeter of the park and afforded a grand bird's-eye view of the wonders it circumscribed, provided one could keep his breath intact and his eyes open.

Because of my tender years, the mama did not permit me to "shoot the chutes" or ride the literally "breathtaking," "scenic railway"; but I was more interested in the animals in the Chutes Zoo, anyway. There were the venerable lion named Wallace, the monkeys, Congo the Gorilla Man, Sally the "only Chimpanzee in America," Greeley the Man-Eating Polar Bear, Kangaroos and Dingoes from Australia, and other wild animals.

Tail 18½ ft. Mane 8½ ft.
Age: 15 years

"Beauty" At The Chutes
Credit: The Archives For The Performing Arts, S.F.

Surpassing my fondness for the wild animals in the zoo, however, was my love for "Beauty." Billed as, "The Handsomest Horse On Earth," Beauty was my favorite. She was a lovely white horse, exhibited against a black velvet setting. Her mane and tail fell to the floor. Beauty's tail was eighteen feet long, and like a bride's train, trailed ever so gracefully behind her. She was magnificent and glossy, for she was immaculately groomed. This equine charmer captured the hearts of grown-ups and children alike. After each performance, Beauty's mane and tail were carefully groomed. To prevent them from unnecessarily sweeping the ground, they were braided and rolled, then inserted into bags. Only after this painstaking ritual, was Beauty moved to her stable.

On June 27, 1897, the Chutes Amusement Park added still another attraction, The Chutes Free Theatre, built on what had once been baseball grounds. It was a real closed-in theater which, at first, presented the animal acts it had featured outdoors, as well as jugglers and acrobats. By the time I played there, about a year and a half later, some changes in format had occurred. The Chutes Theatre, a large sprawling building, featured what I would consider true vaudeville. The acts stayed only a short time, maybe a week, or two at the most. The format was definitely vaudeville, as opposed to the stationary, repertory quality of variety.

The handbill for the Chutes Theater, Thursday, November 17, 1898, the oldest in my collection, delineates well the varied fare presented. With the disclaimer to cover any eventualities, "Program is subject to change," it lists the program of acts for afternoon and evening performances:

> Cotton and Moll—Triple Horizontal Bar Experts
> Little Dody Scholtz—The Youngest Performer On
>   Any Stage (which may well have been true)
> Madame Emily Scheilde—Queen of Equi-poise
> Ed O'Connor—A Tramp of Cox's Army
> Lynton and Whelan—With Their Success, "Light
>   and Shade"

> Famous Projecting Machine, the ANIMATA-
> SCOPE (early motion pictures)
> The Conjuror And The Vanishing Lady (In this, a
> man in full dress waved a baton; a lady in even-
> ing gown appeared; both bowed; he waved his
> baton again; she disappeared; he bowed; and
> that was it, the entire moving picture.)
> Cattle Fording the Stream (cows walking through a
> creek)
> Beach Scene at Monterey (people lying around on
> the sand)
> Morning Exercise of the Light Division (soldiers on
> horseback)
> Automaton
> Baths on the River Rhone, France
> U.S.S. BATTLESHIP OREGON ENTERING
> NEW YORK HARBOR

I recall that this film of the August 20, 1898 event in Tomkins-
ville, New York, was defective or "rainy," and barely showed the
large battleship in the distance; but it was the main feature, and
so it was emblazoned in capital letters on the program. (More on
the Battleship Oregon, later.)

The moving picture in 1898, scarcely two years out of its
cocoon,will be treated in proper perspective, later. Suffice to
note at this point, that the movies shown by the Animatascope
were short, and that their techniques were very crude. To a
child not yet five years old, though, they were fascinating
marvels.

The management of the Chutes Theater announced
proudly that: "This theater is conducted on the same plan as
Keith's famous vaudeville theaters in New York, Boston and
Philadelphia. No refreshments served. Gentlemen will please
refrain from smoking (no need to warn the ladies; no "lady"
dared smoke in public). Among the zoological attractions at the
Chutes is now presented what even the famous New York
Zoological Gardens do not present." And it was a further source
of pride to them that it was the "Only theater in San Francisco

giving daily matinees – Chutes Theater, Admission Free." Once the admission fee to the Chutes Amusement Park had been paid, one could enter the theater without paying an additional charge, unless he opted for a reserve seat for ten cents. When the performance was about to start, a bugle was sounded to alert interested spectators at the park. From all areas of the Park, the audience converged on the Chutes Free Theater.

During my engagement at the Chutes (starting in November of 1898), there was much time between the matinee and evening performances to explore the offerings of the park. I remember well a concession nestled under the sloping roof of the chute on which the boats came down. Here, diabolically it seemed to me, was placed an eerie array of coffins, blinking lights, and weird forms, all accompanied by frightening sounds. It was like a Halloween set or a gruesome horror house. I did not like it and, to this day, I do not like the music from Faust, played there. The concession, with its strange accoutrements and music, seemed quite sordid to me.

Among parting memories is one of Mr. Edward P. Levy, the park's manager, who was also in charge of the Chutes Theater. I was playing there once when the film caught fire in what we called the "lamp house," the modern-day projection room. I did not witness the fire episode, but I recall hearing that Mr. Levy's mustache had been singed.

It would not be the last time Mr. Levy came "under fire." In May of 1899, Manager Edward P. Levy came afoul of the Child Labor Law, and was arrested for "violating the ordinance against employment and exhibition of minors." But it appears that it was a mere formality, for in September, according to newspaper accounts, he engaged "three pickaninnies in Hawaiian grass skirts," and in October, "Major Mite in a 'telephone duet' with Baby Ruth Roland" (later of the movies).

And there was Mr. Bush, the handsome blue-uniformed collector at the turnstile, who was to make a lasting impression. Always pleasant and indulgent with me, he, nevertheless, was once impelled to warn me not to swing on the turnstile or the mama would have to pay for the tickets registered. This early introduction to the intricacies of automatic equipment, put the "fear of God"—or was it "bankruptcy"—in me. I envisioned a terrible financial catastrophe befalling the beloved and innocent mama. Obviously, the torturous guilt resulting from the admonition was a bit out of proportion to Mr. Bush's intent; however, never again did I forget his warning.

Though lacking the glamour and attraction I found in Mr. Bush, the lovable matron in the ladies lounge would leave her imprint on my memory because, of all things, her name—Mrs. Toohey. I thought the name so unusual, I took pleasure in repeating it in a variety of ways, emphasizing first the "Too," then the "hey"; lowering or raising the inflections; and making imaginary introductions between Mrs. Toohey and others. My world of fantasy offered a wide range of possibilities.

And now, after all these years since the Chutes, a thought comes to mind: at the 1915 Panama-Pacific International Exposition, in San Francisco, I wondered what there was so nostalgic about it. Now I know. There was a bit of the quality of the Chutes Amusement Park—albeit more gloriously and beautifully done, to be sure. But the people moved about the concessions, with the same expectant attitude as at the Chutes. The "carnival" atmosphere, in its most delightful sense, was inherent in both. The unmistakable "air" of the Chutes Amusement Park had found its way into San Francisco's incredibly dazzling and sparkling 1915 Exposition that celebrated the 400th Anniversary of Balboa's discovery of the Pacific, and the opening of the Panama Canal.

A theater quite different from the Chutes Free Theater, was the old Olympia Music Hall, located at the southwest corner of Eddy and Mason Streets. It was truly unique. I had never seen one like it, nor have I seen one since. A large brick building with a rounded front, the Olympia had been known as the Panorama in the 1880's, when it displayed a cyclorama of the Battle of Waterloo. In the early 90's it was known as the People's Palace. For a brief time in 1895, it was the Circus Royal; after that, it seems to have fallen on poor times until the Orpheum

Theatre Company took over its destiny. In my recollections of the Olympia, the cyclorama of the Battle of Waterloo had been replaced with that of the Battle of Gettysburg. The updated murals of the Civil War featured life-size figures, and were a great attraction.

Announcements of the leasing of the old building to the Orpheum Company for five years, indicated that, "by doing so (they) have forestalled competition in the vaudeville line in San Francisco." The Figaro's May 25, 1897 article carried the banner, "THE ORPHEUM COMPANY GET ANOTHER HOUSE." From it we learned that a "remodeling of the interior of the theater and . . . the erection of a new stage . . . sufficiently large to accommodate grand scenic dramas for the largest opera companies," were the immediate plans of Secretary Myerfield and his architects, Saalfield and Kolhberg. The management also announced that, "The experiment of giving a continuous performance show will be tried, giving afternoon and evening performances with a combined dramatic and vaudeville company at the popular prices of 10, 20, and 30 cents. The theatre will be christened the 'Olympia'."

Situated as it was, in the theatrical center of the city, it had to compete with such theaters as: the Tivoli Opera House, just a half block away on Eddy Street; the Baldwin and Columbia Theaters, a block away; and a number of others, like the Alcazar, Orpheum, and Grand Opera House, lurking just around the corners. If it were to survive such formidable competition, it had to come up with a quite different fare; and the original plans to "accommodate grand scenic dramas for the largest opera companies" were grandiose and pretentious, to say the least. The Olympia then opted for the "novel."

This unusual theater, with its iron and glass dome, was referred to as a "Box House," a none too complimentary connotation at that time. I daresay, this was a reference to the curtained booths that partitioned the large semi-circular balcony. The booths resembled those once found in restaurants and, in their seclusion, no doubt lent themselves to trysts. Drinks were served directly to these curtained booths, by white-aproned waiters, and it is conceivable the intimate atmosphere of these "Boxes" spawned and perpetuated questionable business executive-secretary relationships.

Admittedly, the prevailing code of morals placed the working girl in a constant state of guardedness. Whereas the telephone girl was supervised by an older woman who acted as a chaperon of sorts, and the domestic was sheltered by the lady of the house when the young son or husband was about, the secretary or office girl did not come under the "moral protection" afforded these and other female workers. Actresses, of course, were beyond the pale.

As a child, I did not understand all this, and so I never questioned the propriety or impropriety of what might have taken place beyond the curtained booths. I'm not at all sure, now, that "nice ladies" of those days went there. But be that as it may, the Olympia was a most unusual theater; and I feel it merits some consideration, and that its description be preserved for the record.

While the balcony had curtained booths, downstairs there were tables and chairs, instead of regular theater seats. The Olympia printed a wine list on the back of each program, offering all manner of drinks to all. Plain drinks were ten cents, "except," and there followed the many possibilities:

Extra Pony Whisky (served in flasks)	15¢
Imported Pony Cognac	15¢
Imported Cordials and Liqueurs	15¢
All Fancy Mixed and Hot Drinks	15¢
Walter's Napa Soda (plain)	10¢
Walter's Napa Soda Lemonade (served in large glass)	15¢
Milk Punch	25¢
Champagne, per glass	15¢

Beers:
    German Lager, per glass, 5¢
    German Lager, per Stein, 10¢
    Wielands Special Brew .... Qts. 25¢
    Pabst Milwaukee .... Qts. 25¢ Pts. 15¢
    Everard's Canada Malt Beer Qts. 35¢ Pts. 20¢
    Val Blatz Milwaukee Import Qts. 50¢ Pts. 25¢
    Alf and Alf .... Pts. 25¢
    English Ale and Porter .... 30¢

Champagne:
    Pommery .... Qts. $5 Pts. $2.50
    Clicquot .... Qts. $5 Pts. $2.50
    Mumm .... Qts. $5 Pts. $2.50
    Dry Monpole .... Qts. $5 Pts. $2.50
    Bouche .... Qts. $4 Pts. $2.00
    Ruinart .... Qts. $4 Pts. $2.00

"Mineral Waters" served included: Apollinaris, Johannis, Bethesda, and imported Ginger Ale, all selling for 50¢ a quart, 25¢ a pint, and 10¢ a glass.

Imported wines were a specialty of the house. The Rhine and Hungarian wines could be purchased by the quart, pint, glass or 1/2 Schoppen.

Accompaniments to the above libations were a choice of oyster cocktails, all kinds of sandwiches and delicacies, and to top it all, cigars were "served in a sealed envelope, with price printed thereon." Patrons were urged to, "Buy our famous 2 for a Quarter Cigar and be surprised." Hm−m!

The dispensing of alcoholic beverages in theaters was not unusual in the Nineteenth and Twentieth Centuries, in spite of an 1892 law forbiding it. Indeed, the Orpheum Theatre, considered the "mother house of the entertainment to cities throughout the United States and overseas" and which presented the highest quality vaudeville in the nation, served drinks until 1904. In March of that year, a notice appeared in its theater program informing its patrons that, "No refreshments will be served hereafter on the lower floor of the Orpheum. Gentlemen will find cafes in front of the theater." Until then, however, the Orpheum's white-aproned waiters walked down the aisles and served beer. I recall the beer was served in schooners and passed along troughs fastened along the back of each row of seats. Patrons pushed the beer along to its destination, and the money, back to the waiter. Everyone was very cooperative and a certain spirit of fellowship prevailed. It was all considered quite proper. Later, however, I never saw beer served in a dramatic theater.

The Olympia Music Hall was a "variety house." Variety was the forerunner of vaudeville, There seemed to be some confusion at the time about the designations, "variety" and "vaudeville." From my vantage point, I offer, based on my personal observations, the following explanations:

In variety, the same people remained at the theater, as a stock company. Each week, they sang different songs, wore different costumes, presented different dances and, in general, varied their acts. By contrast, in vaudeville, different performers *came* to a theater for a week or two's engagement. The formats in both were similar. The vaudevillians were singers, dancers, acrobats, jugglers, et al., doing their specialties for that week. At the conclusion of their engagement, they moved on to yet another theater or town; and a new group would replace them, doing pretty much the same thing, but with new people doing it.

In short, "variety" resembled "stock," with performers attached with some degree of permanency to the theater; in vaudeville, the companies traveled from theater to theater. Variety performers became very popular with their public, and gained a loyal following rarely matched by the transient vaudevillians. But vaudevillians, in spite of their transiency, knew each other or of each other. There was a code of loyalty among them. Before departing a town, they would leave notes for the incoming actors. Dressing room walls were bulletin boards that left all sorts of pertinent information for traveling vaudevillians—an unpleasant situation at a local hotel, unfair prices, forewarnings of undesirable businesses; or perhaps a personal message for a friend.

No account of the Olympia of that time (1898−1899) is complete without mentioning the lost art of the "after-piece." At a rehearsal, the company decided on the skit that would conclude the performance. Would it be the "Irish Justice" or "The Ghost Walks," for example. Everyone knew the fundamental plots of these skits. It was their stock in trade. Some even had manuscripts of their own. These skits were crude and ad libbed, but they were universally used in variety houses—at least on the West Coast.

Let us say they would agree to put on, "The Irish Justice." The spokesman would volunteer to be the bailiff; another actor would choose to be the justice; another, an old woman who beat the dog; or still another, the policeman. In "The Irish Justice," a man is arrested for drunkenness. Throughout the skit, the drunken defendant and the Irish Justice keep sharing a jug of liquor that is supposed to be the evidence. Once when I played in this skit, I was a boy brought in, accused of having stolen a loaf of bread. The Irish Justice gave me "life"; then, when he wasn't looking, I reached up and stole the inkwell. I was caught in this dastardly act and the Justice sentenced me to ten years more.

Just when the art of the"after-piece" had its inception, is difficult to pinpoint. Old playbills of the 1860's include them. The Adelphi Theatre on California Street in San Francisco, listed "The Irish Policeman," with typical "after-piece" characters such as policeman, judge, leading heavy, Bonfanti, and Sangali. The Mercantile Library Hall's program of Easter Sunday, April 1, 1860 ended with "Platt's Hall," a burlesque treatment of the great drama "The Two Orphans," using amusing characters and an insensitive play on words: Louise, the dizzy blind girl; Chevalier de Yaudrey, the masher; Dame Frouchard, the tough old hen; Pierre, the crippled hod-carrier; Doctor Cure-all, the killer; and Joe Blueskin Norton, a villain. Emerson's Opera House concluded its August 1888 program with the after-piece, "Our Politics," featuring a curbstone politician, a hen-pecked husband, and a strong-minded wife.

Though crude and ad-libbed, the after-piece was, nevertheless, an art form that grew among the performers and so had a very meaningful place in the theater history of the time. Sometimes it was a forum for the social ills of the day. Political comment or criticism was treated handily in humor or satire. At times it satirized popular plays of the day, as when MacIntyre and Heath, the blackened twosome, became famous for, "The Worst Born," their satirization of Francis J. Powers', "The First Born." I regret these skits are a lost art.

Familiar names at the Olympia Music Hall were regulars like the Keesings, Carlton and Royce, Dora Mervin, Dolly Mitchell, Josie Gordon, and Snowie Maybelle. As variety gave way to vaudeville, traveling acts began to share billing with the regulars. Names like Kelly and Violet; The Great Freada, Twirling Turkish Dancer; Mulvey and Inman, New York Acts; and Girdeller Brothers, Grotesque Acrobats, began to appear alongside the more familiar names.

Of all the vaudevillians that appeared at the Olympia, none were more popular than Kelly and Violet, "The Fashion Plates." Kelly was a fine, handsome tenor, and his wife Violet, a beautiful, buxom woman. Instead of wearing short soubrette dresses with the full skirts, the style of the day, Violet chose gorgeous evening gowns. And evening gowns then, were truly gorgeous. They did not look like somebody's nightgown. They were made by hand, with meticulous care for detail. Stays were sewn into them to hold their shape. From its inception. the evening gown was a masterpiece of creation. The waist and bust were re-inforced with whalebone stays that almost gave the support of a true corset. Seams were French-seamed by hand, on the inside as well as the outside. Gowns were decollete, and had sleeves that puffed at the shoulder. Since they were so well reinforced at the waist, the dresses could stand up well enough without straps or the short sleeves, or even without a buxom Violet in them.

Passementeries, or ornamentations, for these creations were, as I remember them, patches of lace beaded with pearls and sequins. These elegant trimmings glittered like jewels as the lights played on them; and the grandeur extended to the long skirts, full at the bottom and bearing a regal train. The train was often finished with ruchings—a silk, folded over and pleated, the edges sometimes left raw, and frayed with scissors. The ruchings could be changed easily if they showed the effects of wear or soil.

This was the era just before the Gibson Girl, the lady of the very flat stomach who, because fashion dictated, walked in such a way that her bosom and derrier vied for prominence. In Violet's time, the silhouette was not yet so severely delineated. It was enough that the waistline be small, and Violet's was. Her costumes, of which she had an inordinate variety, were marvels of ruffles, ruchings, and passementeries.

Those who wore the short, knee-length soubrette dresses did not go bare-legged, as they do now. They wore tights. If the soubrettes happened to be thin and sparing of calves, they would wear "hearts," a padding made of felt or flannel. These "hearts," or "falsies," were heart-shaped; and they were placed on the calf of the leg, point down, so that when the tights were put on, the legs looked fatter. It was very important to place the hearts properly, lest they distort the natural shape of the leg. Of course, there was no need for Violet to use hearts, since she wore only long evening gowns.

Kelly's costume, in contrast to Violet's, was the somber evening tails and high hat, in black. But he "cut an elegant and fancy figure," as they put it. Kelly and his lovely Violet sang and did modest dance steps; but their clothes and his beautiful, rich tenor voice were their claims to fame.

My place in the Kelly and Violet act came after they had finished the second verse and chorus of their featured song. Standing on a chair in the balcony box nearest the stage, with the spotlight on me, and visible from all sides, I alternately joined them and sang solo, when they went into the last chorus of their song. The audience was very indulgent, for I was only five years old.

Interesting to note, the fates of the Olympia Music Hall and the Tivoli Opera House would one day be joined. The two theaters were located within a half-block of each other, on Eddy Street.

Second Tivoli Theatre, 1879-1903 – (The Tivoli Opera House)
Credit: Society of California Pioneers

The Tivoli Opera House, where I had played in the special matinee to aid the Maine Memorial Fund, was the second of four Tivoli's, and was located in the middle of the block of Eddy (northside), between Powell and Mason Streets. The theater was near the St. Ann's building where we lived from 1899 into 1903, and had the formal address: 28–32 Eddy Street.

This second Tivoli was housed in a rather unimpressive, three-storied clapboard building, to which the original Tivoli

(1876–1879) had moved in 1879 from the northwest corner of Sutter and Stockton Streets when it was known as the "Tivoli Gardens." After the proprietors/managers, John and Joseph Kreling, moved to the Eddy Street location, their former Tivoli Gardens became the "*Vienna* Gardens" and was operated by Gustav Walter, the same gentleman who later, in June 1887, opened the first of San Francisco's five famous Orpheums.

Though the Eddy Street building looked modest, the Tivoli Opera House gained a reputation for the high caliber entertainment it presented. Its opening bill, July 3, 1879, was Gilbert and Sullivan's H.M.S. PINAFORE, which played for eighty-four consecutive nights. Two leads in this operetta, F.E. Brooks and Harry de Lorne, would make repeat appearances there to celebrate the Tivoli Opera House's tenth anniversary, Wednesday, July 3, 1889.

During the Tivoli Opera House's first year, records show that after the eighty-four nights of H.M.S. PINAFORE, came: THE WRECK OF THE PINAFORE by Mrs. Church. These were followed by a succession of operettas by Gilbert and Sulli-van (THE SORCERER, TRIAL BY JURY); Lecoc (LA FILLE de MADAME ANJOT, GIROFLE-GIROFLA, THE LITTLE DUKE); Offenbach (LA GRANDE DUCHESSE de GEROL-STEIN, BLUE BEARD, LA PERICHOLE); Eichberg's, THE DOCTOR OF ALCANTARA; Suppe's, FATINITZA; and Planquette's, THE BELLS OF CARNEVILLE. None of these played less than two weeks, and most of them spanned three or four weeks of consecutive nights.

A random check of playbills for the decade, 1890–1900, showed that its proprietor, the widow Mrs. Ernestine Kreling, and her manager, William H. Leahy (whom she later married) booked the following: H.M.S. PINAFORE, MIKADO, BAR-BER OF SEVILLE, THE JEWESS, BLUE BEARD, CYRANO DE BERGERAC, THE GEISHA, SHAMUS O'BRIEN, LA GIACONDA, CARMEN, AIDA, MADELEINE, and OR-PHEUS AND EURYDICE. Obviously, the Tivoli outclassed the Olympia Music Hall in every possible manner.

The Olympia Music Hall, on the other hand, as noted earlier, was a "Box House"; dealt in "variety," the precursor of vaudeville; "after-pieces" and, in general, a very light format. From the beginning, it was in heavy competition from several nearby theaters, especially its closest neighbor, the Tivoli. Yet, in spite of all this, the Olympia managed to survive for almost six years.

When the Olympia of the rounded facade closed, the Tivoli, condemned as a firetrap, looked to the Olympia and made a decision. In June 27, 1903, the following item appeared in the San Francisco Dramatic Revue:

Tivoli Lease of Former Olympia

"J.K. Prior has leased to the Tivoli Theatre Company the premise formerly known as the Olympia for one year at $865 per month, with option of a further lease at $1200 per month."

The lease also included permission for the construction of a roof garden and cafe, involving extensive alterations and changes.

In less than six months, my Olympia of the questionable reputation was no more, and the Tivoli had moved in, christening its third Tivoli, "The *New* Tivoli Opera House."

The New Tivoli Opera House opened December 23, 1903, with a "holiday spectacle" in three acts, the musical comedy, IXION, starring the very popular Ferris Hartman, Wallace Brownlow, Bessie Tannehill, and Nettie Deglow among a large cast. IXION was a melange of comedy, singing, and ballets titled, "Greek Pleasure," "Ballet of Love," "Wines of California," "Snow Ballet," and "Early Days in California." The musical concluded with a transformation, "Excelsior."

The third Tivoli, like its predecessor, the Olympia, was short-lived — 1903 to April 18, 1906, when, like the other downtown theaters, it perished under the assaults of earthquake and fire. Scheduled for that night, was the popular SHOW GIRL.

Six years after the disaster of 1906, the fourth Tivoli arose on the same site as the second Tivoli, on the northside of Eddy Street, between Powell and Mason. After the earthquake and until March, 1912, the "temporary" City Hall had occupied this centrally located downtown site.

In 1913, with William H. ("Doc") Leahy again at the helm, the fourth Tivoli opened with its well-known format of musical

The Third Tivoli (The New Tivoli Opera House) — 1903-1906
Credit: The Archives For The Performing Arts, S.F.

drama and greats like Tetrazini and Mary Garden, and the Chicago Opera Company. But, apparently, tastes of San Francisco theater patrons were changing, and the demands for "movies" were clamorous. That same year, the new and fourth Tivoli succumbed to popular trends and became a motion picture house, until its demolition in January, 1950.

In the decade in which I played San Francisco theaters as "Baby Dody," no two theaters bestir the same memories. Each theater was quite different, in its own special way, and this I can also say of The Cineograph Parlors, a quaint, little-known theater in which I played. It was located at 747 Market Street, about three doors above the Call, or "Claus Spreckels Building," as it was known at that time. Though advertised as The Cineograph Theatre, it was not a true theater building, rather a converted store.

Opened in 1897 by Adolphus W. Furst, affectionately called "Pop," the Cineograph Parlors, though primitive, was to hold a special place as the protogenic of the motion picture house in San Francisco. On the street-level floor of this con-

The Cineograph Parlors, 1897-1906 (Arrow)
Credit: San Francisco Public Library

verted store building, "cineographs," or moving pictures, strictly a novelty in those days, were shown to an eager public. Up a flight of stairs, one reached the second floor, more of a loft, where vaudeville was presented.

Refinements at the Cineograph were notable for their absence. In neither the first floor where the movies were shown nor the loft where vaudeville was presented, were there the inclined floors or the elevated seats we have come to take for granted. In the loft, there were rows of benches with a center aisle between, and an aisle on each side. The piano rested on the floor proper, below left of stage. The stage was quite small and included only two pairs of wings, one of which was the "tormentor," and there was no apron. There was precious little attempt at ornamentation or decoration, in either the interior of the theater or the sets. The scenery consisted of four wings and two drops—a garden, and a street drop.

The so-called "vaudeville" at the Cineograph was still of the nature of "variety"; however, the word "vaudeville" had come into vogue, and as do so many new words, had begun to replace the old word, "variety." It was a matter of a short time before the name "variety" lost its old familiar descriptive meaning and came into disuse in theater parlance. Today, it lives only as the banner of the theatrical newspaper which has been printed for years, "VARIETY." I recall, well, that the first time I heard the word "vaudeville," it was misquoted, "waterville" and someone corrected, "No, not 'waterville,' it's vaud-a-vill." The new word seemed to have as many pronunciations as there were dialects.

Into this crude little store-front theater, with its early vaudeville and "new" motion pictures, I came as a bearer of simple child offerings—recitations and song and dance.

My only program of the Cineograph Parlors, 1899 vintage, is a little pink creation, printed on cheap paper. It might well be the only one in existence, for chances are that if there were others, they were burned in the fire that followed the San Francisco Earthquake of 1906. How mine was rescued, quite by accident, will be covered, later; suffice to say, I am very glad it was. In my little pink treasure is a trove of information on the wonders offered at the Cineograph Parlors: "New Scenes Each

Week — Scientific and Refined Entertainment for Ladies and Gentlemen — Continuous Performance — A.W. Furst General Manager — Admission 10¢ — Life-size Moving Pictures Reproduced On a Screen 16 ft. Square — San Francisco Family Resort."

The right side of the program listed the "moving pictures," and the left, the vaudeville acts. Let me, first, address myself to the latter and see where it will take us. It bears the impressive heading, PROGRAM FOR VAUDEVILLE DEPARTMENT, and offers:

> Dick Lester in Fred Helf's latest song, "The Perjured Bride"
>
> Lotta Mancie—"Don't Be So Anxious To Run Down a Woman"—a song
>
> Maxie Mitchell (Lotta Mancie's sister)—Song and Dance
>
> Baby Dody—Saturday and Sunday Evenings Only—"Coon Songs"

No offense is intended in mentioning this. The program records a very popular type of song of that era when, regrettably, the sensitivities of black people were not always a consideration. But it is theater history, and I present the ensuing, in that spirit.

I recall one occasion when I came on stage with two little black dolls in a doll buggy and sang the following two songs:

Mammy Jenny's Carolina Twins
Now close your eyes and cover up your head
The bogey-man will catch you if you cry
Next Sunday morn the bells will sweetly chime
The lords and ladies they will fall in line
They'll dance and sing; the bells will sweetly ring
For Mammy Jenny's Carolina Twins.

My next song on the Cineograph's bill was one I introduced. My picture apeared on the cover of the music sheet. The plaintive ballad was entitled:

Stay In Your Own Backyard

Lilac trees are blooming in the corner by the gate
Mammy in her little cabin door
Curly headed little one coming home so late
Crying cause his little heart was sore
All the children playing round, had skin so white and fair
None of them with him would ever play.
So Mammy in her lap takes the weeping little chap
And says in her own kind way,

"Now honey you stay in your own backyard
Don't mind what the white child do
What show do you suppose they's gwine to give
A little black Coon like you
So stay on this side of the high board fence
And honey don't you cry so hard
Go out and play just as much as you please
But stay in your own backyard."

I felt a deep kinship with this child because I, too, had no one with whom I could play. Each of us was victimized by a barrier—his, color; mine, occupational.

For this act, the mama made me a lovely little dress, floor length, and of alternate rows of lace and lavender ribbon. The skirt hung from a yoke, to the floor. Under the dress, was a beautiful lace petticoat, "real lace," as the mama put it. It had little bows of ribbon that showed when I picked up my dress, slightly, in the dancing. For some unknown reason, I wore a fancy little hat that resembled a Dutch-cap. That seemed a bit incongruous to me, but I was very young and had nothing to say about its suitability.

The dance in my act was a cakewalk—a sort of prancing up and down, with one arm extended forward, the other backward, a step forward, and then a reversal of the arms positions, and another step forward, etc. Since I was quite a mimic, it was no great feat to reproduce any dance I saw.

Baby Dody At The Cineograph Parlors, circa 1899
Credit: Barrett-Miller Collection

Memories of the Cineograph Parlors include a popular form called "Black Art." From the wings, I viewed this very intriguing routine. The backdrop curtain was black. In front of it, about three or four feet, was a black-covered "fence," or "row," in stage parlance, about two and a half feet high. Between the row and black backdrop, was a man entirely clothed in black, including his gloves and black-hooded head. Behind the "fence" and out of sight of the audience, were a number of articles: a bouquet of paper flowers, a vase, and a small pedestal stand. The man reached down, lifted the stand to the view of all the audience, waved it around, reached down again, picked up the vase, placed it on the stand and moved both about. With another flourish, he reached down once more, picked up the bouquet, and placed it in the vase. When he had exploited the mysterious appearances of all the objects, he suddenly lowered everything behind the row and out of view. Because he was all in black, against a black drop, with lighting deftly arranged to eliminate shadows, he was invisible to the audience. This illusion of self-propelled articles moving about in space, "Black Art," was a very popular attraction at the Cineograph.

As with audiences at the Olympia Music Hall and other theatres in San Francisco, the "after-piece" was a great favorite with those of the Cineograph Parlors. Among the many after-pieces in which I played there, was the Garden Scene from UNCLE TOM'S CABIN; but it was played "straight," and was a short version of the original scene. Dick Lester played Uncle Tom; Maxie Mitchell was Topsy; Lotta Mancie, Aunt Ophelia; and I played Eva. Background music during the entire scene was "Hearts and Flowers," played by one of the most engaging piano players it has been my pleasure to watch. His name escapes me, but I can see him in my mind's eye—a plump little man, eager for life, with a mustache that extended well beyond his face.

A familiar name at the Cineograph was Bob Lee, the juggler. He was a circus man, and he tried to convince the mama that I should join the circus, too. Apparently, he was not very persuasive. The mama was not interested in the idea, and so I escaped that sort of life. The nearest I came to it was a very short stint with the Norris and Rowe Dog and Pony Show, on the road.

As the little pink program of the Cineograph Parlors indicates, I appeared on Saturday and Sunday Evenings, only. I had been singing every night, but the Society For the Prevention of Cruelty to Children came to investigate the circumstances of my employment. There was talk I would be removed from the care of my parents because I was being "cruelly treated and exploited." The mama called me to her during the investigator's visit, to show the gentleman that I was a very happy child, well fed and clean throughout. To make her point, she even showed him my underwear, much to my embarrassment. She spared nothing to convince him that I was loved, well cared for, and not abused in any way. And I must concur with mama's insistence. Maybe I was exploited, but it was a way of life; and I was never pushed beyond my endurance. I was happy in my work and ever eager and willing to embark on new challenges and adventures.

During this chapter of my life, an historical drama was unfolding. Absorbing the interest of the nation, were the compelling events of the Spanish-American War. Though I do not remember the sad details, history records that on February 15, 1898, the Battleship U.S.S. Maine blew up in Havana Harbor, with a loss of two-hundred-sixty men, out of a complement of about three-hundred-fifty. Americans were incensed, and patriotic zeal was soon at a high pitch. It was out of this *milieu* that the drive for a Maine Memorial Fund had arisen in San Francisco, culminating in many benefit shows such as the one in which I participated at the Tivoli Opera House, March 1898, dealt with earlier. Perhaps more than most other American cities, San Francisco showed its fervor and appreciation for its gallant sons. It had started the Maine Memorial Fund drive even before President McKinley signed the war resolution against Spain, April 20, 1898.

Of special interest to me, since it is mentioned in my Chutes Theater program, is the Battleship Oregon. She was in Puget Sound when the Maine met her demise in Havana Harbor. On March 6, the Oregon left the Northwest; made her famous "forced-draft" voyage of 14,700 miles around Cape Horn and by May 18, seventy-nine days later, was in Barbados. Soon after, she joined the battleships Iowa, Indiana, Massachusetts, and Texas, and played a key role in the American victory against Admiral Cervera's Fleet in the Battle of Santiago de Cuba July 3, 1898.

The Battleship Oregon, Anchored In Portland Harbor — c. 1916
Credit: Oregon Historical Society

By this time, Commodore Dewey had won his decisive encounter with the Spanish Fleet in Manila Bay (in May), and America's gratitude for her fighting men began to be expressed in many ways.

When San Francisco, the "city that knows how," opened its portals to the war heroes on July 14, 1899, I was at the Cineograph Parlors. From its windows of the second floor, I watched the mammoth parade as it passed below, on Market Street. It was a celebration unequaled in my short years. I recall someone holding onto my dress, lest I fall out the window, as I reached out, waving my little American flag. The joyous welcome San Francisco extended the boys from the Oregon and California Signal Corps included the street parade that started at 8:30 a.m. from the Folsom Street Wharf to Market Street, to Golden Gate Avenue, to Van Ness Avenue where the reviewing stand had been erected at Bush, to Lombard and thence to the Presidio, where it ended three hours later.

That evening, a banquet was held for "the boys" at the Mechanics Pavilion, with speeches of welcome by Governors Greer of Oregon and Gage of California. Following dinner, the soldiers were organized into theater parties and entertained at the various theaters, before returning to the Presidio. Theater programs for the Volunteers included:

Grand Opera House ....CARMEN
Columbia ....LORD AND LADY ALGY
Alcazar ....CAMILLE, with Florence
    Roberts (Courtesy of Fred Belasco and Mark
    Thall)
Tivoli Opera House ....BLUEBEARD
California ....THE LAST WORD
    Blanche Bates Company

Like all other San Francisco theaters, the Cineograph Parlors, too, opened its doors to the soldiers.

Intermittent welcomes for the returning heroes went on for quite some time. The one on August 24, 1899, included a spectacular evening parade from the Ferry Building to the City Hall. To the end of raising funds for this affair, a "Gigantic Benefit" had been held at the Orpheum Theater, the week before. All the local theaters had pooled their talents for, "the biggest performance ever known on this Coast"; and the entire proceeds had gone for this reception given the California Volunteers arriving from the Philippines on the U.S. Transport Sherman.

Finally, San Francisco culminated its tributes to the Spanish-American War heroes with one glorious celebration on the homecoming of Admiral Dewey on his flagship, the Olympia, September 27, 1899.

Having mentioned that the Cineograph Parlors presented both vaudeville and moving pictures, let me now dwell on the latter. The little pink program's right side bears the heading, "Moving Pictures—Entire Change of Pictures Every Day":

Saturday ....The Ghost Show
Sunday   And 20 other Moving Pictures

<pre>
Monday . . . . Cinderella. 35 people take part
          in 20 Tableaus
     And 20 other Moving Pictures
Tuesday . . . . Dewey's Parade
     And 20 other Moving Pictures
Wednesday . . . . Jeffries and Fitzsimmons Fight
Thursday . . . . Dreyfus Court Martial
Friday . . . . Bridegroom's Troubles
     And 20 other Moving Pictures
</pre>

The program might mislead the reader into believing these were complete stories, as we now know them in the modern film; but the era of the so-called "story-film" had not yet begun. These movies were about two to three minutes long, and the entire program hardly lasted a half-hour. The movies I remember at the Cineograph, were made by a French moving picture company called Pathe. The company had a rooster as its trademark. And although the bill advertised, "Entire Change of Pictures Every Day," what they really did was to change their order of appearance.

Movies were hardly out of their infancy at this time. History shows that in 1894, several inventors were experimenting with the projecting machine. In England, it was Robert Paul; in France, the Laumiere brothers, Louis and Auguste, and the Pathes; and, in America, Thomas A. Edison. However, it was C. Francis Jenkins, a clerk in the Treasury Department, who was the first to invent the motion picture projector. And, apparently, his basic concepts were so sound, that some of them are still found in the modern projector. Jenkins showed his first motion picture in Richmond, Indiana, June, 1894.

About the same time, the following dispatch of significance appeared in both the San Francisco Chronicle and the San Francisco Examiner, on Edison's early motion-picture camera and his projector, the Kinetoscope:

THOMAS EDISON AND FIRST MOVING PICTURE
New York, June 15, 1894
A prize-fight in the interest of science is a rather unique

event, but that is what took place in the laboratory of Thomas Edison, the inventor, near Orange, New Jersey early yesterday morning. The mill was between Mike Leonard and Jack Cushing, both of Brooklyn; and Mr. Edison and party of six wealthy gentlemen, all intimate friends of the inventor, were the spectators. Six rounds were fought and then Leonard put his man out with a clever right-hand punch.

. . . . The fighters weighed in at 130 pounds when they entered a twelve-foot ring which had been pitched within the focus of Mr. Edison's last invention, the Kineto-phonograph which was to catch and preserve every move-ment of the pugilists for the purpose of reproducing them later on.

Before the mill it was explained to the men that the rounds would last but two minutes and there would be a 3 minute interval between each round. This was to give the operators a chance to work the machine to good advantage. Mr. Edison expressed himself as thoroughly satisfied with the negatives obtained during the fight.

The kineto-phonograph is arranged to take 46 pictures a second and it had never before been capable of acting continuously for more than 20 seconds. . . . It was learned that 100 new instruments are about ready for sale. At present there are only 25 in the world; ten in this city, ten in Chicago, and five in San Francisco. These kinetoscopes were set up by Messrs. Holland Bros., who are managing the exhibition at 644 Market Street and come with the following endorsation from the great inventor himself.

'Orange, N.J. May 1, 1894 (to)
Holland Bros., Ottawa, Canada
I am pleased to hear that the first public exhibition of my Kinetoscope has been a success under your management, and hope your firm will continue to be associated with its further exploitation.

Yours,
Thomas A. Edison'

Predictably, competition in the evolution of the moving picture projector was not only international but intranational, as well. Mr. Edison and his laboratory worked assiduously not only to perfect his Kinetoscope (a cabinet with an eye piece or "peep-hole," limited to one viewer at a time), but to eliminate the competition in America. In time, he was to use the talents of other inventors like Thomas Arnat who had been associated with Jenkins in the development of his projector, and Woodville Latham who invented the so-called "Latham Loop."

By 1896, Edison had bought the rights to the Latham Loop and the Arnat-Jenkins gearshift mechanism, which he combined in the projector he called the Vitascope. With it he showed a motion picture at the Koster and Bial's Music Hall in New York City in April 23 of that year. This was the first time a moving picture was shown in any theater in America.

Meanwhile, in France, the Laumiere brothers, on March 22, 1895, showed a newsreel film of employees of their Lyon factory in their lunch period. By June 1896, using the projector they had invented, called the Biograph, they showed French pictures in New York. In October 1896, their Biograph Company presented a film in Hammerstein's Olympia Music Hall showing William McKinley, the candidate for president of the United States, on a rocking chair on the front porch of his home in Canton, Ohio.

Yet another projector, the Vitagraph, was developed by J. Stuart Blackton and Albert E. Smith.

It was inevitable that these competing companies would become involved in a patent war and that Edison would finally win it. Mistrust seemed to be the keynote of the game, and conspiracies and piracies were their "modus operandi." Cameras and projectors were kept under lock and key. It was not uncommon for theaters to buy a popular film at regular prices, then have what came to be known as "pirated copies" made. These, they would sell for less than the original price. Another practice, was to rent a movie, pay the price of showing it at one theater; then hire someone to rush over with it to another theater or more, nearby. It could be lucrative.

Although the Kinetoscope had been demonstrated in San Francisco in 1894, it was in 1895 that our "Pop Furst" of the Cineograph Parlors saw an advertisement in a New York paper that aroused his curiosity. From the Oakland Tribune's "Knave" column of June 18, 1944, comes the following:

> *There has been a good deal of material printed this year in connection with the 50th anniversary of the motion picture as an entertainment agency, but somehow the name of Adolphus ("Pop") Furst hasn't entered the lists, so far as I have seen, yet it was he who gave that city its first cinema. It was in 1895 that Furst picked up a copy of the New York Clipper and saw an advertisement by Lubin, who was then taking pictures in Paris. Furst became interested, sent for a machine and one picture, for which he paid $250. At that time films were not rented, but purchased outright. The picture he received was a fake of the Fitzsimmons-Corbett fight (staged in Carson City, Nevada). The Orpheum had ordered the film, but there was only one original, and the pseudo fight picture arrived earlier. Unaware that he was duping the public, Furst opened the first moving-picture theater in a shack at 1747 Market Street (actually, 747 Market Street). He ran the film for three weeks, and averaged $100 a day. He followed it with a picture of a Spanish bull fight that stayed on for nine months. The films averaged 50 to 60 feet in length. Three years after he got underway, Furst hired Sid Grauman as a ticket taker. Not long after that, Grauman opened his own theater, the Unique on Market Street (actually, it was his father, Dennis J. Grauman, who opened the Unique; Sid was only in his teens). Furst's theater was called the Cineograph and he used a foreign-made projection machine because Edison had not yet perfected his projector. Furst's biggest day of record was Admission Day in 1900, when he ran 92 shows.*

The article raises a point bearing on chronological sequence. Pop Furst may have read the advertisement by Lubin in 1895, but it was two years later that he opened the Cineograph Parlors. City directories of San Francisco bear this out (listing him as an auctioneer, prior to 1897), as does the date of the Fitzsimmons-Corbett fight, March 17, 1897.

Another statement open to clarification comes in the article's penultimate sentence, indicating that Pop Furst used a foreign-made projector because Edison had not yet perfected his projector. As noted earlier, Edison and his French competitors were in a neck-and-neck race in the field of research and development of the projector. Both had shown their films in theaters in New York in 1896, Edison using his Vitascope and the Laumiere brothers, their Biograph. The strong possibility remains that the film mentioned in the article was a Pathe film, the only ones I recall ever being shown at the Cineograph. I'm inclined to conclude that Pop Furst's use of the foreign projector was by chance. Our American projectors and films were at least as good.

But I am delighted that the Knave corroborates my contention, "I shall maintain with my last breath that the Cineograph Parlors was the first moving picture theater in San Francisco." And, according to Pop Furst, it was also the first 10¢ vaudeville house in the west.

It would be about three years later, circa 1900−1901, that Dennis J. Grauman opened his Unique Theater at 1132 Market Street. It, too, showed movies and vaudeville.

Mr. Grauman had a son named Sid, a tall, skinny boy with bushy disheveled hair. Like most boys in their early teens, Sid was more comfortable in his unkempt appearance and "street-urchin" demeanor. I wonder why I particulary remember those black, ribbed stockings he wore below his knickers!

Perhaps the reason I remember Sid so well is that I got a strong and well-deserved reprimand from the mama on his account. She was very selective about my playmates, and rarely permitted me the joy of playing with children, for fear I might come under bad influences or soil my immaculate clothes. Somehow, Sid coaxed me to get on the back of a dray, a low-slung horse-drawn truck of those days. When the mama came upon our escapade, she was furious. Not only was this an un-ladylike caper, it dirtied a beautiful white dress; and it resulted in my receiving an unforgettable rebuke. Needless to say, that was the first and last time I fell victim to Sid's exhortations. And I shall never forget how he led me into that predicament.

This was the same Sid Grauman who later went to Los Angeles and established the famous "Grauman's Chinese Theater," where the prints of so many movie celebrities are imbedded in cement, for posterity. Sid became a well-known and well-touted man in the movie world. For some reason, he always maintained that his father had opened the first moving picture theater in San Francisco. I trust I have laid that contention to rest, once and for all.

As the relentless progression of my status from amateur to professional unfolded, with appearances at the Chutes, Olympia, and Cineograph, the Nineteenth Century drew to a close. The new century would end, for me, the tyro stage and open the door to "my first love." There would, however, be two other noteworthy appearances before this truly fulfilling adventure took place—the first, at Glen Park, San Francisco on April 29, 1900.

Situated at Chenery and Diamond Streets, just southeast of Diamond Heights, Glen Park had opened on October 16, 1898. Promotionals for the grand opening appeared in the news media of San Francisco. Terms like "Sensation of the Century" were accorded Professor J. Williams, the "World Renowned High Wire Athlete"; and the question was, "Can he do it?" The great "professor" would attempt "the hazardous and unprecedented feat of walking a wire cable 1000 ft. in length across Glen Park Canyon, 300 ft. above the ground, for a wager of $500." Other attractions would include: "A Grand Balloon Ascension and Parachute Descent (very big in those days); a concert by the Fourth Cavalry Band, 20 pieces, mounted; Morro Castle, Full of Interesting Animals; and a free Childrens Playground with plenty of Swings and Seesaws." Admission would be 10¢, with "no further charge" and soldiers in uniform, free.

Centrally located in Glen Park, their open-air theater had a covered stage, and the audience sat on benches and chairs, al fresco. The Glen Park Theater's format resembled the Chutes's, with animals, vaudeville, concerts, and "spectaculars."

When I was engaged to play at the Glen Park Theater, an event of special interest to San Franciscans was soon to take place. For weeks, notices appeared in the local publications, reading in part, "Grand Opening Sunday April 29 — Tunnel Day — Mammoth Show At The Theater — Continuous Vaudeville." The Federation of Mission Improvement Clubs was to hold a celebration at Glen Park to commemorate the opening of the Bosworth Street Tunnel that had been built by the city at the then stupendous cost of $30,000. It was also to mark the inaugural run of the new Bosworth Street Electric Line, and so the improvement clubs went all out to make the dual event a memorable one for residents of that part of San Francisco.

Accounts following the event were effusive about how "fireworks and bombs exploded to give notice to those in the park" of the approaching car with its coterie of dignitaries — one hundred prominent delegates, led by Mayor Phelan. The car's first run through the tunnel was a joyful one, marked by the noisy merriment of its occupants. When they reached the west terminus at Sunny Side Drive and Glen Park, the merrymakers were joined by "several hundred others and including many ladies," and the impromptu parade marched to the cafe for the banquet. A.S. Lillie, the president of the Federation of Mission Improvement Clubs, presided. There were the usual speeches by the luminaries, and music to make them more bearable. Mr. Lillie noted that, "The Bosworth Street Tunnel will shorten the trip for the people who travel to and from Ocean View and San Mateo."

Following the banquet, the crowd repaired to the park's outdoor theater where manager C.F. Kapp had arranged for the mammoth vaudeville show, details of which are recorded in a little green program I prize among my collection. The long two-part program started with two familiar faces with whom I had played before: Dutch Walton, the "Inimitable Musical Comedian," and Snowie Maybelle, the "Up-to-Date Singer."

After Snowie's renditions, there followed an intermission during which Professor C. Romaine made his "Most Sensational Slide-For-Life, on a Bicycle," from the dome of the theater to the ground, a distance of two hundred feet. Because he accomplished this feat on a wire, the mama would not let me watch the great Professor Romaine's act. She was always fearful of a mishap that might prove traumatic to this young six-year-old.

After his performance, there followed two more acts, the Oura's Royal Japanese Troupe of equilibrists, acrobats, jugglers and gymnasts, and a "Comedy Sketch Team" with their "Comedy Spanish Dance."

Again, Professor Romaine made his "Awe-inspiring and Hazardous Slide for Life," and so ended Part I.

To herald the start of Part II, the audience was alerted to listen for a bugle call and a shot from the famous "Baby Dewey Cannon." When it came, there was no escape or excuse; and Part II was off and running with another overture, followed by Mae Tunison "Queen of Song" and Baby Dody, "Wonderful Child Artist." My song and dance over, there came the great attraction, the Grand Balloon Ascension and Parachute Drop by Professor C. Vosmer. Here again, the mama's protectiveness prevailed. The "professor" may have inspired all the awe of our modern astronauts, but the mama set the rules. I was allowed to watch his ascent, but could never get too close to the smoking fire that created the hot air that started the balloon's ascension. His parachute drop, I do not recall, so I can safely deduce that the mama ruled that wild adventure verboten.

Anything that came after Professor Vosmer's act could only be anticlimactic, but Part II was not to end with its finale until the Oura Troupe had repeated its act and Moulton and Moll the "Triple Horizontal Bar Experts," theirs.

It had been a memorable day at Glen Park, this celebration to honor the opening of the Bosworth Tunnel and its electric train, but Glen Park like its counterpart, the Chutes, was known for its spectaculars. Tunnel Day was drawing to a close, but already the fanfare was sounded for a Monster Vaudeville Show to be given the following Sunday. This one added: Hali Adali, the Terrible Turk vs. A.G. Olsen, the Ferocious Swede in a "catch-as-can wrestling match, for the purse of one thousand dollars, on the open-air slope in the center of the park." At the conclusion of this match, the winner would give "one dollar a minute to any three men, respectively, coming before him in a wrestling bout." Needless to say, it conjured a formidable picture, and this was not the type of bill the mama and I would watch.

The last engagement before embarking on "my first love," would be the result of a telegram I received, dated June 2, 1900. It came from Sacramento, California and read as follows:

B. Scholtz
Room 67 St. Ann's Bldg. 6 Eddy St. S.F.
Will engage baby dody see letter
Geo. W. Lowe

Mr. Lowe engaged me to play Little Eva in a roadshow version of UNCLE TOM'S CABIN. My first attempt at drama had been in "after-piece" presentations at the old Olympia. This was followed by others, including a straight version of the garden scene from UNCLE TOM'S CABIN, at the Cineograph Parlors. This engagement with the George W. Lowe Roadshow, however, was to be my first one playing a lead in a full, legitimate play.

Although I was not really a sad child, I was a serious child, dedicated to my art. Since, physically, I was tiny and inclined to be pale, I was a "natural" to portray Little Eva who was dying through almost the entire part.

After weeks of rehearsal, we were on the road, playing small towns around the San Francisco Bay Area, then east to California's "Gold Country," and a return by way of Tracy, California. It was in the theater of the little town of Crockett, on the Straits of Carquinez, that I was startled when I came upon the loveliest marionettes I have ever seen. They were stored under the stage, in the basement of the theater. Each was beautifully carved of wood and painted in bright colors. Some of them, in gorgeous medieval costumes, were on horseback.

George W. Lowe, c. 1900
Credit: Barrett-Miller Collection

The marionettes had rods running perpendicularly through their centers. When in use, the rods extended into the flies, where they were skillfully manipulatd by the artists. Because the exquisite figures were as big as I, I was awestruck whenever I found myself next to them. Looking back on that unforgettable encounter, I have often wished I could find them again. The marionettes were of European origin, meticulously carved, and, for all I know, may have come "around the Horn."

The small-town theaters in which we playcd on the George W. Lowe tour were not always very elegant, nor up to date. We were barnstormers, working on inadequate stages with, sometimes, outmoded equipment. Some of the theaters still had sconces around the candles used for footlights. Others, had replaced the candles with gas lights. The latter were, in turn, to be replaced, later, with the electric lights. But we "made do" with what each little theater had to offer.

Remembrances of the George W. Lowe Roadshow include Bob Lee, the juggler and circus acrobat with whom I had played at the Cineograph Parlors and who still had visions of me as a bareback rider in his circus. Though the mama liked this very personable man, she continued to disabuse him of the notion that I would ever join him.

Another member of the cast, was a very stout man who had the improbable name, Pearl Allen. I have often wondered that a man could be called "Pearl," but that was his name; and that was the crux of a very confusing problem for me. In the death scene of Little Eva's, there is a line in which she says, "I see the beautiful gates ajar and behind them it is all mother-of-pearl." I did not want to say that line, just as I had always resisted "Little Tommy Tittlemouse lived in a little house and caught fishes in another man's ditches." Since "fishes" and "ditches" don't rhyme, I always rendered the line in my own fashion, "He caught fishes in another man's dishes." Everyone thought I lisped and hence, "dishes" instead of "ditches." So it was with saying, "I see the beautiful gates ajar and behind them it is all mother-of-pearl." In childish misinterpretation, I obstinately said, "Behind them is the mother of Pearl," or, "Behind them is Pearl's mother." Since I was usually quite cooperative, the elders could not understand why I was so stubborn on this point. It took much querying on their part, but they finally extracted my reasoning. They explained to me what mother-of-pearl was. And that, thank goodness, solved the puzzlement that plagued me, namely: "What was Pearl's mother doing up there in the clouds, anyway!"

Hotel accommodations for the roadshow were woefully inadequate in the Gold Country towns. They were, for the most part, a far cry from the relative comforts of the San Francisco of that era. Typical room appointments in these primitive little hotels included an all-purpose cabinet covered with an oil-cloth runner on which stood the matching porcelain washbowl and pitcher, the soapdish, and vase-shaped holder for the toothbrush. Below, were two or three drawers; and on the side of the cabinet, hung the towels and face cloth. At the back of this washstand, rose an ingenious appurtenance called the "splasher." It was usually a white muslin cloth, hemmed top and bottom, and threaded on two horizontal rods attached at each end to the curved arms of the cabinet. The "splasher," of course, was intended to protect the wallpaper from splashes, in those days before laminated plastic became a household convenience. In more creative hotels, the splasher was embroidered in bright "turkey-red." Designs like reeds, cattails, storks, cranes and other waterfowl, were used to carry out the aquatic theme.

Next to the washstand, on the floor, stood the matching porcelain "slop-jar," a container into which one poured the waste water from the washbowl. And, of course, there was the ubiquitous receptacle under the bed. The hotel receptacle, however, was not adorned with the "husher," a crocheted cover that fitted over the lid. This genteel piece of handiwork, intended to silence the lid's rattle, was found in homes, but rarely in any but the most elegant of hotels.

The wooden bed could have either a straw, a horsehair, or a feather mattress. I found the latter an abomination into which I sank almost to the point of suffocation. The mama always made a nightly ritual of inspecting the bed to be sure the sheets were fresh, and that no uninvited "guests" were sequestered therein.

Dining in these hotels, more often than not, proved to be an unhappy struggle to, somehow, "get it over with." To better appreciate my dismay, let it be known that my tastes in food were rather sophisticated. The devoted papa had always catered to the delicate mama's whims by bringing her "goodies" like fresh shrimp, mussels, clams, cracked crab, and oysters on the half shell. To accompany the coquillage, there would be a pièce de résistance, the "water biscuit," a round, puffy and airy delicacy. Another special treat the mama and I relished was the oyster loaf. It was a loaf of French bread, well buttered and filled with oysters in a well-seasoned binding sauce. We sliced the loaf at an angle. It was a meal in itself, served with a salad and a drink. The mama and papa enjoyed beer with it, while I was served milk.

Since the mama was no cook, we ate out most of the time. I had developed a palate for the French cuisine served at restaurants like Delmonico's, Techau Tavern, the Poodle Dog, and the dining rooms of our fancy hotels. I was accustomed to full course dinners that included soup, salad, appetizers and choice of entrees. Desserts included a wide range of choices: from cakes and pies, to French pastries and mouth-watering mousses and frappes.

One always "dressed" for dinner at the more elegant dining rooms. Some of these temples of haute cuisine did not serve children there. Instead, the "young fry" were served at the "second table," in a separate room where they were supervised by the help. The mama never subjected me to this indignity. She simply would not patronize a restaurant where I could not eat with the adults.

When it came to table manners, the mama exercised the strictest discipline; and as a result, I learned table etiquette at a very tender age. It never occurred to me to disgrace her by being anything but circumspect at the table. I can never forget the occasion when dining out one evening, the mama slapped me across the mouth. I was bewildered and mortified; I did not know why she had done it, much less what I had done to merit it. But her training had been so thorough that even though she had created a "scene," I did not react in kind. It was not until a week later, when we were alone, that I summoned the courage to ask her what I had done. She explained I had put my tongue out to receive the spoon.

In contrast to what I was accustomed in San Francisco, what I found in the small hotels in the Gold Country was dismaying, indeed. Typical desserts included nauseants, for me, like rice pudding or tapioca pudding bulging with its "fish-eyes" or, worst of all, bread pudding. But before I reached this final encounter, I had had a go-round with unseasoned stew, or bland casserole whose contents were forever intended to remain a mystery, or roasts that surely "came around the Horn"; and I had gagged on the greatest bane of all, for me, "squashed squashes." The mama finally took pity on me and excused me from the torment of the "squashed squashes." With family-style serving the mode there, all manner of food unpleasantries passed my way; and etiquette and training decreed I must eat what was placed before me. I was always relieved that etiquette also demanded that I leave something on my plate.

With these taxing encounters in the dining room over, we would repair to the porch, common to most country hotels then, where we sought respite from the heat inside. It was quite pleasurable—except for mosquito bites—sitting on the porch chairs and watching the people stroll by on the wooden side-walks. The high porch roof usually rested on pillars beyond the outer edge of the wooden sidewalk and afforded an inviting shady stop-point for strollers. On the porch of one of these hotels where we stayed, a monkey was kept fastened on a chain. He was an attraction for guests and passersby, alike. I was fascinated by him, but the mama would not allow me to touch him, for fear he might bite me.

During this roadshow of Mr. Lowe's, we played in still familiar Mother Lode towns such as Jamestown, Sonora, Angels Camp, Mokelumne Hill, Jackson, and Placerville which once bore the telling name of "Hangtown." This fabulous area of California, just a half century earlier, had really hummed to the tunes of gold and silver mining.

Nevertheless, it was my pleasure to observe two types of gold mining still extant. There was the placer miner with his "cradle," a box with two uprights at one end for handles. The miner was working on a stream, and from behind large rocks or boulders where he was most apt to find worthwhile deposits, he scooped the stream gravel into his cradle, tilted at the most advantageous angle possible. Across the bottom of the carpeted cradle, were cleats, narrow strips of wood about four inches apart. The stream's current washed over the gravel as the miner rocked the cradle by its handles. This rocking motion washed away the lighter, unwanted materials and sifted the gold dust onto the rug where it clung to the pile, while the heavier nuggets of gold were caught by the riffles. This method was only a degree more sophisticated than panning from an ordinary pan.

Perhaps a step more advanced, was the stamp mill I saw in operation. In a tall wooden shed on the side of the hill, were housed the stamps used in the mining process. The ore came down the hill in six chutes or sluices, to within the confines of the shed. For each chute, there was an enormous metal-capped tree trunk that served as the stamp. The six stamps stood on end and were activated by a camshaft rotated by a "donkey engine." As one huge trunk rose, another came down, crushing the ore with such a force that everything around shook as if an earthquake had dislodged the surrounding hills. As the ore was crushed, a flow of water in each chute carried it on down. On each of the sluices, below the point of impact, a box built around it was padlocked and entrusted to one man, whose job it was to unlock this "holder" at the appropriate time. I recall watching such a privileged occasion, as he opened the "sanctum sanctorum." Inside, was a disk coated with quicksilver; and as the worker scraped it, he informed us he was scraping off the quicksilver that had caught the gold. He then placed the scrapings from the box in a chamois bag. He showed me how by deftly squeezing the bag, the quicksilver would come through the pores of the chamois skin and leave the gold in the bag. This sluice-box method of mining gold was one of the first mechanical methods used. But, apparently, some gold escaped the traps; for, much later, it became a worthwhile business just to work these tailings or castoffs from the stamp mills.

Modes of travel with the George W. Lowe Roadshow were exciting for me. The adults, however, did not always share my childish enthusiasm. There were places where the only means of transportation was the stage coach, drawn by four horses. These coaches were not the ones we associate with western films, cradle-shaped and with the two seats facing each other. The type we rode had several rows of seats across, and accommodated nine to twelve passengers, compared to the western coach's four.

Roads were very bad. They were unpaved, gulley-ridden, dusty, and rough; and they seemed to have been purposely charted through the worst hill terrain available. It was small wonder then that the adults in our company complained of backaches when they traveled in these coaches, and that they dreaded the trips. But I was still that youth of Wordsworth's ode, "who daily farther from east/ Must travel, still is Nature's priest/ And by the vision splendid/ Is on his way attended." From my vantage point as a child, it was a wild, wonderful adventure everytime I rode the stages and watched the magnificent animals in a breathtaking rhythm of force and speed. Could not the adults see what I saw and feel what I felt! Alas, for them all had faded "into the light of common day."

Less spectacular than the coach but, none the less, one I adored, was the caboose at the end of a freight train. This was the form of transportation we used whenever regular passenger train service was unavailable or inconvenient to our schedule. The caboose was rather bare, but very cozy and comfortable, with wooden seats along the sides, below the windows. On the left rear corner, two steep steps led up to a lookout where a railman could sit to observe the progress of the cars. The crewmen were very friendly, so I enjoyed every one of them very much. As a child, I had a peculiar trait of not seeing people I did not like, but the friendly freight crewmen did not come under that designation.

Indeed, an incident during one of the caboose rides is a fitting tribute to these crewmen who extended their very best in behalf of my welfare and happiness. The mama, always so particular about how I looked, kept me dressed in the fastidiously cleaned and starched white dresses, even when riding the caboose. Her constant admonitions of "don't get your dress dirty" were her hue and cry. I must not get my clothes soiled, and I must be a little lady, under all circumstances—these were the first two commandments of my childhood. This was not always easy for a young child, especially one riding in a caboose with a pot-bellied stove in the middle. It followed that the mama's fastidiousness would apply even to the toys with which I played. They had to have a certain degree of respectability. Alas, my dear, darling, old and dilapidated doll, Binna, did not measure up to my mother's standards. Binna was truly disgraceful, and the mama could no longer abide her, so she cajoled, "Dody, dear, you don't want to be seen with that old doll, now, do you?" And she, somehow, maneuvered my parting with dear old Binna. Having talked me out of my precious old doll, the mama, much relieved, placed it in the pot-bellied stove in the caboose. Happily, the weather was quite hot and there was no need for a fire in the stove.

With mixed emotions on my part, we proceeded to our stop in Tracy, California, the so-called "Division Point," where the change of crews took place. We detrained and went to our hotel for much needed baths and changes, after the long, hot trip. Later, feeling fresh and revived, we descended the stairs and started our way to the dining room for dinner. As we passed through the lobby, a man approached us, tipped his hat to the mama, and presented me with my old friend, Binna.

"Here, " he beamed, "the little girl must have been playing with her doll and put it in the stove." "I knew she would miss it," he added, solicitously. I grinned like a Cheshire Cat as I accepted the doll. The mama, with all the graciousness of a queen, told him it was so kind of him and, "Thank you, very much." Actually, I know she could have choked him. And I, I marched triumphantly into the dining room of Tracy's best hotel, with my ragged, disgraceful Binna safely cradled in my arms, and the dignified but mortified mama gritting her teeth.

Disarmed by the turn of events that brought the pitiful Binna back to me, the mama capitulated. Binna was to see me through the remainder of the tour of the George W. Lowe Roadshow and return to her honored niche in my room at home, in San Francisco.

Chapter Three
Aerie Of The St. Ann's

During my most active, creative, and fruitful years as "Baby Dody," I lived at the St. Ann's Building, at the corner of Eddy and Powell Streets, San Francisco. Centrally located as it was, in the greater theatre community of the city, it was to be our home from early 1899 to 1903. My parents had selected the St. Ann's to better accommodate to the mama's physical problem. She was a small, delicate woman who was ill most of the time with symptoms that had been diagnosed as rheumatism. The mama's illness proved to be a small tumor in the base of the brain. This condition caused her much discomfort, with sensations of pain at the nerve endings of the legs and feet. Since she always accompanied me wherever I went, it was imperative we reside within a short walking distance of the theaters.

Built in 1878 and part of the E.W. Hopkins Estate, the St. Ann's Building served some of the commercial and housing needs of its immediate environs. It was situated on the present site of the Bank of America Branch where Eddy, one of the many so-called "gore" streets, meets Powell. Totally destroyed in the great fire of 1906, the St. Ann's was truly a fire trap, but that thought never occurred to us while we lived there. My personal recollections of this venerable old building, confirmed by recent acquisitions of photographs, are happy ones.

Architecturally, it was a six-storied wooden building with numerous tall narrow windows, and with turrets and cupolas atop its furbelowed roof. The main turret rested squarely at the angle of Eddy and Powell, and its dome was topped by a weather vane that dominated the shorter buildings adjoining it, the Columbia Theatre on the Powell Street side, and the Tivoli Cigar Store on Eddy. Between the roof's two cupolas on Eddy Street, was a smaller structure that resembled a Doric temple. From the latter, a flagpole rose prominently, an arrangement duplicated on the Powell Street side.

St. Ann's Building 1878-1906, Architect David Farquharson
Credit: California Historical Society, San Francisco

At the canopied entrance of the St Ann's building, on Eddy and Powell, a few curved, marble steps with brass hand-rails, led up to the large Michaels and Crosby Tailor Shop. The shop catered to the more affluent customers who could choose their material and have their suits made to order. Incidentally, those were the days of the baggy pants, when fashion did not decree the knife-edged trouser pleat. This tailor shop had once housed the California Savings Bank, and had inherited its large plate glass windows.

Near this front entrance, on both Eddy and Powell Streets, were stairs leading down a half floor to the Louvre Restaurant. From the sidewalks, the passerby could look down through the transom windows and see the restaurant's lovely appointments—round pedestal tables with white tablecloths, ice-cream-parlor type chairs, and potted palms on black and white marble floors. The Louvre proudly advertised itself as the, "Leading Restaurant and Family Resort Exellent Cuisine Imported Wines and Beers   Prompt Service." It held evening concerts by an Hungarian orchestra, and was a fitting place for after-theater parties. But I best remember that light refreshments, such as sandwiches and beer, were served to its patrons. It was considered genteel enough for ladies—no saloon, this.

Originally, the Louvre was called "St. Ann's Restaurant" when it opened August 12, 1879, with Smith and Butler, Proprietors, H. Gates, Manager, and W. Stuckenholz, Musical Director. At its grand opening it offered Eichberg's comic opera DOCTOR OF ALCANTARA, an "Opera Bouffe at Popular Prices," and proclaimed itself, "The Most Elegantly Appointed Family Resort In The City." When I lived at the St. Ann's, however, the Louvre had long since discontinued presenting opera.

At the northwest end of the St. Ann's, on Eddy Street, was a billiard parlor operated by Jesse E. Marks. A wide stairway led to its upper floor, another one, to its lower level. I had no occasion to recall much of that end of the building, for we always used the main entrance to the upper floors of the St. Ann's, located at the center, Number 6, Eddy Street. The entrance's marble steps led up to a short entry hall, where the rickety old Otis elevator waited for its innocent prey. But, it was the first elevator I had ever seen, and it was not without its charm.

The next three floors of the St. Ann's were occupied by all manner of businesses, so we simply by-passed them on our way to the sixth floor, apartment 67, where we resided. The sixth, or top floor, consisted of a hodgepodge of what today we would call "apartments."

One of these, larger than the rest, was occupied by a dress-maker, Miss May Campbell, who employed many poor, weak, sickly-looking girls. It saddened me to see these pathetic young women, victims of their physical disabilities. Together, however, they created and literally built gorgeous dresses. With small waists de rigueur, a dress had to be meticulously form fitted. Most dresses were made of silks, stiffened with whalebone featherstitched into French seams, and, of course, painstakingly decorated with passementeries. These creations from Miss Campbell's establishment were designed and destined for society matrons, actresses, and "others."

Like St. Ann's, the Baldwin-Hotel-Theater Building, across the street, was another of the many firetraps that seemed the rule rather than the exception in pre-1906 San Francisco. It had been dubbed, "Lucky Baldwin's firetrap." Baldwin himself is said to have turned the first shovelful of dirt in 1873, but actual construction began February, 1875.

Baldwin's partner, Thomas Maguire, had bought part of the site fourteen years earlier, and the remainder of the property on a twenty-year lease, at $1200 a month. He was very much a part, if not always a recognized partner, of this business venture. Maguire was the showman, with years of business experience to his credit in both theater production and management. Some referred to him as the "Napoleon of the San Francisco stage," when in 1875 he "proudly surveyed the rising of a fine new San Francisco theater," The Baldwin's Academy of Music. Earliest programs list him as proprietor, Al Hayman as manager, and J.A. Herne, stage manager.

When the Baldwin Hotel-Theater Building was completed in March of 1876, it was the epitome of elegance in every detail.

Baldwin Hotel-Theatre Building 1876-1898
Credit: California Historical Society, San Francisco

Through the hotel's enormous and magnificent rotunda lobby, with handsome carved pillars and huge chandeliers, passed the renowned in nobility, politics, and sports, as well as the greats of the entertainment world. The Baldwin Hotel had over five hundred rooms, and could accommodate six hundred guests, in first-class style. From its souvenir booklet, published circa 1876, we learn:

> *In connection with every suite of rooms are bath-rooms and closets. Every room is in direct connection with a perfect system of electric signal service to call house servants or messengers. There is a large core of carefully trained servants, waiters, and stewards. The rooms are elegantly furnished. There is not a dark room in the house. There are three complete elevators in the building, all of the latest French design and noted for their ease, safety and speed.*

Assurance that, "There is not a dark room in the house," was likely prompted by the fact that some hotels and rooming houses of that era had what were termed "inside rooms." The windows of these, opened only into the hallway. As a result, such rooms were dank because of poor ventilation, and the air, fetid, to say the least. The mama, I know, always insisted on an outside room wherever we traveled.

The Baldwin's exterior was an imposing architectural gem of French Renaissance design, with countless windows "so designed as to carry up each window projection a completeness in itself." It was the city's most up-to-date creation in hotels. It was bounded by Market, Eddy, Powell, and Ellis Streets; and its famous Baldwin's Academy of Music was sandwiched within its confines, between the Baldwin Hotel on the west and the Baldwin Annex on the eastern end of its Market Street side. On its mansard roof, was an enormous dome 168 feet from the pavement, at Market and Powell; and several smaller ones rimmed its perimeters. The Baldwin Hotel-Theater Building covered an impressive address, ranging from 946 to 932 Market Street. The Academy of Music's canopied entrance was at 934 Market, and the theater itself ran through to Ellis Street, where its stage entrance opened. Within the hotel building, were various business establishments that opened either on Market, Powell or Ellis Streets. Entrances to the hotel proper were also found on each front, with the main one on Powell Street.

When the building opened in 1876, attention was mainly focused on its Baldwin's Academy of Music. A gala preview was held on Friday, March 3, and on Monday, March 6, the dedicatory program offered the Maguire Dramatic Company's presentation of RICHARD III, with Barry Sullivan in the title role,

Mr. Cathcart as Earl of Richmond, and Mr. Lewis James, the Duke of Buckingham.

Reflecting Thomas Maguire's tastes, ornateness was the keynote of this famous theater, according to all accounts and descriptions of its interior. From its entrance, paved in bright patterned tiles, one approached a foyer with Italian furnishings, Italian marbles, lovely plate glass mirrors, and curtains of red velvet. Throughout the theater, rare California woods were used for the woodwork. Filigree, gilt scrollwork, and elaborate frescoes were surpassed only by the sparkling crystal chandeliers that were said to be valued at sixteen hundred dollars each. Included in this ambiance of opulence, was the six thousand dollar curtain made of crimson satin. Innovatively for the time, it parted in the middle to drape at the sides, instead of rolling up.

The theater's main staircase was of white marble and black walnut, and rose past elegant mirrors to where a chandelier hung from an arch of the frescoed ceiling.

Seating for the patrons ran the gamut of: mezzanine boxes in walnut and crimson; parterre, orchestra circle and dress circle, with opera chairs; and the family circle, with seats upholstered in red plush. Altogether, there were about eight hundred seats in the family circle and one thousand in the rest of the theater. There was no gallery.

One reviewer best summed up the elegance of the Baldwin Academy of Music when he waxed eloquent over the "sensuous satisfaction, the warmth, richness of design and grace of execution." The walls, he described as "painted to look as though hung with folds of figured tapestry." Dedicatory credits in the first week's programs, list the following prestigious names of the times:

G.G. Gariboldi . . . . Frescoing
V. Togetti . . . . Figures
Celebrated House of Potriel and Stymus . . . . . . Drop Curtain and Upholstery Decorations, under the supervision of Mr. Stymus
Chandeliers, Opera Chairs . . . . . . By Composite Iron Works, New York

<pre>
Alex Macabee . . . . Superintendent
Thomas Maguire. . . . . Proprietor
     (and Business Manager)
J.A. Herne . . . . Stage Manager
Al Hayman . . . . Manager
</pre>

This grandiloquent mansion to the muses of the theater, was managed by Thomas Maguire who just happened, as stated earlier, to also own the building site. This strange business relationship in which "Lucky Baldwin" owned the building, and Maguire the site, was to lead to acrimonious exchanges between the two. Maguire's young and diplomatic secretary, David Belasco, often acted as intermediary, but to little avail. Eventually, Mr. Baldwin gained sole ownership of both the site and the building.

By January 1877, Maguire's fortunes were beginning to tumble. Due in part to the business crash of that year, his two other theaters (Maguire's New Theatre and Maguire's Opera House, both on Bush Street) were temporarily closed, and he "was compelled to relinquish his hold on the Baldwin's Academy of Music." Mr. Baldwin replaced him with John McCullough as lessee and manager and Barton Hill, acting manager. McCullough, who came from his post as manager of the California Theater, shortened the name "Baldwin's Academy of Music" to "Baldwin's." Eventually, it was to be known as "The Baldwin Theatre," the name it retained until its end by fire, November 23, 1898.

McCullough's association with The Baldwin Theatre was short-lived. His first presentation, the Hess Opera Company on March 2, 1877, was not very successful. He followed this with himself as HAMLET, and when the next show, SHADOWS, turned a dismal failure, McCullough bowed out of the Baldwin Theatre.

Born John Edward McCullough in Coleraine, Ireland in 1837, he came to America in 1853. In 1857, he made his first American appearance in THE BELLE'S STRATAGEM at the Arch Street Theater in Philadelphia. Famous as a tragedian in plays like HAMLET, MACDUFF, RICHELIEU, SPARTACUS, and many others, his personality seemed to have absorbed somber and eccentric notes that were to affect his outlook on life and culminate in his insanity by 1884, and his death the following year.

I recall attending a dramatic recitation called THE RAVINGS OF JOHN McCULLOUGH, in the early 1900's. It was a very strong philosophical rendition , chock-full of Shakespearean quotations and allusions that best befitted this unusually iconoclastic man. Of course, the recitation was beyond my comprehension at that time in my young life.

After McCullough's departure, the Baldwin Theatre was closed until Maguire returned at the end of 1877 and opened it with the Union Square Company of New York. He presented numerous plays with both this famous New York company and another he formed soon after. It was a happy resurrection for the Baldwin Theatre, that was to flourish, once again, under Maguire's management until the mid-1880's when Maguire moved to New York. He died on January 20, 1896 and was spared the pain of seeing his beloved Academy of Music crumble to ashes, two years later.

When we moved into the St. Ann's in 1899, the Baldwin Hotel-Theater had met its fiery demise the previous year. The fire started in the hotel's basement kitchen on the Ellis Street side, at about 3:30 a.m., Wednesday, November 23, 1898 and, "soon shot up to its sixth floor. The narrow hallways and absence of ladders on its fire escapes, made escape difficult and resulted in the loss of five known lives. An explosion in the theater caused a cave-in that extinguished the building's lights." Several other explosions followed, and in spite of the valiant efforts of firemen manning thirty fire engines, the building was soon consumed.

Recriminations followed in the wake of the holocaust. Although advertised as, "The Leading Theatre, Absolutely Safe" (Program, March 29, 1897), many had foreseen the tragedy, not the least of whom was Mrs. Drew, the famous actress. On August 28, three months before the fire destroyed the Baldwin-Hotel-Theatre, she wrote concerning the Baldwin Theatre: "The collection under one roof of a theater and a hotel is cramping to the former and full of danger from fire to the latter."

Mrs. Drew reminded San Franciscans later that, "This was taken by some . . . as unnecessarily alarming. Within three months the theatre was burned down with considerable loss of life. This is just what might have been expected. It does not need expert testimony to show that a theatre-hotel construction violates every principle of common sense. No sleeping-rooms, tailor shop or such occupations should be permitted in a building used for a place of amusement." Her excoriation ended with, "Insurance companies should refuse to insure a theater-hotel at all."

In all fairness, however, it must be said that serious thought had been given, in its design and construction, to making the Baldwin Hotel-Theater Building safe and fireproof. The basement of the building was entirely of brick and iron. The Souvenir gives detailed accounts of the walls:

> *The outside walls with a thickness of 3 ft. 2 in., and footings 9 ft. wide; interior walls of the same thickness, with footings 7 ft. wide. All cross and partition walls and interior supports are of brick, laid in cement and 10 inch cast-iron heavy columns, no woodwork whatever being used in the basement. The first story is entirely of iron. Rear walls, cross-walls, and walls of all permanent divisions are of brick, laid in cement, and are 2 ft. 2 inches, 21 inches and 13 inches thick; from the first story, iron lintels course upwards.*

> *Every contrivance has been taken advantage of and contingency provided for to prevent, guard against and extinguish fire. In the fire-proof vaults and engine-rooms are located the fire pumps—four in number—independent of the house supply of pumps. Each story of the hotel has 7 fire plugs, with 150 ft. of hose, located in positions to command all parts of each story and stairway. On the outside of the building, 5 lines of galvanized wrought iron pipe extend from the lower level of the sidewalk up to and over the roof of the building, and these are supplied with fire plugs, and*

*on the level of each story and on the roof there are many
hundred feet of hose attached, coiled and ready for instant
use. By pipe connection with the pumps below, the whole
building, in case of fire, could be drenched in a moment.*

*The vast structure is supplied with the latest designed traps,
drain pipes, etc. known to sanitary science. Two artesian
wells, supplying 71,000 gallons daily, are in the basement.
These, with a reservoir of 60,000 gallons in the basement,
and tanks on the roof, holding 82,000 gallons, give an
immediate supply of 205,000 gallons of water.*

The accounts speak for themselves.

In theater announcements of the week of the fire, the
Baldwin Theatre advertised, "All This and Next Week, Special
Matinee Thanksgiving Mr. Charles Frohman Announces the
Prominent Success of the Period, SECRET SERVICE with William Gillette and a Great Cast. Extra: Sunday Night November
27 Joaquin Miller in Lecture Upon Experiences in the Klondike." Reserved seats went for 50¢, 75¢, and $1. But, with the
theater's destruction on the Wednesday, Joaquin Miller's engagement at the Baldwin was never to take place.

The day following the fire, the California Theater advertised: "NORTHERN LIGHTS   Extra, SECRET SERVICE
with William Gillette; Seats for Baldwin Can Be Exchanged."
Exchange courtesies between theaters, in moments of adversity,
were not unusual in those days.

During the ensuing months, it became apparent that Mr.
Elias Baldwin would have to put the site up for sale. The
Hibernia Bank held the mortgage of $1,600,000 on the proper-
ty, and Baldwin was liable for the yearly interest bill of some
$96,000 on it.

Almost a year after the fire, Mr. James Flood made an offer
of $1,600,500 for the whole site, exclusive of the adjoining
Baldwin Annex on Market Street. On November 10, 1899, the
news broke that Mr. Flood had bought for $1,100,000 a piece of
the Baldwin site with frontage of 186 feet on Market, 22 feet 8
inches on Eddy, and 175 feet on Powell. By December 5, city
papers carried the announcement of a second transaction, in

which Mr. James Flood had bought the full lot of the Baldwin Hotel-Theatre, bounded by 187 feet on Market Street, 275 feet on Powell, and 137 feet 6 inches on Ellis, for the sum of $1,425,000. Mr. Baldwin retained the Annex Building with 65 feet on Market Street, and running diagonally back to Ellis, with about 27 feet on that street.

Speculation in the San Francisco Examiner that Mr. Baldwin had lost some $437,800 by holding out too long, fit into the following calculations:

Highest offer made for lot $1,700,000
Interest $300 a day for 376 days $112,800
Presumptive Maximum Value $1,862,800
Sold to Mr. Flood for $1,425,000
Loss Borne by Mr. Elias J. Baldwin $437,800

With the completion of the transaction, Mr. James Flood announced that, "No theatre, no hotel will be built. My present idea is to put up a modern office building. The site and the building on it will belong to the Flood Estate." And, according to news reports, the "fine fireproof structure" would cost over a million dollars.

After we moved into the St. Ann's, the process of dismantling and tearing down the ruins of the Baldwin Hotel-Theatre began. From our apartment windows facing Powell, we looked directly across the street to the charred ruins below. A high board fence enclosed them for some time, as work went on intermittently. I watched the dismemberment of the Baldwin's skeleton, and then the excavation for the new building that was to be erected there. Steadfastly at the windows, I was mesmerized as they dug enormous cavities on which the foundations were laid. In wonderment, from my special "watchtower" on the sixth floor of the St. Ann's, I followed the horses as they pulled the wagons, loaded with a yellowish soil, up the ramps from the gaping holes to the street level.

At that time, in 1901, a Teamsters' strike was called, adding still another dimension to the drama I witnessed. As the wagons were filled with earth by the non-union men who then tried to drive the horses up the inclines, the union men standing at the sidewalk level, yelled down to the horses, "Whoa!" Of course, the horses would stop. Again, the non-union men urged the poor beasts on, only to be frustrated and thwarted by more, "whoas." This amusing performance went on all day and each day until the labor dispute was finally resolved.

My sympathy throughout this strange comic-drama was with the horses, as they alternately strained against their collars and then lapsed into an "at-ease" stance, after each "whoa." The labor problems that attended, were no concern of mine. It seemed like a silly bit of business, even after the papa had explained it to me.

In time, I saw the laying of the foundations. From them arose the steel skeleton that gradually reached my eye level. It was a framework of beams and cross-beams on which the men walked with the poise and skill of tightrope walkers. One man heated the rivets and then threw them, one at a time, to another worker who caught it in a can, while balancing himself on the cross-beam. The red-hot rivet was then inserted into place and the process repeated, over and over. How I loved to watch this skillful, rhythmic game.

Skeleton Flood Building—St. Ann's Towers, left. c. 1901
Credit: California Historical Society, San Francisco

As each step of construction continued, the building evolved, ever so miraculously, into one of the wonders of that day. It was the Flood Building, still in use today, standing defiantly at the corner of Market and Powell Streets, to attest to its invulnerability even through the Earthquake and Fire of 1906. At that time, it was gutted by the fire; but its framework withstood the earth's convulsions and, in time, the Flood Building demonstrated its Phoenix-like persistence as it rose from the ashes within. Today, it is one of San Francisco's historic landmarks, still handsome and very useful. I am pleased to have been a witness to its creation, and to have sequestered many precious memories of the event as it unfolded.

Of course, a very young child then, I was not privy to the full story of what had taken place on one of San Francisco's most famous sites—the personality clashes, the struggles for supremacy, and the business transactions. But, unknowingly, the Messrs. Baldwin, Maguire, and Flood had been the instruments of a play, to the conclusion of which I was to be one of its most privileged spectators. All the gripping components were there:

Flood Building—Post 1906
Credit: California Historical Society, San Francisco

Act I   The intrigue and competition between antagonists, oddly enough with but a single goal, the raising of an elegant edifice.

Act II   The birth of the temple to Melpomene and Thalia, nurtured under circumstances both propitious and, at times, less so.

Act III   The ravagement by flame of the lovely temple and the yielding of its site to a new fate.

I had missed all of the first two acts and part of the third, but the denouement of the compelling drama was played for me, alone. A child can shut out the rest of the world as he builds his dreamstuff, and I was unusually adept at this game. So, on my special "throne of plush and gold," I was the imperious queen. I waved my wand from my castle window at St. Ann's, and the final scene of Act III took place before my eyes. But, one of the three leads, Mr. Thomas Maguire, was missing. He had left at the end of Act II, yet I'm sure he was watching from his own special "celestial throne."

Before the Flood Building arose to obstruct it from view, I was able to look out on the very large and colorful General Arthur Cigar sign painted high on the west side of the seven-story Knoth-Behrend Building on Market Street. This picture of the general with the sideburns and short neck, oddly enough, had much significance in my childhood. In my eagerness to learn to read and write, I would sit at the window, with my pencils and papers, with which I was always amply supplied, and meticulously trace the letters of the cigar sign. Education for girls, in those days, was not considered necessary; but I was not satisfied with that opinion, for I wanted to learn to read and write. The General Arthur Cigar sign, then, was my first introduction to the letters.

By the papa, I was to be led into the world of arithmetic. During those periods between plays with child parts, time hung heavily for me. In the evenings, while my parents played cards, usually casino, I would come to the papa and ask him to write a column of numbers for me. He showed me how to add them; and I recall his forbearance as I came, time after time, in search of more mathematical columns to conquer. After this indoctrination, I was taught subtraction, and so whiled away many an otherwise dull evening away from my world of make-believe. I was to wait until I was twelve years old before I was introduced to the public school.

From Mr. and Mrs. Richard C. White, an elderly couple who lived on the same floor of the St. Ann's, I was to add to my learning experience. The Whites were lovely, kindly people who seemed like grandparents to me. They showed much interest in me and in my career. In fact, Mr. White, a playwright, wrote a play for me, called SPRAY. In it, I was a child cast upon a beach by the ocean waves; and whence I came, no one knew. It was supposed to be a very romantic and idyllic vehicle, but the play was never produced. My poor mama had even gone to the trouble of having a sea-green dress, trimmed with moss, made for me.

Dear Mrs. White, whose hair, appropriately enough, was very white, in contrast to very dark eyes, wore her glasses high on her pompadour most of the time, and a triangular shawl around her shoulders at all times. She volunteered to tutor me; and to that end, purchased a reader and embarked on her noble mission. Since their apartment was at the far end of the building, on the Eddy Street side, and ours was at the far end, on Powell, it was quite a trek as I skipped along the wide hallways to "school," with my books tucked under my arm. Poor Mrs. White was soon to become a rather frustrated teacher. Having decided on the page for my study, she opened the book and prompted me through the lesson; then she would say, "Now, read it again." With that, I would *close* the book and "read" it all back again. Mrs. White had not reckoned with Baby Dody's memory— that mischievous faculty of my childhood.

Leonore, the Whites's beautiful daughter, was an artists' model. I remember her pictures, in which she was beautifully draped with yards upon yards of overlapping layers of satin, wound round and round to delineate her voluptuous form. The encasing started under her arms to outline a large firm bust, a very small waist, large hips, and a tapering to ever so small delicate ankles. This mummy-like vision in brilliant shiny satin, to suggest the female form at its quintessence, was the epitome of fashion art for the model of those days. Miss White's pictures appeared in various art publications.

Among publications devoted, in varying degrees, to the theater of the West Coast, were Music and Drama, San Francisco Dramatic Revue, the San Francisco Mirror, The Wasp, Figaro, The Argonaut, and, of course, the newspapers. In time, the first two were to merge and become the San Francisco Dramatic Revue. The mama and I occasionally had reason to go to the office of Music and Drama, 40 Ellis Street, where Mr. Beers R. Loos was on its editorial staff. On those occasions, I enjoyed playing with his little daughter, Anita, while the mama attended to the business end of the visit.

These cherished times when I shared playtime with my peers, were infrequent. For the most part, while at the St. Ann's, I played alone. Many provisions for quiet pursuits were provided me—paper, paste, scissors, pencils, and crayons. With these I created all manner of paper dolls and their raiments. Among my treasured paper dolls, was a large one that Leonore White had made for me. She drew it on, and carefully cut it out of cardboard. I spent many happy moments both playing with, and making dresses for, this beautiful but nameless paper doll.

Judy, however, was my first real doll. She was made of rubber and, when new, sported a loud squeaky whistle incorporated in her torso. She received all the tender loving care a small child is capable of exercising. Eventually the years extracted their toll, reducing poor Judy to a whistle-less, faded rubber plaything.

Then there was Sally of the bisque head with painted hair, whose body was made of horsehair covered with cloth. Her cloth legs had red and white horizontal stripes to simulate stockings, and her feet were made of leather. Sally's hands were also of bisque. She had belonged to the foster-sister, Bertha. The paint on Sally's face was pretty well gone, for she had been washed too often. Though she had lost her glamour, Sally never lost her place of esteem among my prized possessions; for she was extra special.

Still another doll, was one given to me by a close friend of the mama's, Etta Whaley Dean. Etta, from a poor family, had married Peter Sager Dean, son of Elisha B. Dean, a very wealthy lumber baron. Peter had offices on Sansome Street and was president of the Merchants Exchange Bank of San Francisco and the Sierra Lumber Company. In her nouveau-riche status, Etta could spend money, with impunity; so, she gave me a spectacular doll that was as big as I. The doll wore clothes that fitted a four-year-old child. Etta had purchased them from San Francisco's leading fashion store. Thoroughly enjoying her new affluence, Etta went all out and bought a complete and elaborate wardrobe for the doll. I called the doll Daisy Dean, and I hated her. She was so big it was like struggling with a bear with rigor mortis every time I picked her up. I could not cuddle it. In fact, I felt more like setting her on a chair and sitting on *her* lap. The doll, therefore, was relegated to a position of lesser importance in my doll hierarchy, much to Etta's consternation. Etta soon took a violent dislike to me, for she thought I was a very ungrateful child. How little she understood a child and its basic needs. Could it be, Daisy Dean was pretentious beyond my comprehension?

The Peter Deans lived in one of San Francisco's better hotels, where we visited them occasionally. The beautiful Etta with the lovely red hair, displayed unusual hand mannerisms that fascinated me; so, being the mimic I was, I adopted and sported all of them for some time. I was also awed by her beautiful clothes. On one of our visits, miraculously, Etta appeared with a baby—her own—in her arms. I was allowed to hold the baby, but I wasn't too impressed with it, all the grown-ups' admiration, notwithstanding.

When months later Etta wanted to accompany her husband on a trip to New York, she asked the mama to take care of the baby for her. Little Peter was brought to our home at St. Ann's, accompanied with mounds of clothes and baby paraphernalia; but as far as I was concerned, the poor little thing might have been better off had be been left at the pound. One day the mama was diapering the baby when I observed, "Oh, look!" She replied, "Yes, little boys are different from little girls." Unconcerned by what might have turned into a dissertation on the "birds and bees" routine, I simply said, offhandedly, "Oh," and walked away. Actually, the only thought that went through my mind was that now I knew why the mama would not allow me to be a boy. When I played boy roles on the stage, I had always enjoyed such freedom of movement, dressed in trousers—no admonitions about keeping white starchy dresses clean, only blessed freedom to climb around and be like a boy. Now I understood, and I could never ever again fault the mama for her exhortations to me to be a little lady—there was no alternative. Little Peter had served some purpose, after all.

Such thoughts, and others, however, quickly gave way to those of an exciting impending event of not only local, but global import—time was consuming our Nineteenth Century. With the approach of the new century, San Franciscans were in a frenzy of anticipation. Noted for its wild and riotous New Year's celebrations, San Francisco, "the city that knows how," was about to outdo itself. For weeks the imminence of the Twentieth Century kept San Franciscans coiled in readiness for the great touch-off, the stroke of twelve, that finally released their pent-up emotions. From the windows of the St. Ann's, I watched a celebration, the likes of which I know I shall never see again. The town went mad. Streamers and confetti soon covered the horn-blowing, serpentineing celebrants. The din of shouting, horn blowing, bell ringing, and cable car clanging, was but a glorious delirium. As frenetic a crowd, I had never witnessed from my grandstand seat at the St. Ann's.

Directly below us was the cable-car turntable, at the foot of Powell Street. In sheer childish delight, I watched the revelers seize the cable car on the turntable and spin it around and around and around.Today, as then, the conductor and grip-man get off at the table and, with a hand from eager and ever ready passengers and spectators, turn the cable car around so that it can start its ascent on Powell. That memorable night, however, the cable car was to do a "whirling-dervish" dance for an eternity before the merrymakers finally released it.

Typical coverage of the joyous insanity of the turn of the

century celebration, was that of the San Francisco Examiner, January 1, 1900:

> *Raucous Rattle of Bells and Roar of Tuneless Horns Mingle in Riotous Welcome of Another Glad New Year. Every Man, Woman and Child Had a Horn and There Was No Lack of Effort to Increase the Tumult.*
>
> *Closing night of 1899 in San Francisco was the noisiest in its history, the wildest, the jolliest, most hilarious and withal good natured. The entire city was out for a good time, and it had it. The "roughhouse" play, unfortunately, so customary on carnival nights in Western cities, was noticeably lessened, save by a few enthusiastic lads. However, after the crowd had thinned out and the women had gone, "roughhouse" was instituted among the men and boys, but the police kept it in subjection, double watches being on duty on Market Street. The watch that usually goes off duty at 11:30 being kept on until 12:30.*

Now that the century had turned, life at the St. Ann's resumed its familiar pattern of theatrical engagements and travel to and from theaters. Transportation in downtown San Francisco was by cable car or, for the most part, by horse-drawn vehicles. Rarely did one see a "horseless carriage." After a night's performance, the mama would sometimes call a horse-drawn cab to take us home. The cab was always dark inside, and I was afraid there were spiders in it. Was the fear based on fact, or had the black spider on the lovely china cuspidor on the hearth of our Tremont Avenue home left dormant impressions, aroused by my vivid imagination? I only know that while riding was more convenient and expedient, especially in inclement weather, I preferred walking home.

On these occasions the mama would put my coat over my hair because there was some professional jealousy toward me, and she was afraid someone would cut my long blond curls. With the mama holding my hand on one side, and the papa on the other, the three of us would walk home; and I, all the while, literally sleeping as I walked. When we reached a curb, they would lift me by my hands, ever so gently, and I responded automatically by stepping up or down, as the occasion demanded.

On our arrival home there was always a bottle of milk and Jenny Lind bread for a snack. The bread, speckled with raisins, was somewhat loose-textured and easily gave way as the mama tore it apart and gave it to me in a bowl of milk. As automatically as my "sleeping-walks" home, I somehow managed to consume the mama's offering. I thought the concoction was a very unpalatable one, but I had long since resigned myself to eating bland, innocuous Jenny Lind bread and milk. The bread was purchased a few doors away, at the Tivoli Bakery on Eddy Street. The bakery and ice-cream parlor were part of the Tivoli Cafe, named after the Tivoli Theatre, two doors west, and were owned and operated by C.G. Larsen.

With the ordeal of the Jenny Lind mishmash out of the way, came the usual childhood pre-sleep routine that concluded with the prayer, "Now I Lay Me Down To Sleep." It seemed meaningless in itself, but I did enjoy the opportunity to bless my loved ones, especially the mama, papa, and Bertha, and a lesser heirarchy that grew nightly. When the mama at last interrupted, "That's enough," I was quite ready to be tucked in and fall into blessed oblivion.

Since formal religion was not a part of my every day life, I knew practically nothing about it. We were not church-goers and the mama was sparing in religious instruction. My religion was nature, wherein I was to find the embodiment of the concept God. In time, I was to restring the bits and pieces of information on nature's order and wondrous creations, into a personal sense of religion that transported me to another plane. I expressed this religious awareness in poetry, my humble way of honoring and exalting it.

Among these "wondrous creations," were all the animals so dearly loved by children. I had come to adore the performing dogs, horses, and various wild animals I met in the theater acts. And then there were the ubiquitous cats that served the theaters well in controlling the mice and rat populations. I championed the cause of the poor horses, when the cobblestones were removed on Market Street and replaced by a pavement that would better serve the encroaching era of the automobile. The horses had been happier with the cobblestones, into which they could dig down with their hooves as they pulled their loads. As they tried to adapt to the smooth surface, many of them slipped and fell. During one such incident, in front of the Emporium Department Store, my distress over the horses' predicament would impell me to upbraid the driver with, "Take off their harnesses." The pleading of a little child was not to be denied.

To this love affair of mine with animals, the papa was instrumental in adding still another set of "friends." The papa, I know, felt sorry for me because I had no coterie of playmates; so, he made every effort to help fill in those times when I was not preoccupied with the stage. He would take me for walks—long walks down to our wharves to see the ships. On the way, he always stopped at Mr. Thomas M. Ferguson's Old Crow Saloon on 719 Market Street. There, in an enclosure at the large front display window, were live crows hopping about and peering at their captive audiences. Before leaving me for a libation, the papa would pat my head lovingly and say, "Now, Baby, you look at the nice crows and papa will bring you a pretzel." I became very well acquainted, indeed, with these intriguing bird friends; and I spent many moments watching their unpredictable antics. And, sure enough, I was always rewarded for my patient waiting, with a pretzel. In retrospect, it was a fair exchange—the papa had his "nip" and I, a visit with my comical "friends."

Our peregrinations continued down Market Street to the Embarcadero, where all the piers, with their many ships, spread before us in scenes still vivid and dear. The highlight came when, on occasion, the papa would take me aboard one of the ships. He had been a sea-going man who had participated in the Charleston Blockade during the Civil War, and ships were a strong magnet that frequently drew him to San Francisco's beautiful, busy waterfront. I shared his love of ships and the sea. He took great delight in showing me a ship and pointing out the names of its various parts. When we came to the metal ships, however, he would shake his head skeptically and sputter, "Anybody knows metal doesn't float." He forever maintained

San Francisco Waterfront c. 1890
Credit: C.P. Heininger — Barrett-Miller Collection

grave reservations about them. Only wooden ships, especially sailing ships, held his regard.

On the way home we always stopped at the Haas Candy Shop at 810 Market Street. He would buy only a small amount each time because the mama did not permit me to eat much candy. I often received presents of boxes of candy, backstage; but she allowed me only one or two pieces of candy a day, for she was convinced candy was not good for me. And, the mama insisted that one always took the nearest piece of candy from the proferred box. Somehow, the candy purchased at the Haas Candy Shop during our walks was really special—any little girl can understand that.

Newbegin's Book Store, in the old Flood Building at the corner of Market and Fourth, was another favorite stop on our walks. Since the Newbegins were personal friends of the papa's, we often stopped in the store for a book or a visit. I always looked forward to these stimulating pauses because the New-begins daughter, Pansy, whom I idolized, was a very charming young lady who was very kind and attentive toward me. The Newbegins encompassed, in great measure, my world of books, and they helped influence my taste and appreciation for the written word. For this I shall always be grateful, as I continue to reminisce fondly about them. The well-known San Francisco book store has survived several locations, as well as the direct descendants of the original Newbegins, in its long history.

Whereas "papa outings," by virtue of their nature and infrequencies, were something special, no less memorable and cherished were those with the mama. Not only was she my constant companion in the theater, but, naturally, it was she who took me on shopping adventures. We often walked to Weinstock-Lubin Company, on Market and Taylor Streets. It had opened its doors, according to the records, at 10 a.m., Monday, April 5, 1898, the year before we moved into the St. Ann's. Weinstock-Lubin's was an exciting department store that offered a wide variety of merchandise and bargains.

But, for me, the monarch of them all was the Emporium in the 800 block, just a half block away and in view of the St. Ann's. The famous store had been built in 1894 by Mrs. Abbey M. Parrott. Her husband, John Parrott, had come West during the gold rush and had acquired considerable property in the 1800's. Among these, were a corner at Sutter and Montgomery Streets; the northwest corner of Montgomery and California Streets, known as "Parrott's Granite Block"; and the site on Market, between Fourth and Fifth Streets, on which the Emporium was located. While being built the Emporium promised to be "the largest and best equipped store in the world," and it had kept its promise.

In time the Emporium absorbed Davis Brothers' The Golden Rule Bazaar, 21-23 Geary Street, and became known as "The Emporium and Golden Rule Bazaar" for a while, until it dropped the latter appendage. In 1906, the lovely store fell victim to the devastating earthquake and fire. For about a year or so, it was temporarily located at Van Ness Avenue and Post Street, until the present Emporium opened in 1908.

While still known as "The Emporium and Golden Rule Bazaar," April 1898, it advertised the usual bargains; but, more interesting, was the announcement below its heading: "Musical Program 7:30−10:30 tonight. Orchestra, John Marquardt; Soloist, Frank Coffin, Tenor." What a lovely custom! But imagine our modern stores offering such a musical format for the edification of its customers.

Although I do not recall attending these musical programs, I have other happy memories of frequent shopping excursions with the mama to the Emporium, pretext or no. As now, Christmas shopping in their toy department, when we lived at the St. Ann's, was an unforgettably delightful lark. The selections offered had not yet been mechanicalized in ways so familiar to us now; but we were, nevertheless, regaled in spite of our deprivation. Of course, there was Santa Claus whom I could take or leave—and chose the latter. I knew too much about make-up to be impressed by him and his false whiskers. I decided it was a custom, and I accepted it as I did superstitions, namely: that was the way the world was when I came into it.

When it was still known as "The Emporium and Golden Rule Bazaar," the mama had me photographed in their studio. These photographs, with their identifying imprint stamped on the back, are still among my picture collection.

Other San Francisco studios whose services we used for my theater photographs included: the Stanford Studios, 731 Market Street, near the Cineograph Parlors; Alisky, 916 Market Street; Coover and Rasmussen, 724 Market Street; and Schulze, at 116 Stockton and 46 O'Farrell Streets. It was at the latter studio that I posed for calendar pictures—and, I hasten to add, these are not to be confused with present-day adult "cheesecake" offerings.

Incidentally, among my calendar pictures was one I favored most; but how it got on the calendar is still a source of irritation, even after the passing of over seventy years. The photograph has me seated and holding an armful of roses. As I posed for it, I was not aware of its ultimate disposition. Months later, to my disgust and dismay, I saw it on a brewery calendar—how incongruous a setting, and what fiendish mentality in the advertising medium could have conceived it.

Happily, that was the only vexation I experienced in the field of commercial photography. Photogenic as I was then, I was photographed more than any child in San Francisco. One picture, with happier results, was taken by Schulze's, for a jeweler's ad. In this two-panel photograph, I'm a little boy who has just taken his clock apart and is crying as he looks at the hopeless mass of wheels, springs, assorted metal pieces, and screws on the table before him. In panel two, the clock is all put together and I sit cross-legged, smiling, with my hand extended and forefinger crooked. The photographer had superimposed

Baby Dody c. 1900
Credit: Barrett-Miller Collection

Baby Martine   Baby Dody   Eleanor Gordan   Wlliam Lamp   For Christmas Supplement — San Francisco Examiner c. 1901
Credit: Barrett-Miller Collection

an oversized watch, hanging by its ring, on my crooked finger, so that the face of the watch was turned toward the viewer—"trick photography" in its infancy, perhaps? Schulze's also made casts of my hands. These were widely used by art classes in studies of children's hands.

Posing for theater pictures at that time could be an abomination. These were the days of the tripod on a standard, and glass slides instead of film. Clamps were placed behind the victim's head to hold it erect and steady, but they rendered the poses stiff and unnatural. The subject looked, for all the world, as if it were facing a firing squad. I rejected all attempts to entrap me in these devices; and there was no need for the "look-at-the-birdie" nonsense, either. The results, needless to say, were very natural. If there were a theme to a picture, I either acted it out or posed it. Posing took longer, for these were the days before the instant camera. The photographer, poor chap, bobbed in and out from under the black cloth draped over the camera. Nervously and temperamentally making precise adjustments, he would say, "Now, move a little this way, Baby"; flutter back under his "canopied aviary"; then coax me to, "Lift your chin, Baby." Then, when all was perfection, he threatened, "Hold it," and the masterpiece was a fait accompli.

Not all the "mama outings" were business or frivolity. She had a deep concern for my education, and she often took me to places where I might enrich it. Our travels away from San Francisco were always a source of knowledge in history and geography; while at home, she frequently escorted me to the Museum and Academy of Science on Market Street, a few doors west of the Emporium. The museum's center of attraction was its stupendous dinosaur skeleton that rose from the first floor and extended up into the second level. The museum proper had all the usual offerings found in a museum of natural history, and I whiled away many happy hours within its halls. It was the dinosaur, however, that made a lasting impression because, by deduction, it occurred to me for the first time that people, too, had skeletons that supported all that skin and flesh.

When outings were impossible, there were other preoccupations to help pass the time between theater engagements. The mama was an accomplished seamstress; and she patiently taught me how to make dresses for my dolls. I learned to cut patterns and insert sleeves, and to master the countless other intricacies of dressmaking. At age five, I learned the precise art of hemstitching lawn handkerchieves.

A more challenging art the mama mastered very well, was that of Battenberg Lace making. First called "Renaissance Lace," or guipure, it had no ground mesh and the pattern was held in place by connecting threads. Its history dates back to the Middle Ages. Old guipure could be a gold and silver thread lace. The term, however, also applied to a gimp (braid) made with "cartisane," a little strip of thin parchment or vellum covered with twisted silk, gold, or silver thread. Because it was so costly, "guipure was worn only by the rich or on the livery of the king's servants."

From such limited usage, the lofty guipures were in time available to almost anyone. Gold and silver were replaced by silk and cotton. In parts of Germany and other European countries,

Battenberg Lace Collar — By "The Mama"
Credit: Barrett-Miller Collection

as well as Russia, in the Eighteenth and early Nineteenth Centuries, peasant laces were made of cotton braid. It is assumed the Germans learned the technique of Battenberg Lace making from the Flemish who fled to Saxony during the Spanish Inquisition. Of all the guipures made in Europe, the finest, it is said, came from Genoa and Venice, Italy and from Flanders. The Belgians' tape-lace was considered a very special type, with "close workmanship and exquisite fineness of thread"—still characteristic of Flemish lace today.

The mama's Battenberg Lace could stand comparison with the best. Her style of execution was the accepted method of the time. She followed the pattern stamped on cotton cambric by basting the delicate braid over it with a tacking stitch. Wherever the design crossed, such as in a loop, the braid was always tacked to the braid only. She then gathered the puckered inner edge of each loop so that it would lie flat. In the open spaces or interstices between the loops, she wove all manner of designs with needle and thread—the possibilities were limitless. When all this was accomplished, she then pulled the bastings, leaving the finished lace intact and free of the cambric. Because the tacking of braid to braid, and the fill-in workings were so masterfully done, her resulting, delicate lace had no right nor wrong side. Various degrees of texture were achieved by the type of braid used—cotton, mercerized cotton, or silk. Collars and boleros of Battenberg Lace were very fashionable in the early Twentieth Century. I still have one of the mama's black silk lace boleros, a completed white collar, and one she had only partly finished when she died.

No less admirable was her crochet, for she was a perfectionist at that handicraft, too. For this work, she used the finest thread available and produced the most delicate crochet possible. The mama was fond of showing my long christening robe she had made entirely of alternate bands of tucks and hand-crocheted lace. For this lace, she had used gossamer-fine #100 thread. In such finery, was I christened in an old Lutheran church in San Francisco. Captain Schroeder, later lost at sea, was my godfather and his daughter, Binna, my godmother. In deference to the latter, I was to name one of my dolls "Binna," she of the pot-bellied-stove adventure when we traveled by caboose, during the George W. Lowe Roadshow.

The mama's clothes, most of which she made herself, were very much in the current style of that period—long skirts with horsehair-braid stitched around the inside of the bottom of the hem, for example. The braid protected the edge of the skirt as it rubbed the floor or street, while milady went about her work or travel. The braid was easily replaced when frayed or soiled. These wide skirts were usually gored to make for freedom of movement. The days of the "hobble" skirt were yet to come. With the skirt, went the long puffed-sleeve blouse. Dresses, also, had long puffed-sleeves that tightened abruptly below the puff and gradually onto the wrist. Over black cotton stockings, went the high-laced or the buttoned shoe. The mama wore size-two shoe. On dress occasions her tiny feet were adorned in lovely, pointed slippers with high heels. At the other extremity she wore the very large hat, so fasionable but such an abomination in theaters. This towering headdress was secured by one or two very long hat pins—long enough to penetrate the crown of the hat, find its way through the mama's expansive coiffure of high brown pompadour and large bun, and pierce through to the opposite side. Women were known to use these millinery daggers in self-defense. On windy days, not uncommon in our lovely San Francisco, she wore a feathered toque with a fine nose veil.

No account of ladies' hats of that era is complete without dwelling for a moment on their effect on theater-goers. The massive silhouettes of milady's chapeaux were constant irritants to those sitting behind them. It was inevitable that the suffering (especially male) patrons' complaints would be heeded. The crescendo of outcries finally reached the right ears, for on May 25, 1897, an article of much interest appeared in Figaro:

A SAN FRANCISCO HIGH HAT ORDINANCE

The Rotanzi ordinance prohibiting ladies from wearing high hats and bonnets in theaters during a performance was finally passed by the Board of Supervisors, without a dissenting vote, and will soon become a law unless the Mayor vetoes it.

The ordinance is an excessively stringent one, and it will be difficult to enforce it. It requires the managers of theaters to print the provisions of the order upon their programmes and they are charged with its enforcement. If a manager violates the order by permitting an objectionable hat to be worn he will be subject to fines of not less than ten dollars nor more than twenty dollars; or imprisonment in the County Jail for not less than ten nor more than twenty days, or by both such fine and imprisonment.

Apparently, it did not take long for Mayor Phelan to act upon the Rottanzi ordinance, for very soon all theater programs carried a notice similar to the one of Morosco's Grand Opera House of August 16, 1897:

> *To Lady Patrons of Morosco's Grand Opera House*
>
> *The order of the Board of Supervisors signed by Mayor Phelan, Thursday June 3, compels all persons in a theatre wearing hats of such size as to obstruct the view of those seated behind them, to remove the same. There is an arrest and fine for non-compliance with this order, and the person offending will be subpoenaed as a witness. All persons who do not care to comply with this ordinance can have their money refunded at the box office.*
>
> *Respectfully yours*
> *Walter Morosco*

Although gallantry of that era dictated the onus be placed on the management of the theaters, the message was abundantly clear. Most ladies responded, albeit reluctantly by some, by removing their hats and holding them on their laps.Of course, the very ladylike and law-abiding little mama was no exception. Pertinently, I might add, the rigidly corseted costume of the day restricted a woman's ability to raise her arms high enough to freely remove the hat. For this reason, some women continued to resist compliance with the law; others removed their hats either in the lobby before entering the auditorium or just before sitting down. I recall an incident when a woman, a few rows behind us, had chosen to keep her hat on, perhaps thinking she could avoid detection; but the vigilant usher politely asked her to remove it. With the assistance of friends with her, she finally managed to get the obnoxious headdress off her head and on her lap. Out of sheer convenience, and probably in response to the changing fashion, milady's hats in San Francisco gradually shrank in size—at least those worn to the theater.

While the mama's stylish outer garments were impressive, her under-raiments were formidable. She wore a white knit undershirt under a corset made rigid, almost to the point of inflexibility, by metal or whalebone stays; for that era antidated the brassiere. The only breast support employed was that of pulling the undershirt down below the corset and allowing the edge of the corset itself to act as the "uplift." Over the shirt, corset, and long voluminous underpants ruffled at the knees, went the "corset-cover," a short garment adorned with finery, like embroidery and ribbons. This bounteous array was topped by a "chemise," the equivalent of our full-length slip. Then, after long, black lisle stockings had been secured to the corset's garters, the mama was ready to add the outer garments.

But, a word on the garter, if I may. Compared to our modern-day garter, the one of the mama's day was ingenious for its time; and that is the kindest description I am willing to accord it. The "business end" of the garter on the corset was all metal, with a hole that tapered to a slot at its lower end. The mama pulled a pinch of the top area of the stocking through the hole and drew it downward through the pointed or slotted end, which held the hose quite securely. The device, however, was very hard on stockings, especially the silk ones the mama wore for special occasions.

With the completion of the final step of dress, came the consideration of makeup—a very simple one for the mama. Since the only women who wore "paint" on their faces advertised they were "ladies of the night," nice ladies never used rouge or "paint," as it was called. Actresses wore it *only* on the stage. The mama used a rice powder applied with a chamois skin—the powder puff of her day. Seemingly with a sense of guilt and always somewhat embarrassed, she would apologize, "It's only to take the shine off my nose."

Apologies completed, she donned her coat—a large, full, wool coat in winter, a grosgrain silk one in summer. Colors were generally tan, brown, or black. Accessories were the gloves of kid or silk, while with evening dress, went the long white kid gloves. Style decreed the "chatelaine" purse that hung at the waist. The soft cloth bag was covered with either gathered ribbon or with beads, and its lower end was trimmed with a long, beaded fringe.

Bruno Scholz — "The Papa"
Credit: Barrett-Miller Collection

Finally, came the choice of what jewelry to wear. The mama eschewed cheap costume jewelry. She wore only "real" jewelry, as she put it—diamond brooches and rings, gold chains, a pearl ring in an elegant mounting, and gold lapel watches of the utmost delicacy. When she stepped out of St. Ann's, she was always the regal Southern matron.

The papa's dress, on the other hand, was considerably simpler, though equally dictated by the fashion of the day. No matter what he wore, his appearance was one of neatness and nattiness. Born in Breslau, Germany, he had migrated to America to avoid the draft. Yet, once here, he joined the United States Navy. A gentleman in every way, he had traveled worldwide as a sea-going man, both in and out of the Navy, and had acquired an impeccable sartorial sense. He was a short, dapper man with a small, well-groomed mustache; and he always wore a conservative suit of either blue serge or salt-and-pepper grey. As fashion decreed, his pant legs were not creased. Fastidious, he wore under his vest only spotless-white, stiff-bosomed shirts, fastened with studs. To the neckline of the collarless shirt, he applied a stiff, white removable collar fastened by collar-buttons; and added a black bow tie. His headgear consisted of a fedora, a soft black hat with a reasonable brim. Later, he replaced the fedora with the derby, or bowler, a stiff, round monstrosity I thought quite hideous. I still prefer to remember him bareheaded. He wore black high-laced shoes over black cotton socks. His under "raiments," we leave, discreetly, behind our mental curtain.

These two lovely people shared a beautiful relationship. The unusual devotion of this "odd couple" was, at times, touching. The papa, so gallant, so kind and solicitous toward his true love at all times, constantly reminded me to be nice to the delicate little mama. The mama's frailty, however, never affected her ability to give orders, even from the sickbed. This demure, Southern matron, steeped in all the social graces, had all the instincts of a general; and when she spoke, she spoke! There was not a mean bone in her frail frame, yet in her inimitable way, she could move mountains. Needless to say, things, somehow, got done around our house.

Lovingly, to me, they seemed like characters out of a Dickens novel. Their equanimity and patience were sorely tried, however, as when I persisted, "If I had been born someone else, would I still be me?" I wondered if I would still have the same identity of consciousness, but I could not reduce the concept to their level of comprehension, as incongruous as that may sound. I doubt they knew what I was talking about—the "shades of the prison-house" had long since closed in on them. And while I dearly loved my parents, I early came to regard them critically. They could not answer my questions, and I could not learn from their conduct or speech the things I yearned to know. They were inconsistent, and it seemed they contradicted themselves continually. Their words came with the occasion and would not fit into a solid philosophical or logical structure. I think they, too, must have regarded me with knitted brows; but they loved me and I loved them; so, outwardly, I was obedient. To describe the quaint human atmosphere that dwelt with us, would require the mauve and gray of Dickens; and my palette is rather meager.

Time and again, I would try the mama's forbearance, though sometimes in more down-to-earth ways than the above. Frequent visitors at our apartment at St. Ann's were friends of long standing, Mr. and Mrs. Barney Meyers. Mr. Meyers was a small, lean man whose occupation at the racetrack could be called, "bookmaker," since bookmaking was legal then. His wife, by contrast, was a big woman. She was given to wearing black taffeta skirts and dresses, whose rustle sounded like a rain storm, with each step of her large frame. On one occasion, she made a formal visit to the mama, who always extended typical Southern hospitality. As usual, Mrs. Meyers was dressed in black taffeta, this time with a lace overdress in a floral design. The two ladies were engaged in chitchat over their tea when I was irresistibly drawn to the beautiful flowers on our visitor's full skirt. Unfortunately, I still held the scissors with which I had been cutting paper dolls. Without realizing what I was doing, much less contemplating its dire results, I quietly and deftly cut one of the beautiful flowers from the lace overdress. I was startled out of my hypnotic trance as the mama yanked me to

my feet. In utter mortification, the mama apologized apoplecti-
cally to Mrs. Meyers, while the very understanding lady sooth-
ed, "There, there, she didn't know what she was doing." My
punishment was of the worst possible kind—the mama's consternation and disfavor, and the penetrating realization I had
done something quite horrendous.

With the theater my world, and actors and actresses my
surrogate "playmates," I could hardly escape these influences.
My daily life, however, mostly detached from my peers, had its
lonely moments, and I sought my favorite outlets to lighten and
fill them. I played by myself, especially when the mama had to
take to her bed, with pain. The St. Ann's apartment, with its tall
windows and wide window ledges closed off by wooden shutters
that opened into the rooms, provided a perfect stage setting for
my play. Often, I made up plays which I staged and directed,
and in which, of course, I starred. I was fond of taking one of my
mother's blue-checked aprons, fastidiously embroidered in
cross-stitch a foot deep, tie it around my waist, backward, with
the panel trailing behind me. (Incidentally, I don't know why
the mama had aprons; she never cooked a meal for me!) Beautifully costumed, I would climb my building blocks onto the side
window ledge and pull the shutters closed in front of me. After
a few moments' dramatic pause, I pushed the shutters open
and, voilà, the great star mesmerized her devoted following of
millions. I descended the "magic stairway," crossed the room,
made a turn while kicking the trailing apron, moved to the
other side of the room and, again, kicked my "train," with all the
grace and majesty of the queen I affected. So engrossed in
kicking my train about was I, that I fear my "play" suffered
badly. But, no matter, Miss Florence Roberts would have been
flattered to see herself mirrored in my great performance—a
poor little mimic, aping her mentor.

Sometimes my building blocks would lend themselves to
another diversion. I loved to turn one of the boxes on edge and
pretend I was "Kitty" astride her horse at the head of my
regiment—a rough soubrette, "Jeanne D'Arc," urging her
forces on to victory through the power of her valor. There I was,
bounding along—a sublime commixture of Jeanne D'Arc and

Teddy Roosevelt—"Charge!" But we never got to the wars because the din of battle disturbed the sick mama; and I soon found myself seeking more quiet pursuits with paper, pencil, and crayons.

How dear to the heart of childhood, is this game of dramatization; and how can one forget the childish ecstasy of being part of a story. Surely, we cherish this sense of participation throughout our lives; for to be a part of something is to derive constant nourishment for our souls. All children are actors when they play house, or store, or soldier, or school. In this way, do they transport themselves to planes unobtainable in any other manner. Even animals have a great sense of the dramatic. I have watched my dog pounce upon his Teddy Bear and shake it as though he had caught an arch enemy. And who has failed to observe animals' and birds' dramatization for survival.

My own play-acting took still another unusual direction. I had been taught by the director on stage the precise art of smiling and being happy at the appropriate time, and, conversely, when to look disappointed or sad, and even how to cry. I found that the best place to practice these moods was before the mirror. Since I was a pretty little child and often praised, the mama mistook these antics, for vanity. So, to curb these seemingly vain activities, she warned me that if I kept looking in the mirror, I would see the devil. Thinking it one of her quaint expresssions, I laughed it off. Remember, I had seen the devil in SORROWS OF SATAN, earlier; and while he did not frighten me, she now planted a seed of curiosity about this character.

Curiosity and anticipation finally resolved themselves one day when Mrs. Meyer (she of the flowered overskirt I ruined) visited the mama at the St. Ann's. While the ladies were at tea, I amused myself before the mirror, practicing moods. Again the mama remonstrated I would see the devil if I did not stop. She turned to her guest for confirmation, "Isn't that so, Mrs. Meyer?" Of course, Mrs. Meyer replied in the affirmative. I was delighted. Could there *really* be some truth to this? I quickly glanced up to the corner of the mirror frame, first one side, and then the other, hoping very much to catch a glimpse of the devil. I turned to my mother and asked excitedly, "Which way will he come from?" Bewildered and exasperated, the mama brushed me off. The two ladies went on with their conversation, while I was left with a life-long unrequited search for the character with the brilliant red-lined cloak I had seen in SORROWS OF SATAN. Through the years, the nearest I have come to him is on the label of the well-known can of deviled ham.

Closing thoughts on this era of the St. Ann's compete with each other in their feverish efforts for recognition. From my "castle window" at the St. Ann's, I observed the passing parade which was but a microcosm of my beautiful San Francisco. Without my observation tower at the St. Ann's, life could have been dreary, indeed. But what little child could be bored as she beheld the panoramas of city life below her—myriads of peoples, moving at various paces, and in various ways.

Enamored as I was with animals, the horses I watched had their own stories to tell. Since the advent of the cable cars on Powell Street about 1886–1887, horses were not seen there often; however, they were plentiful on Market Street. There were castes among my equine friends, from the elite to the toilers. The fashionable bang-tailed coach horses were objects of both concern and pride to me when I watched them pull their flashy vehicles—concern over what I considered the cruelty of the check-reins fastened between their heads and backs to keep their heads high and rigid; pride, in their majestic mein as they pranced high of gait, their glossy, cropped and knotted tails enhancing their royal stature. At the rear of the carriage, ran the spotted coach dog, the Dalmatian, taught to run between the two back wheels. Altogether, the melding of handsome horses, beautiful coaches with elegant passengers, and coach dogs in synchrony and harmony, created what I felt was the epitome of magnificence.

While the lovely "Bangtails" were things of beauty, to me the real aristocrats were the fire horses. These massive but graceful specimens in either matched brown or dappled gray, would fly three or four abreast, their steaming nostrils distended and their manes and tails flying, as they sped to their destination. It seemed that the clang of the bells on the engine spurred them to greater frenzy, and only the arrival at the fire itself, could sate them. In the firehouses, their harnesses, hung above them, were released at the sound of the alarm and dropped over their broad, anticipating backs. These sleek and well groomed, beautiful brutes were ever eager to spring into action and carry their chariots with them. Only the long hook-and-ladder maneuvering around a corner could reduce their relentless speed. And who could forget the sight of the Dalmatian or the White Bull mascot perched high on the fire chariot, for all the world as if the excitement of the flight had been ordained his and his alone! Now, fire horse has yielded to horse-power, but the memories will always stir my soul.

Admittedly no match for the speed and class of their "elite cousins," the coach or the fire horses, the horses at the lower echelons had their special functions to perform, too. These were the work horses on which business of all kinds, and wheels of industry relied. Those that pulled milk wagons learned the location of each customer, by rote, and made their rounds with scarcely a hint from the relaxed drivers. The Chinese Laundry wagon and the French Laundry wagon, each catering to his own special clientele, were pulled by the work horses. For the heavier work, there were the ponderous dray or draft horses, heads held low as they pulled their prodigious loads.

Working horses required regular feedings to maintain their level of productivity; and so it was not unusual to observe, hanging by a strap over their heads, their canvas feed-bags with the breathing holes. In shape, the bags resembled the shoulder purse women use today. Watching the horses eat from their feedbags was a fascination, with the plum reward coming as they ate their way down to the bottom. At that level the grain was harder to reach, so my resourceful friends would give a jerk to the bag, thus rearranging the grains' distribution, the better to get every last seed flipped into their hungry mouths.

Accommodating to the horses' physical needs, were the many wooden watering troughs the city maintained on most side streets, off Market Street; while, on Market, there was the famous Lotta's Fountain that included a big water basin for horses. Some drinking fountains had drinking bowls for the coach dogs, too. I recall that the brass faucets and tin cups on chains, to serve the people's needs, were the most important services rendered by Lotta's Fountain. The mama considered the tin cups unsanitary and so she always carried collapsible cups in her purse, one for her, the other, for me.

Lowest on the heirachy of horses, it seemed to me, were the cab or hack horses. How I pitied them, for they always looked very tired. Theirs was the thankless mission of constantly transporting the indifferent passenger; but the poor beasts did what was expected of them. I often wondered if anyone thought of giving them a grateful pat.

Because the city was so dependent on the horse, stables were scattered, strategically, throughout the city; and "rent-a-horse" livery stables were everywhere.

Paralleling, somewhat, our present-day concern with the automobile accident, was the problem of runaway horses. Many pedestrians were injured by them or the carriage wheels; and an overturned carriage could result in death or injury to its passengers or passersby. Often, the horse was frightened by the "horseless carriage"—that new-fangled mechanical monster that threatened his world. There was potential danger in the "runaway horse situation." And the mark of heroism was his, for the brave one who rushed out to grab the fleeing horse's bridle and brought him to a halt.

It followed that in an era when horses provided most of our transportation needs, there would also be attendant obvious problems, chief of which was the one so adroitly handled by the white-uniformed street sweepers. They were on the job at all times, with their white metal boxes, and their push-brooms and long-handled dust pans. Without their services, our beautiful windy city might have been somewhat unbearable at times.

In the "canvas" below me, every street corner had its "leatherlunged" newsboy, each with his unique and nearly unintelligible call. His sing-song air was couched in decibles high and low, and successfully aimed at his passing, captive clientele. Who could resist the spell of implied murder, intrigue, and mayhem the news vendor broadcast through his "leather lungs," at a time when he alone disseminated the only news available to curious, news-hungry people.

On my "painting" I must also place my most beloved of all, the Powell Street Cable Car. In 1886, history records, "The newly incorporated Powell Street Cable Company, whose line is now in course of rapid construction will run its cars to the Powell Street entrance of the Baldwin Hotel." When we moved into the St. Ann's thirteen years later, the Powell Street cable car was an established San Francisco landmark, and it has lost none of its charm through the years. Today, thanks to the Administration of President Lyndon Baines Johnson, our San Francisco cable cars were designated a national monument in 1964, with the implied protection in perpetuity.

While other children had toy trains on tracks, I had a real one that clanged its way up and down Powell. It was small, but it had all the authority of a juggernaut as it moved along and came to rest on the tracks on the turntable below my window. Here, it discharged its passengers, but not without one last ritual. Whether the men passengers were leaving or boarding, or even just strolling by, they vied for the privilege of helping to turn the car around on the table before it started up Powell Street again. When the tracks on the table matched the tracks with the cable once again, there was a fairly audible click. I listened carefully for this reassuring click that the track was now locked in place. The car was then pushed off the table by the volunteers, far enough for the "grip" to engage the cable through the slot. It was only then that I knew my little car could safely scamper up Powell once again. The pride of "personal possession" was no greater than when I perceived grown men competing for the favor of hanging on the outside of my cable car, and I observed, with some degree of disdain, that only the "cream-puffs" sat inside.

My cable car depended on an array of underground cables whose dimensions and mechanics were formidable, but reduced themselves to the car's simple operation of its clutch gripping the ever-moving cable through a slot—an operation ably executed by the "grip man," who else! It was this peerless paragon's further duty to keep up the clanging of the bell, in response to my exhortations. And just to insure my investment, there was the conductor gathering all manner of manna, to be deposited in my coffers at the end of each journey.

My street-scene-on-canvas lacks a few more entries. Let me first add the round-hatted policeman in his belted, blue suit. He was held in high esteem, this symbol of law and protection to San Franciscans; and his reassuring presence was respectfully accepted by most. Whether he was walking his beat or directing traffic, there was no gainsaying his value to our burgeoning city.

My masterpiece is becoming a bustling panorama as I include the frenetic pace of the messenger boy. Although telephones were in existence in San Francisco then, they were not so numerous, nor so universally used as now. The most widely employed means of local communication was the messenger boy. He could be seen at any moment of the day, sometimes night, darting here and there carrying messages. From my "golden tower" I could conjure all manner of messages, bad and good, that he carried to a victim or a happy recipient. Only the limits of my imagination could put "finis" to the possibilities. When he came to our door, it meant a message from one of the local theaters to appear for yet another engagement. He never knew the joy he brought with his communique, nor the gates to fulfillment he opened. There would follow a whirl of activity, and another one of those omnipresent white dresses would be brought forth as we speculated what the new part might entail. Then, too, there would be money for the rent or, perhaps, we might now call in that new doctor about whom we had heard such hopeful promise—would he be the one to help alleviate the poor mama's suffering? Regardless, at last the little mama would limp down to the theater with me for my rehearsals.

And what of color in my growing scenograph? Nothing compared with nature's own, such as in the flower stand below my window of the St. Ann's. Flower stands were, and still are, a "sine qua non" of my beautiful San Francisco. Tourist and native alike shared the joy of a stop at my colorful flower stand to choose white or velvety red roses, violets, gladioli, carnations, and other choices, too numerous to mention. It seemed that no one was ever too poor to resist the temptation of a flower or two, if need be. In the midst of the muted browns and grays of the tall buildings of downtown San Francisco, the bright colors of the flower stands and flower wagons were a welcome relief, by contrast. I observed the change of expression on the hurried passerby as he approached the multicolored flowers. I saw facial tension give way to relaxed smiles, and I felt a certain pride of identification as he finally moved on, with a bouquet to gladden the heart of a loved one. I thought of how often the papa stopped to purchase a floral token of love for the appreciative little mama, and of the great joy the simple gesture brought her.

As I complete my San Francisco street scene, there is but one element missing: from my "castle window" at the St. Ann's, I would observe the eternal ways of "man with the maiden." In the prevailing social and moral codes of behavior, ladies must never show their ankles. But, did it not seem to me the ladies purposely invited responses from the gentlemen? Oh yes, indeed! They would gingerly grasp their bustled skirts from behind as they stepped up onto the curb on the opposite side of the street. I noticed that it was during this interval that some of the "demure sex" intentionally beguiled the "girl-watchers"; and I'm positive they took guarded delight in provoking the latters' attentions. I wondered then why grown-ups acted so peculiarly, for this strange game seemed so "childish"—ah me. Could it be that the wisdom of childhood will forever lie in its innocence?

Chapter Four
Open sesame, My Moorish Gem

As regular engagements at the Chutes, Olympia, and Cineograph Parlors were drawing to a close with the end of the old century, the newborn century was ushering in a new world for me. I would progress from the "cute baby" parts to far more serious and demanding roles. It was time I bid "adieu" to the trysts with my frescoed cherubs on the ceiling and the little things that attract a young child's eye, because the "shadows of the prison-house" would approach, in due time. I was now, contradictorily, both a sad and a happy child. Perhaps my sadness stemmed from the necessity of leaving behind me the things I can no longer recall; and happiness, from the excitement of looking forward to a challenging world, a world of great experiences and new adventures. And so I say, "I was now both a sad and a happy child."

I still beheld "the light and whence it flows," and I must travel farther from the East, on my way attended by the vision splendid. May the day never come when my perception of it dies away and fades completely "into the light of common day." It is a person bent with age who tries to recapture the things of life as seen through the eyes of a child. And if it sometimes sounds like a harlequin assortment of representations, the reader must know that, through this magic called "memory," I am retrieving impressions of seventy years and more.

The great new adventure started when a little girl named Ollie Cooper, member of the well-known Cooper family of thespians, was not able to appear in a play because, of all things, a toothache. A search was made for a child to replace her. Perhaps it was my many appearances in song and dance acts at the Chutes, Olympia, and Cineograph Parlors that had catapulted me to someone's attention. Whatever it was, I was "discovered," and the world opened up to me through the beautiful

Alcazar Theatre 1885-1906
Credit: Barrett-Miller Collection

Lobby of The First Alcazar Theatre 1885-1906
Credit: California Historical Society, San Francisco

doors of a "Moorish Castle." This "Moorish Castle" was the old Alcazar Theatre at 116 O'Farrell Street, San Francisco. Here, was about to transpire one of those moments I would have wished to last forever, etched like the figures on the vase in Keat's "Ode To A Grecian Urn," so precious and unforgettable was the experience. How sublime, could it have been carved on the vessel at that precise instant, not one step later.

On that magical morning, the very affable man with the dark mustache took my hand and opened the doors to the castle, and the mama followed closely behind. As we walked in, the silence echoed from the domed ceiling, conveying more of a cathedral-like atmosphere than that of a theater. We entered a theater where there was no play, no audience, and all was dark except for the "bunch light" shining on the stage. Thereafter, I never entered an empty, darkened theater with only the bunch light burning to light the rehearsal, but what I experienced much the same feeling one senses upon entering a house of God at noon, when few are there and the only light comes from the candles burning on the altar. The bunch light, used in all theaters during rehearsals, is a standard with a reflector and numerous lights. The rehearsal was now in progress, as I found myself skipping down the aisle, the better to keep up with the brisk pace of the gentleman who was leading me toward the stage. He was Mark Thall, who together with Fred Belasco managed the Alcazar Theatre. (More on these two gentlemen and the house itself, later.)

As Mark Thall led me down that aisle, the skip and hop I took for every step of his, soon brought me to the railing around the orchestra pit. There he called, "Miss Roberts," and Florence Roberts, who was the leading lady in every sense of the term, stepped to the footlights and answered, "Yes!"

"We have found a child for the part," announced Mr. Thall. He then took me around to the steps at one side, leading up to the stage. The cast stood about, looking at me appraisingly but without comment, as Miss Robert's face registered utter dismay. As young as I was,I undertood her consternation when, in a high-pitched voice she snapped, "Huh, couldn't you find an infant!"

Mr. Thall replied, "Well, this is the only child available." So, she lifted me up and stood me on a high-backed, so-called "throne-chair," used in many theater productions. The throne-chair was always very ornately carved and was upholstered in red velvet. Somewhat resigned, Miss Roberts said to me, "Now Baby, say this," and she gave me a line to say. I would give anything to remember what it was, but it eludes me. In all likelihood, it was a line from Shakespeare. But whatever the line, it must have been rendered with some degree of promise; for, more hopefully, she urged, "Now, say it real loud, *real* loud." So, I took a deep breath and, from somewhere in the middle of me, I repeated the line.

"Oh, my gracious," she exclaimed, "they'll evidently be able to *hear* her, anyway. But will she be able to memorize the part?" Preliminary rehearsals had already taken place, with dress rehearsals scheduled for the next day.

Stepping forward, the mama assured, "Oh, I'm quite sure she can memorize the part." Of course, *I* was quite sure, too. It was explained to me that I would play a little boy whose devoted mother was a very beautiful lady, and that I had been living with peasants, outside of Paris. I was a little young to know why or to understand the implications of such a living arrangement, and I did not question it. The play was SAPHO and I played little Joseph.

When SAPHO, the four-act play founded upon the novel of the same name, by Alphonse Daudet, appeared at the Alcazar two months earlier, it was described as, "a play which has been praised and condemned more times than any play." The management of the Alcazar was quoted as promising, "There will not be a word or an act that invites a base thought; there will not be one suggestive scene that doesn't at all times uphold the right and condemn the wrong."

A few days before our run began, the same publication announced that the Alcazar was, "to give us another glimpse of 'naughty' SAPHO." It added that there were "preparations to revive the play upon the same scale of magnificence which marked its former triumphant run." Further, it noted that at that time the play had closed a four-weeks' run to "houses packed to the door." Obviously, the theater-public's preoccupation with titillating stories is nothing new. But, gracious, I don't recall that there was anything "naughty" about "Miss" or "Auntie Sapho," as I thought of her; but then, how could a six-year-old have known or cared about that.

When I was given the part of Joseph, the script was handed, with instructions, to my mother because I could not read at that time. They then walked me through the part saying, "Now Baby, you come on here, and then you say this, and then you go out there," as they described the part of Joseph. To me, this was like a lovely game with "beautiful people." In this fashion, I tried to assimilate as much of my part as I could. Finally, the rehearsal was over and I was told to return the next day for the dress rehearsals and the opening performance. Incredulous over our great fortune, the very happy, delighted mama and I left the theater for home.

At home, I stood excitedly at the mama's knee as she read my part to me about three times. She had been instructed on the cues and lines. After the third reading, I became bored and tired and the mama suggested, "Go play a while." This I did, all the while mulling over in my mind the part of Joseph. When I returned to the mama, she read me just the cue and I recited the line that followed. When I faltered, she prompted me. After three such readings, I was again released to play. That evening, we went through the procedure again, the mama giving me the cues and I repeating the lines.

The following morning, we went to dress rehearsal and I knew my part. I knew it "cold." No prompting was necessary. There was stunned silence and much awe among my colleagues as I went through my part. They seemed amazed I had learned it overnight. I went on that night of August 20, 1900 and played little Joseph in SAPHO for a one-week run.

On the day following the opening of SAPHO, their faith in me was demonstrated when they gave me the part of Georgie in FROU FROU, their very next play. I began rehearsing for FROU FROU in the daytime and appearing in SAPHO, evenings. Fortunately, I never confused the characters. While in

Baby Dody as Joseph in "Sapho"   Alcazar Theatre 1900
Credit: Barrett-Miller Collection

SAPHO I was dressed in peasant clothes, in FROU FROU I
played Georgie Sartorys, elegantly attired in velvet and lace.
FROU FROU had a Nineteenth Century setting, when little
boys wore fancy shirts adorned with lace collars and cuffs, velvet
britches, and curls. Since my own curls were a bit longer than
the part called for, the mama rolled them over the length of my

head, rendering the remainder the proper boy-length.

White Whittlesey, our very handsome leading man, played my father. We lived in a beautiful house where, in one memorable scene, I sat on his lap as he told me a fairy tale. It was a story about a beautiful princess who went away, leaving her prince with a sad, sad heart. In effect, my father in FROU FROU was alluding to the fact that his wife, Georgie's mother, had left him and that he was very lonely and unhappy without her.

Near the end of the rehearsals for FROU FROU, I made a perplexing discovery. As she sat in her rocker reading my part to me for memorization, the mama skipped over a section with several scratches across it. When I quizzed her on what that was all about, she explained that the part of Georgie had been cut down for me because I was quite young. At my persistence, however, she finally read the deleted section. It was a very lovely embellishment of the fairy story of the beautiful princess and her sad prince. Loving fairy tales as I did, the story intrigued me; so I blurted, "But why cut out the best part of the story?" To appease me, the mama read the part several times.

The following day, I approached our director, Mr. Charles Bryant, and in great indignation asked, "Why have they cut out the beautiful part of this fairy story?" Appearing rather compromised, he replied, "Well, I thought I would make it easier for you." His answer only distressed me further—the very idea of making it easier for me, how dared he! I had the entire part committed to memory and I insisted on demonstrating my point. To humor me, he permitted me to recite the deleted part. Convinced, he agreed, "Why that's fine, we'll put it back in then." While *I* was now mollified, poor Mr. White Whittlesey was dismayed over the prospect of memorizing cues and lines that had been eliminated. But since it was unanimous that I knew my part, everyone agreed with the director that I should be allowed to play the entire part.

After only one more rehearsal, we went on that night of Monday, August 27, 1900, in the opening performance of FROU FROU. In due time we came to the scene in which Georgie was sitting on his father's knee, listening to the story of the princess and her prince. When we reached the section

White Whittlesey in "Frou Frou"   Alcazar Theatre 1900
Credit: Barrett-Miller Collection

that had been originally deleted, Mr. Whittlesey jumped the cue; so I nestled my head under his ear, whispered what he should say, and he said it. Then, I rose up gloriously and gave my response. He gave me a vague, vapid, glassy look that spelled he was still in dire trouble; so once again, I nestled against him and whispered his next line. By now, the other actors, in the wings, were convulsed with repressed laughter over the strange plight of the famous White Whittlesey being prompted by the little tyro on his knee. We went through the entire beautiful scene in this fashion. In retrospect, I'm sure he would have been justified had he choked me. It certainly had not been my intent to embarrass him; but I *was* committed to presenting that lovely story in its entirety.

When it was all over, Mr. Whittlesey appeared unsure just how he should react to the ignominious episode; however, when he saw how well it had been accepted by the rest of the company, he took it good-naturedly and wound up carrying me on his shoulders to my dressing room. All was forgiven. And the next night, to be sure, Mr. White Whittlesey knew all his lines. There was no need, ever after, for me to nestle under his chin and prompt him—I rather missed that.

Florence Roberts in "Sapho"   Alcazar Theatre 1900
Credit: Barrett-Miller Collection

Our leading lady, Florence Roberts, was at the zenith of her career, and rightly so. Earlier she had played leading lady at the Alcazar in a repertoire of very heavy dramas that featured her husband, Lewis Morrison, in plays such as FAUST, MASTER OF CEREMONIES, FREDERICK THE GREAT, and YORICK'S LOVE. By the time I met her, however, she had already become a star in her own right. Although she still appeared with her husband on occasion, I never played in any vehicle in which they both participated. Miss Roberts held the high esteem of her colleagues and the devotion of a large following. By now she had also reached the prestigious social level of maintaining a constant traveling companion—a devoted black maid in uniform, who dressed her and waited on her, hand and foot, anticipating her slightest needs. Miss Roberts was not very tall, but amply compensated for that in talent and regal bearing. To her, went the best dressing room of all, for she was the star. Some thought her affected and a bit of a "prima donna," with more than a modicum of temperament. I'm sure she was skeptical about my suitability, at first, and tolerated me in a patronizing way; but I liked her, and I'm grateful for the many fond memories of having played with such a great actress.

Among others in the casts of SAPHO and FROU FROU were: Clarence Arper, a kindly man who saw to it that I made my entrances at the right time; Carlyle Moore; both Edwin Emery and Ernest Howell with whom I was to make many appearances later; George Webster (more about him later); Lorena Atwood; and Marie Howe.

Marie Howe, our character woman, was an older, very motherly kind of person whom I liked very much, save on one occasion. She and the mama had become good friends, and so on this particular occasion when Miss Howe had to take a short trip, she asked the mama to take care of her parrot. The mama was delighted to accommodate her dear friend, and the parrot was brought to us. I tried to talk to my new friend, but he mocked every word I said. One day I was crying, I know not why, for I had not much reason for crying. The parrot mocked me, even then, and after that I hated him. I hasten to add, I would never harm one; but to this day, I would not own one.

With SAPHO and FROU FROU I had received my baptism, and passed from the probation period to the legitimate stage. I now knew the crew and cast of the Alcazar's company. In a way, I was now "launched" as a "real pro." But even before that, I had had experience with audiences, and they had never frightened me. They had always appeared to like me; and in turn, I liked them and always have.

Still, I was now into a new experience. When the play was prepared, when I was properly costumed, and the curtain about to rise, there was an indescribable, joyful intensity. Once upon the stage, I was free, free. I was beyond the reach of instruction or correction. The only restraint I knew was the words which the playwright had written; and they usually made sense and allowed for a range of emotional interpretations. Now it was mine to say just how Joseph reacted in his strange environment; or how Georgie Sartorys felt about his doting but unhappy father. And, it was mine to see the heavens open for little Eva, and to comfort those about her as she lay dying. I even knew what it was like to die. It was mine to say just how little William in EAST LYNNE felt when, at last, he recognized his own mother. Mine, all mine, was the experience of actually being little Anna, in Tolstoy's RESURRECTION when, at the end of an act, she sobbingly pleads, on her knees, with the obdurate Siberian guard to release her dying father from the stocks.

In my new adventure, I developed a kinship with my friends beyond the footlights, and I learned to reach out to them. In time, I played more dramatic parts that carried the range of emotions, from joy to grief. It was like mastering the musical instrument, to reach out over the footlights and play the emotions of these people—to make them laugh, to make them cry. These were great and wonderfully exhilarating moments. Small wonder then, that under such fulfilling and reassuring conditions, I never knew stage fright. Indeed, I have often wondered how performers could enjoy their work if they were frightened by it.

Gradually, I grew to become the character I portrayed. I played child parts, both girl and boy. I could be a very thoroughgoing little boy, for I learned and lived each part—witness,

Joseph in SAPHO, Georgie in FROU FROU, and many more, later. I always enjoyed the freedom I felt, dressed as a little boy. I could affect the deeper voice of a boy, and swagger with the best of them.

Since these were the days before microphones and other electronic aids, voice projection was a very important technique. Earlier, in ancient times, over two thousand years ago, actors wore huge painted canvas masks with wide mouths fitted with devices to increase the resonance of the voices. These tubes, or "megaphones," aided in projecting the voice a considerable distance. In many instances, the actor wore a buskin, a half-boot with thick soles, giving him the added height and size that further helped project the sound, as well as increase his visability throughout the large amphitheater. But, all this was thousands of years ago. When I was a child, of course, none of these aids were in use. The art or technique of voice projection was one of the most important tools for communication with the audience. This was achieved by speaking from the diaphragm, with always a reserve of breath.

Nowhere could I have found a more fitting environment for learning the tools of communication and the enrichments of theater life, than at the Alcazar. Our managers, Mark Thall and Fred Belasco, had the distinct advantage of the influence and guidance of the latter's brother, David Belasco, the well-known New York impresario, playwright, and innovator of scenic productions. Plans for many of David Belasco's innovations were sent to his brother Fred, who reproduced them on the stage of the Alcazar. With this advantage, the Alcazar was not only up with the times, but ahead of other theaters of San Francisco and the nation, according to many leading critics.

One ingenious device, employing a crock of salt water into which an unfathomable, bizarre contraption was lowered and raised, acted as a prototype of the modern "dimmer." It was regularly used to create lovely scenes, such as in a beautiful sunrise, when a bird call was struck by the orchestra and then, ever so gradually, the lights came on to simulate daybreak. Often the scenery and lighting effects were so beautiful, the audience went into rapturous applause, even before the actors appeared.

In the footlight trough along the apron of the Alcazar's stage, was a row of multicolored electric lights controlled by various switches. Depending on the effect desired, different combinations of colors were used adroitly. To fully appreciate how advanced the house was for the times, one must remember that, much earlier, candles set about eighteen inches apart and protected by sconces, were used as footlights. Later, a great achievement came with the introduction of gas lights to replace the hazardous candles. In turn, the gas lights were replaced by the electric bulbs.

Like the other better theaters, the Alcazar had an outstanding orchestra. When I played there, Edward B. Lada was its musical leader. The "Music Programme" was always of the highest caliber, with selections from grand opera, operettas, the classics, and original compositions for some of the plays. The orchestra in the pit made its contribution to my eager soul—rhythm, and a friendship with the better quality of music. This was the only kind of music that surrounded me in my childhood. It must have seemed strange to see and hear this little tot going about humming snatches from the great marches, waltzes, and overtures.

Dressing rooms in my "Moorish Castle" were located under the stage. In fact, since the theater's floor was on an incline, the rooms were at *quite* a low level, below ground. They were small and cozy and located off a hallway. Of course, it was not as pretty down there, underground, as it was upstairs, but there was always an air of compactness in which none of the essentials to our comfort were missing.

Herbert Farjeon was our "book boy." Usually stationed at first entrance right, he followed the script and acted as prompter. But, to me, his role as our "call boy" was more memorable. Herbert would come through the dressing room hallway and call, "Half-hour *up*," with an emphasis on the word "up." In due time, he called, "Fifteen minutes *up*"; and after fifteen minutes, "Overture." By this time, the orchestra, which had been in a special room, tuning up their instruments—ah, the beautiful

Baby Dody as Master Cooke in "The Adventures of Nell Gwynne"
Alcazar Theatre 1901
Credit: Barrett-Miller Collection

sounds, sounds that have no equal—left by a small door under the stage for their places in the orchestra pit. Next, the "call boy" announced, "Five minutes *up*," with even greater stress and urgency on "up"; "places, curtain"—and we had better be there in our places, for the "show must go on."

While still a novice I was guided, mostly, by the mama's direction, relative to time limits proscribed. But my fellow actors and actresses were very kind, and they, too, especially Clarence Arper, helped me in many ways. To them I owe a debt of gratitude for making my new life in the theater a happy and smooth one. They made it possible for me to go on stage, joyously, and do what was expected of me.

After this auspicious beginning, there followed an interval during which there were no child parts in plays at the Alcazar until the end of the year. I returned then for rehearsals in THE ADVENTURES OF NELL GWYNNE, by Charlotte Thompson. The title role of the well-known story of Charles II's protege who was considered far below him in social station, was played by Florence Roberts. Prior to becoming an actress, Nell Gwynne had sold oranges in the streets, prompting the famous scene still vivid—Miss Roberts wending her way across the stage singing, "Oranges, oranges, who'll buy my oranges?"

Howard Scott played the enamored Charles II who strutted in elegant clothes, and carried a tall cane with a gold knob. He wore knee britches and a matching pale-green brocade coat that flared just above his knees. His silk shirt with lace-cuffed sleeves, had a cascade of lace down the front. His costume was enhanced by a powdered wig with long curls, a tricornered, braided dark hat, and a jeweled snuffbox—all, trappings that went with the king's artificial mannerisms.

My part in THE ADVENTURES OF NELL GWYNNE came in the scene that featured the Green Room of the Drury Lane Theater in London. The "Green Room," the social room where actors and actresses met for talk and relaxation, was also where they entertained guests. In this scene in which I appeared, Miss Gwynne was now the successful actress who had the great favor and patronage of Charles II. I was Master Cooke, a street urchin with long shoulder-length dark hair, brought in because of his ability to recite Shakespeare. Once again, I stood on a throne chair and recited Shakespeare—this time, to entertain those gathered in the Green Room. The part was neither long nor vital to the play, and it seemed to have been dragged in by the heels.

Since I had to be at the Alcazar at least a half-hour before I was called, it gave me time to do some exploring backstage. On one occasion, an actor who wore a beard in the play was still in his dressing room. His door was ajar, so I stepped into his room. Spellbound, and standing on tiptoes, with my fingers clinging to the edge of his dressing table, I watched him make up. I was very intrigued by, and asked many questions about, the false beard he was soon to apply to his face. I observed that after he ran a comb through the crepe hair (bought by the yard, it was braided tightly and came in different human hair colors), he cut it with scissors along the edge of the comb to insure that all ends were even. In the meantime, having already put on the grease paint, he applied a smelly mess of spirit-gum to his face and firmly pressed the beard against it. Once properly shaped, the beard could be used numerous times, until it became noticeably scraggly. Removing it, each time, was a matter of peeling it off carefully. Having watched many actors put on beards, I'm sure I could dispense this tonsorial service today to any man who needed it. One of my childhood frustrations was that I could never wear these marvelous chin whiskers.

My incursions into dressing rooms were always quickly terminated by the mama's admonition, "Now Dody, come here. Don't you bother anyone!" Invariably, my indulgent colleagues would reassure her, "She's no bother. I don't mind."

Another wonderful place I discovered in my explorations backstage at the Alcazar, was a very special, large room at stage level. In it reposed a most amazing array of things: little gilded chairs, upholstered pieces of furniture, statues, vases, palm trees in pots, and other articles too numerous to recount. Like our present-day Flea Market, the room housed everything imaginable. This fascinating repository was the "prop room." The man who presided over it was Harry Glendinning, a genius, it seemed, who could produce anything from it. How clearly I still see him, limping about the prop room and pointing out to me its many delights and their uses. In themselves, these experiences in this magical storeroom were an education—treasures all, of my beautiful Alcazar.

Among others in the Alcazar's brilliant stock company, of whom I became particularly fond as I grew to know them, were familiar San Francisco theater names like: Kitty Belmour, whose husband, Louis, had once been its stage manager; Frank Bacon, who left our company for a very sucessful starring role in New York in LIGHTNIN: and George Osbourne, my unforgettable favorite, whom I can still see, climbing to the top of the Christmas tree (set up by the company for me, backstage) to get the woolly lamb pulltoy that said "baah" when I pressed his head down, and which I preferred to the big doll they had already given me.

Frank Bacon   Alcazar Theatre c. 1900
Credit: Barrett-Miller Collection

Still another dear friend was Polly Stockwell, our ingenue, daughter of the well-known San Francisco actor-manager, L.R. Stockwell. Her father went blind in his later years, and a benefit show was staged to help him over a financial crisis—the only way theater people took care of their own before the advent of actors' beneficial organizations. I'm happy to have been part of the L.R. Stockwell Benefit Show. Mr. Stockwell himself participated in the performance. Much to the admiration and respect of his faithful audience, this seasoned actor put on a very poignant presentation in a sketch. He won our hearts, too, from the time we started him out from the wings. After that, he was on his own. He took some numbered steps forward, turned right to face the audience, and then proceeded some steps downstage. As we spoke our lines to him, he turned toward the speaker and addressed him on whichever side the latter might be. So accomplished an actor was Mr. Stockwell, that one could scarcely believe the flawless performance was executed by one totally blind.

Since Mr. Stockwell's financial predicament was not unique, an interpolation on the plight of the destitute or sick actor in those days seems fitting at this point. Countless well-known actors, and sometimes managers, found themselves in dire financial straits, and benefits were the only recourse. Actors, like other artists, were individualists. They recognized their own special importance to the total world of the theater. Such being the case, one can appreciate how difficult it must have been to organize these disparate, independent, and proud personalities, even for their own protection, as when illness struck or companies broke up for lack of finances and could not pay salaries.

For years after the Theatrical Syndicate was established in 1896, it had a stranglehold on bookings and financing; and some managers could, in a sense, take advantage of imposed restrictions by sustaining the intolerable working conditions of the actors. The latter never knew in advance what to expect, for since there was no standard contract, each manager's was the final word on free rehearsal time, number of appearances, and salary.

Although the two weeks' notice of closing had always been the accepted custom, since the Syndicate, actors were lucky to receive a week's notice, for many were fired without any forewarning.

Costs for transportation and costumes were generally absorbed by the actors, and working conditions backstage were often impossible. Regarding costumes, I recall that many actors indicated in their ads in trade publications,"wardrobe" or "extensive wardrobe," especially for period plays. One's wardrobe could be an important consideration by managers working on limited capital. In my own case, the elaborate costumes I wore were either created, ordered, or rented by the mama, at our own expense.

Further vicissitudes came when "ghost walks" did not materialize, leaving the artists in unlikely places and broke, to boot. Often, they found themselves stranded in the middle of nowhere, at the mercy of unscrupulous or indifferent managers, or unfriendly local townspeople. For these hapless actors, security and freedom from exploitation were cherished goals.

The earliest attempt to organize actors and actresses against these conditions was by the Actors' Society of America (May 1896), some of whose well-known members included: David Belasco, Fanny Davenport, Nat Goodwin, and Mrs. Fiske. After an unsuccesful petition to the American Federation of Labor for a charter, the Actors' Society of America lost its impetus, as well as its membership.

A more promising New York organization was the one that called itself the White Rats Actors' Union of America, or simply, "White Rats"—"star" spelled backwards. It was granted a charter by the American Federation of Labor, one that covered both vaudevillians and dramatic actors and actresses. Its moving force was Harry Mountford, International Executive; and, in time, the organization spread nationwide. It was while I was living at the St. Ann's that, about 1901, I was elected, because of my tender years, an "honorary" member of the White Rats—an honor I have held dear these many years.

But the rise of Actors' Equity Association in 1913 would, in time, spell the demise of the White Rats. Actors' Equity Association sought a charter from the American Federation of Labor, but were told that they would have to join the White Rats, of course on the latter's terms. For years, there were confrontations and stand-offs between the White Rats and AEA, with the latter always holding out for complete independence.

In November, 1917, the Committee on Adjustments of the AFL proposed revocation of the White Rats' charter and the substitution of a new International; but Harry Mountford held his ground for the White Rats. An acrimonious period continued between Equity and the United Managers' Protective Association, and Equity and the White Rats.

The resolution of the squabbles is well delineated by Alfred Harding in his "The Revolt of The Actors":

> *The terms finally worked out were in the nature of a compromise. Equity had not the International Charter for which it had been asking; but neither had it been required to become a Branch of the White Rats Actors' International Union of America.*
>
> *The White Rats agreed to turn in their charter to the Federation (of Labor) which would issue a new international charter to cover the entire amusement field. Within the international would be a number of unions, each of which would be autonomous in its own field. So, instead of being subordinate to the White Rats, Equity stood on an equal footing; and because of the system of representation on the International Board by which each union was entitled to one representative for every three hundred members in good standing, Equity was likely to be the dominant factor in the new international.*
>
> *July 18 (1919) . . . there was created the Associated Actors' and Artistes of America, the Four A's.*
>
> *The officers of the Four A's indicated the nature of the compromise. Equity had been conceded the Presidency and Treasury; the White Rats had reserved the Executive Secretaryship and Vice Presidency for its own officers, at least on this first board.*

The "compromise" proved to be an emasculation of the White Rats and, in time, with the increasing rise of Equity, the White Rats Actors' Union of America gradually faded away.

The long sought-after reforms, however, especially the standard contract, came to fruition; and the actor and actress of the succeeding decades have been the beneficiaries.

After THE ADVENTURES OF NELL GWYNNE, came a change of pace. I left the Alcazar for a two weeks' engagement at the Orpheum Theater in THE LITTLEST GIRL, Robert Hilliard's dramatic adaptation of Richard Harding Davis' short story, HER FIRST APPEARANCE. Mr. Hilliard played Van Bibber, friend of Mr. Carruthers, who was played by Mr. St. Maur. I played the title role of the "littlest girl" in the ballet company; but the part in the sketch called for no lines. It was enough for the role that I be sleepy, pretty, and all tarlton and sparkle.

In this strange play with social overtones, the child's brokenhearted father, having rejected his faithless wife, casts off their child, too. The little girl is left with an aunt who, in time, places her in a ballet company. Van Bibber's mission, having seen the tyke dance in the ballet, is to , somehow, convince Carruthers, her bitter and unyielding father, to accept his innocent, abandoned child and spare her the rigors of work at such a tender age.

As the play opens, the scene is the elegant New York drawing-room of the Carruthers mansion. Van Bibber, still attired in the evening clothes, top hat, and cloak he wore to the ballet, enters carrying the sleeping cherub in his arms. He crosses the stage to a large chair where he gently places her. Drawing a screen before her to conceal her from the father who enters stage left, Van Bibber turns toward his friend, Carruthers. The two men settle in comfortable chairs center left, and the dialogue takes place. I found two weeks' repetition of this lengthy exchange rather boring, because I had to remain silent and motionless during the play's entire denouement. I also had to be very careful lest the garland of roses round my head be canted askew. A bundle of tarlton, I continued my angelic slumber while Van Bibber launched his noble undertaking. He

Baby Dody Title Role, "The Littlest Girl"   Orpheum Theatre 1901
Credit: Barrett-Miller Collection

pleads the child's cause with his intransigent friend. When all else fails, he pushes the screen aside, revealing the sleeping child. Lifting the drowsy child from the Land of Nod, Van Bibber places her on her feet, before the startled father. Of course, this disarmingly exquisite, sleepyhead melts her father's heart and reduces him to putty. Carruthers embraces his winsome cherub, indicating she will never again have to dance in the ballet for a living—so ends the tedium!

Reviews about this tearjerker were, for the most part, tart. An especially caustic one by Josephine Hart Phelps in the Argonaut opined, "I do not think that Mr. Hilliard's play takes with the Orpheum audience. There was a steady accompaniment of coughs, sneezes, and rustlings, which is the bored auditor's unconscious and involuntary testimony that his soul is absent." She put herself squarely on the audience's side that the play was monotonous (and I concur) because it consisted entirely of long exchanges between the two men. Her comments on the child's part were only somewhat more flattering; "We have two fugitive glimpses of the child, a pretty little creature, all snow and sparkle of tarlton and tinsel, but not another glimpse of femininity to light up the waste of words." After observing that she thought it was a disappointment that the action had not transpired, like the first act of ZAZA, "behind the scenes of a theater," she added: "And to those who like child-acting, it was no doubt a further disappointment that the child did not lisp some few lines of baby prattle. When we pause to reflect, however, that Mr. Hilliard would be obliged to carry a day-nursery over the continent in order to be able to take a fully trained child actress with him to the several Orpheum stands, and that he would probably have several hair-raising experiences in grappling with the various infantile outbursts of measles and chicken pox, we must commend his good sense for restricting the appearance of his leading lady to the two glimpses aforesaid."

Obviously, THE LITTLEST GIRL had hardly caused a positive ripple, but it did have the questionable distinction of "playing" concurrently with two events—one of local, the other of nationwide interest. San Francisco's popular Techau Tavern, which had burned down some months earlier, was announcing

Papinta, The Myriad Dancer   Orpheum Theatre 1901
Credit: The Archives For The Performing Arts, S.F.

with pride that the "restored and renovated" eatery had purposely chosen a memorable date for its second opening, May 4, 1901—Inauguration Day of President William McKinley's second term. While the date proved an auspicious one for Mr. R.J. Tehau's second start, the same cannot be said for Mr. McKinley's. Six months later, September 6, the president was shot while attending a reception that followed his address at the Pan-American Exposition in Buffalo, New York, and died eight days later.

Among those sharing the vaudeville bill at the Orpheum during THE LITTLEST GIRL, was an unusual act, "Papinta and Her Serpentine Dance." Papinta was well known to San Francisco audiences. Seven years earlier, May 1894, she had made her San Francisco debut at the California Theatre with the Hopkins' New Trans-Oceanic Star Spangled Specialty Company. At that time, she was billed as "Papinta, The Marvelous Danseuse, In the Myriad Dance. The present craze in Paris and London. Positively produced for the first time in San Francisco." The playbill further elaborated:

"NOTE   The dance production of costly mirrors, calcium lights, a bewildering illusion, in which the audience is forced to believe that it is witnessing a grand ballet ensemble, when in reality only the graceful Papinta is entertaining with her dance. Particular attention is called to the harmonious blending of lights and the many rainbow effects produced. The sole property of J.D. Hopkins, H.C. Miner and Herr von Prittwitz Palm, the inventor."

As with her Myriad Dance, Papinta's Serpentine Dance drew much favorable attention. Although she could not lay claim to being the world's greatest dancer, Papinta's Serpentine Dance was different, perhaps even "gimmicky." To the best of my recollection, however, mirrors were not employed in this dance.

Draped over her head and covering her entire body, she wore an enormously voluminous tent-like costume. It was made of white silk and fell in myriad folds, to her feet. Underneath, attached to each side of her dress, was a wand. From under her massive robe, Papinta grasped a wand in each hand and slowly raised her arms to a horizontal position, sparking the first response from the audience. Gradually, she then raised her arms above her head, fluttered them, and ran about the stage, while multicolored lights played on the very supple Papinta, creating the illusion of a butterfly in flight. When she held the wands high above her head and pirouetted, she created the illusion of a white lily. Thus, with her sinuous movements in this simple "prop-less" act, and with only the enhancement of the colored lights, Papinta presented a large repertoire of illusions.

While the San Francisco Argonaut's drama critic, Josephine Hart Phelps, had given THE LITTLEST GIRL a well deserved caustic review, about Papinta she wrote the more complimentary appraisal that follows:

> *"And then Papinta came. Life is full of coincidences. Next week Loie Fuller, upon whose beautiful color-dances Papinta's special line of work is founded, and who has only come to San Francisco once before, will be in town. And I dare say that many who have seen Papinta at the Orpheum for fifty cents will be surprised to find that the famous Loie can offer nothing better. How amazingly and bewilderingly and incredibly beautiful these color effects are. The dancing is nothing: a mere drop lost in surges and seas of glorious, swelling, towering wave bursts of light, and radiance, and color. The human figure in the centre is merely a standard-bearer, from whose active, tireless arms roll and ripple countless billows of silk, upon which the varying hues shimmer and bloom and burn. The eye is ravished by the sight, and we sit like enchanted children watching giant bubbles tossed off by that most potent wizard of our day, electricity."*

Papinta, born Carolyn Holprin in 1867, was a resident of Contra Costa County (east, across the Bay from San Francisco), where she owned a farm. In 1907, while touring Europe, she died in Dusseldorf, Germany—her career thus abruptly ending when she was only forty years old. Her body was returned home and buried in the Pioneer Cemetery in Martinez, California.

A parting profile on the Orpheum seems a fitting digression at this time. Building for the first (there were five)

Orpheum at 119 O'Farrell Street, San Francisco, was started in November 1886 by Gustav Walter—the same gentleman who earlier had managed the Vienna Gardens (Sutter and Stockton Streets), the Fountain (Kearney Street), and the Wigwam Theatre (Geary and Stockton Streets).

On June 30, 1887, the first Orpheum opened with a program that featured Rosner's Hungarian Electric Orchestra from Budapest, at the then outrageous cost of six thousand dollars. The bill also included a variety of vaudeville acts:

"A Practical Joke" (with Harry Le Clair and W.J. Russell)
Silvo—The World's Greatest Equipoise Artist
Ouda—The Parisian Aerial Marvel
Mlle. Garetta And Her Wonderful Bevy of Fifty
    Performing Pigeons
"A Night Of Terror"—A Comic Pantomime By The
    Original Phoites Company

First Orpheum Theatre 1887-1906
Credit: The Archives For The Performing Arts, S.F.

This opening bill played for six months, setting the tone for the typical vaudeville-drama format at the Orpheum until 1891, when it became the Orpheum *Opera* House and its playbills for 1891 and 1892 included such operas as THE RABBI, BOHEMIAN GIRL, and (January 16, 1892) ERMINE by the New York Opera Company. Other opera companies engaged during this period were: the C.D. Hess Opera Company, three Spanish opera companies, and the Columbia Opera Company.

This venture into opera was short-lived, however, for in 1893, the Orpheum returned to the vaudeville-drama format for which it became nationally famous. Indeed, by 1897, Gustav Walter was listed on the Orpheum playbills as Director General of the Orpheum Circuit (San Francisco, Los Angeles, and Sacramento). Soon after, however, he had to forfeit his lovely Orpheum to two creditors, Morris Meyerfeld and Dan Mitchell, to whom he owed $50,000 for the liquor sold in the Orpheum's bar.

This Orpheum of my misadventure in THE LITTLEST GIRL was still presenting vaudeville when it fell victim, along with its "across-the-street" neighbor, the Alcazar, to the ravages by earthquake and fire in 1906. The bill on the marquee that week was: Vaudeville (Motoring) and Orpheum Motion Picture.

Undaunted, on May 20, 1906, a month after the earthquake, the second Orpheum set up business in San Francisco's only surviving theater, the Chutes, located on the north side of Golden Gate Park, Fulton Street (between 10th and 11th Avenues).

About eight months later, January 21, 1907, a third Orpheum opened, located on Ellis Street, west of Fillmore. I recall that at that time it was thought the Fillmore District could become a better location for theaters than the former "downtown" area of pre-earthquake times. This notion proved fallacious, as other theaters—the Alcazar, included—would learn. San Franciscans were not about to accept this change from the accustomed downtown theater-row. Nevertheless, this Orpheum held out at its Ellis Street location for almost two and a half years.

On April 19, 1909, the Orpheum moved back to more familiar surroundings, for me—O'Farrell, between Stockton and Powell Streets. Again, San Francisco had a downtown Orpheum Theatre—this time, the fourth one.

On September 29, 1929, the fifth location for the Orpheum was established on Market Street, near Hyde, when Radio-Keith-Orpheum (R.K.O.) purchased the former New Pantages and changed its name to Orpheum. Since then, the Orpheum has presented an assortment of formats: vaudeville, vaudeville-movies, "talkies," CINERAMA, CINERAMA HOLIDAY, and AROUND THE WORLD IN 80 DAYS (1954—1956).

Then, according to Russell Hartley, Director of the San Francisco Archives For The Performing Arts, in his paper, A SHORT HISTORY OF THE ORPHEUM THEATRE, San Francisco 1876—1977:

"When the construction of Bart (Bay Area Rapid Transit System) tore up Market Street, a station was constructed near the Orpheum, which necessitated the removal of the theater's marquee. Most of the theater life along Market Street was seriously affected, and this situation led to the shutting down of the Orpheum's activities."

After Bart's completion of the Market Street work, A.C.T. (American Conservatory Theater) took over the house for two runs of the popular musical HAIR. HAIR was followed by a concert version of JESUS CHRIST SUPERSTAR, BIG SHOW OF 1936 (presented August 1972) by Barney Gould, and MAN OF LA MANCHA.

On May 10, 1977, the Orpheum's interior was remodeled to accommodate the San Francisco Light Opera and, as of this writing, still functions for this purpose.

This digression from my appearance at the original Orpheum in THE LITTLEST GIRL in 1901 has been long, but it was felt that because this famous playhouse has been a part of San Francisco's theater history over one hundred years, the interpolation was justified. But now, let me return to 1901.

True, my engagement at the Orpheum was a "ho-hum" interlude that left few worthwhile memories. This bout with mediocrity in THE LITTLEST GIRL was greatly mitigated by the fact that I was rehearsing, at the same time, for a much more rewarding adventure at Belasco and Thall's new theater, the Central, on Market near Eighth. These were busy days, full of promise, for there was much excited chatter in the San Francisco theater world over the Central's pending presentation of Harriet Beecher Stowe's UNCLE TOM'S CABIN; and I was to be little Eva once more.

Promotions for the great event were well-touted in the newspapers and magazines. The play had been in preparation for several weeks as the management announced, "It will be the most elaborate presentation of this great play ever presented in this city. The cotton plantations, with the slave laborers at work, the negro festivals, the breaking of the ice on the river, across which Eliza flees with the savage bloodhounds in pursuit, the slave mart, and a beautiful transformation scene of some fifteen minutes duration are among the scenic features."

For me, this was to be a different experience from the other two when I played little Eva in the "afterpieces" at the Cineograph Parlors, and in the G.W. Lowe Roadshow. The difference was created by the immensity of the house itself. The Central's elaborate stage was intended to accommodate to limitless spatial and scenic demands. Further, the script not only was unabbreviated, it had been expanded wherever an addition improved the production. I had to unlearn the versions I had played before. Lines and cues had been altered to adjust to the necessary pacing the huge stage dictated. With nothing to restrict or hinder the best possible artistic expression, the great feeling of freedom on such a vast stage was to afford me the most delightful experience in acting I had ever known. I became better acquainted with my little friend, Eva, in the garden scene on her father's plantation. So flawless were the acoustics of the theater that the slightest nuance was carried effortlessly out over the vast auditorium. This was particularly so when I sang to my father, pleading for the freedom, by release, of Uncle Tom:

> *When your daughter is taken away*
> *And your heart is filled with care*
> *When with angels I will pray*
> *For your peace and comfort there*
> *Uncle Tom! Oh set him free*
> *Father, promise this to me*

I sometimes wonder how many people are left who remember the words and music to this, then, very moving song—Eva's plaintive appeal to her father.

In the famous transformation scene, memories of what its effects may have been on the audience were lost in the mechanics of it all. In particular, I recall the great incline from about "second-upstage" up to the flies. There, in a white robe with flowing sleeves, my curls draped over my shoulders, arms extended down to Uncle Tom, head slightly to one side, and a look of compassion on my face, *I was hauled away up into the flies!*

One thing always troubled me, however: the large glittering wings I wore. They seemed like an extra set of arms that made me a six-limbed creature—an attribute I could never reconcile with an angel. While I felt like a monstrosity, I accepted all this "angel business" as just another one of the many superstitions of my mentors—a comfortable answer to many situations throughout my career as Baby Dody.

Whatever my reservations about the wings, reviews proclaimed, "Baby Dody is a clever little girl and enacted the role of Little Eva in such a natural way that she brought tears to the eyes of many in the audience." I was truly among very good company, for our excellent cast included seasoned artists: James M. Ward as Uncle Tom; Fay Courtney, Topsy; Myron Leffingwell, Simon Legree; and Lorena Atwood as Eliza. If, as noted, "the balance of the cast was in clever and capable hands and all acted in a convincing way that entirely won the audience," then I was, indeed, a privileged little girl.

The revival of UNCLE TOM'S CABIN across the nation was inspired, according to the San Francisco Examiner's Ashton Stevens, by the W.A. Brady production in New York, with L.R. Stockwell as Marks and Wilton Lackaye, Uncle Tom. Not to be outdone, Belasco and Thall went all out to present the best

UNCLE TOM'S CABIN the city of San Francisco had ever seen. That they succeeded, was attested by the packed houses during its entire run.

From this spectacular version of UNCLE TOM'S CABIN at the Central Theater, where all was on a grand scale and expression had no limitations, I went to still another version, my fourth. I had been little Eva on the Cineograph Parlor's cracker-box stage; on the more expanded, but still "make-do" stages of the small towns, during the George W. Lowe Roadshow; and on the Central's expansive stage, where I am very glad I played the role as it should be played. Now I was rehearsing the part under still another somewhat different frame of reference—under canvas, in the Harry Connors' Mammoth Pavilion Show. Again, there were different lines and subtle changes employed, to best adapt the play for its rendition in a traveling tent show. And, again, I had to unlearn much of what I had learned before, posing, at times, some difficult challenges. Added to the frenzy of rehearsals were the many fittings for my costume: a high-waisted, long, white silk dress with lace pantalettes showing below; dainty slippers over white stockings; white bows on my long blonde curls; and a white straw (Leghorn) hat.

As usual, the pressures of deadlines had their effect of eventually restoring order out of chaos, for the obstacles were conquered, the blur of confusion was dissipated, and all was readied for the "shakedown" performance in Berkeley, California, starting April 15, 1901. The premiere was preceded by a big parade, a procedure to be duplicated at each stop on our tour.

Mr. Connors was commended for his selection of a "very capable company—(with) undoubtedly one of the finest propositions on the road." Notable among the leads in this tent version of UNCLE TOM'S CABIN were:

      Uncle Tom—George M. Hermance
        (also our stage manager)
      George Harris—John F. McDonald
      St. Clair—John F. McDonald
      Phineas Fletcher—Charles King

    Shelby—Charles Tonnie
    Eliza—Celine Archer
    Ophelia—Laura Adams
    Topsy—Pauline Shayne

Including those who played the lesser roles: Walter Miller, Bert Vanson, Ed C. Barton, Herbert Clarke, William Douglass, T. Daniel Dougherty, Paul Crimp, Henry Dority, Little Bertie, and Ione Everett, our cast numbered some twenty people. Because each performance was followed by a concert, there were a few added names, such as: my old friend Dutch Walton, Gus Tate, and Eva Leslie who joined T. Daniel Dougherty, Bert Van Cleeve, Pauline Shayne, and me in the closing offering, or "added attraction," as it was billed.

If for no other reason, a look at the list of the "Executive Staff" of the Harry Connors' Mammoth Pavilion Show tells the story of some of the problems that accompanied an undertaking of such proportions: Harry Connors, Lessee and Manager; E. Block, Business Manager; Frank Herrell, Treasurer; George Hermance, Stage Manager; William H. Simpson, Musical Director; T. Ehrman, Band Master; Walter Pollard, Master Mechanic; James Schneider, Property Man; Jerry Prince, Gas Man; Fred Roads, Boss Canvas Man; C. Neville, Master Transportation; G. Doolittle, Steward; Bert Van Cleeve, Press Agent; McClelland and McClelland, Attorneys-at-law.

With our Berkeley engagement over, the Harry Connors' Mammoth Pavilion Show left San Francisco by special train for a tour of the San Joaquin Valley and Southern California cities of: Stockton, Lodi, Modesto, Merced, Madera, Fresno, Porterville, Visalia, Hanford, Tulare, Bakersfield, Pasadena, Pomona, Ontario, Redlands, San Bernardino, Riverside, San Diego, Santa Ana, Anaheim, San Pedro, Santa Monica, and Los Angeles.

Dimensions of the giant tent we carried were impressive for the times: a 100 x 80 foot auditorium, with a 54 x 40 foot stage; a raised platform that extended from the orchestra line to the main entrance, a distance of 90 feet, and accommodated 1000 folding-back, reserved chairs. On either side of this, in tier style, were "circus seats with a capacity of 1400, so that the theater (would) accommodate a total of 2400 people."

Adding to the giant logistics feat of our "combination," were all the paraphernalia for: "a parade, consisting of large floats representing cotton-picking scenes, the old cabin, the whipping-stake, besides a Shetland pony and cart for Little Eva, jubilee singers in carriages, a pack of immense bloodhounds, three donkeys, not to speak of the band chariot and the indispensable drum-major. When the combination arrives in a city or town on its royal route, with glittering banners, flags, music, parade and great white canvas, it will be 'circus day ' indeed." It was truly a "traveling theater with stage scenery and all the accessories."

Personnel for the spectacular Connors' Roadshow was on an equally large scale. As already noted, the company included some twenty members in the cast, as well as an executive staff of about sixteen. But added to these, were workers of all descriptions: musicians, stage hands, property men, canvas men, transportation men, stewards, cooks, waiters, mechanics, "gas men," laborers to assemble and dismantle scenery, sets, and the tent itself, and advance press agents who traveled in uniform.

From the start, our train seemed to be divided into an accepted caste system, with actors and staff, the "aristocracy," in one Pullman car, and the workers, in others. The remaining cars carried animals and the mounds of equipment. The cooking was done in a separate car, and the meals were served on trays to each section of the actors' Pullman. Workers ate in the cook car. Mr. Doolittle, our steward, was in charge of all the buying—food and supplies— and managed the assignment well, considering the thankless job. The caste system, it seemed, prevailed among the workers themselves. Tent men, skilled in their craft, directed the "roustabouts" who did the heavy work. Thus, implied and accepted dichotomies existed among both actors and workers. The mama and I had our own section in the Pullman, and we were as comfortable as could be expected, considering the confined quarters in which we traveled.

Upon arriving at a destination, the train pulled to a siding. For reasons of convenience, it was always near the site chosen for the tent. There followed a well-perfected plan for transporting all the equipment to the tent site, and a miraculous assemblage began. Usually, we did not approach the tent till all was set up; but on the rare occasions I was permitted to watch the assembling of the great canvas house, I marveled at the wonderland that unfurled before my eyes. Each step was synchronized into a flowing movement, until the enormous traveling pavilion's metamorphosis was completed. The stage that had been dismantled into sections to facilitate its portability—but which still took up much space in the cars—was now rejoined in place. In time, the 90-foot-long platform for the reserved seats spread to the main entrance.

Ingenious for the times, was the special lighting system used in this mammoth canvas theater. Calcium lights hung from above at variously spaced points, imparting a bright, white glow inside the entire tent.

Mr. Connors had adopted a recent innovation, the so-called "Ad Curtain." It was sectioned off into various advertisements for well-known products of the day such as Sarsaparilla, Hire's Root Beer, Sapolio, White Owl Cigars, and Borden's Condensed Milk. I suppose if there were "ad-curtains" today, they would be advertising colas, razor blades, and deodorants. Since our "ad-curtain" was also the drop curtain, it was an excellent source of revenue.

Backstage, conditions were not so glamorous as out front. Performers lived out of their trunks, so these portable closets were clustered about, for the convenience of their owners. Canvas was spread on the ground for a "floor-covering." The mama had our trunk very well organized, so that our dresses hung free; and to insure their impeccable appearance, there were the ubiquitous sadiron and "ironing board" (the lid of our Taylor Trunk till).

For me, nevertheless, there was a very special attraction backstage: the pair of dogs used in the famous escape scene when Eliza, carrying her young son, Harry, flees from Kentucky, across the frozen Ohio River. In this breathless scene, Eliza is spurred onward, intent on saving her son from Haley, the slave trader, who had just bought him from Mr. Shelby, the plantation owner. Though hardly compatible with the book's treatment of the episode, like most dramatized versions this one, too, used dogs. Indeed, audiences expected them in this very tense scene when Eliza is driven by the frenzied hope of preventing her son from being wrenched from her and sold at the auction block by Haley. Her wildest dreams are that one day they will be reunited with her husband, George Harris, in blessed freedom in Canada. She leaps from one cake of ice to another, as the frozen river breaks under her. The "ice" used in the Connors' Show consisted of little platforms on rockers, whose movements simulated the river's motion as she jumped her way across. I was always amazed that Eliza, so ably played by Celine Archer, did not break her legs while on her nightly leap-dance. During this escape, she not only rendered her dramatic lines superbly, she maneuvered "ice block" after "ice block," as the pursuing men and barking dogs closed in on her.

According to the dramatic versions of UNCLE TOM'S CABIN, bloodhounds were used because of their known tracking sense. But since the bloodhound is not a very large dog, contrary to some popular beliefs, the management decided to substitute two Great Danes, the better to impress the audience. The dogs were enormous, and their impact on the audience so overwhelming, that their authenticity as bloodhounds was never questioned. The two beautiful, soft beige Great Danes, Don and Silver, were tied to a stake backstage, until time for their appearance with the men chasing poor Eliza.

Don and Silver were extraordinary animals, and I adored them. As they sat chained, and I stood before them, our eyes would meet on the same level, for the dogs were very big, and I, very small. It was for them that I saved my sugar-coated cookies the mama always brought along to assuage my hunger pangs between meals. Considering the mama's usual restraint in dispensing sweets to me, the sugar-coated cookies were special prizes, indeed; and parting with them, truly an act of sacrifice prompted only by the greatest devotion. But, Don and Silver were worthy of my unqualified love, so I gave them the sugar-coated cookies and ate the less desirable plain ones—greater love hath no child. My two giant friends of the cavernous mouths swallowed each cooky with one gulp, while I watched, transfixed. I wonder if they knew how much I loved them and how tremendous, my sacrifice—perhaps. Even now, as I look back on the Connors' Mammoth Pavilion Show, the most cherished memories still center around these two Great Danes, the Honorables Don and Silver. I hope that some day I shall once again give them sugar-coated cookies, when I "ascend."

During most of my scenes as little Eva, the orchestra in the pit played the usual soft, sad music. It could hardly do otherwise, for the specter of little Evangeline St. Clair dying of "consumption" called for nothing short of tunes calculated to bestir the deepest emotions—the familiar "Hearts and Flowers" and "Angel's Serenade." The music helped perpetuate the mood of impending death that was the burden of her song, later.

First of the three most memorable scenes in which she plays, was the garden scene. In it, little Eva appears with her beloved Uncle Tom, her constant and devoted protector-companion. Uncle Tom held a special place in the dubious "social order" of the slaves on the St. Clair plantation. While the field slaves were quartered in a separate area, Uncle Tom, a household slave, had his own little cabin and worked only in the mansion, for the master and his family. Implied was the presumption that household slaves received more privileged treatment than the field slaves.

Uncle Tom had been aboard the same boat that was transporting Northeasterner, newcomer Aunt Ophelia to manage the St. Clair household. Little Eva and St. Clair were accompanying the latter's sister to the plantation. When the little girl falls overboard, it is Uncle Tom who rescues her. When the grateful father hears, later, that Uncle Tom is on his way to be sold at auction, he responds to Eva's pleas to buy the lovable slave and spare him the risk of going to a cruel master. And while ostensibly bought as a coachman for St. Clair's wife, Marie, Uncle Tom spent virtually all his time as Eva's companion. All the foregoing facts are implicit in the garden scene. In it, the very humble and religious attendant shares his love of the Bible with his charge. They are seen strolling hand-in-hand in the beautiful garden, where the sick little girl has been taken for fresh air and sunlight. When Eva asks, "Where do you suppose New Jerusalem is, Uncle Tom?" he solemnly replies with the famous line, "Up in the clouds, Miss Eva, up in the clouds." When her father joins them in the garden, the ailing little Eva pleads with him for Tom's freedom, in the memorable song, "When Your Daughter Is Taken Away."

Eva's second well-known scene takes place when she lies on her death bed, surrounded by her father, mother, Uncle Tom, Aunt Ophelia, and the irrepressible Topsy. It is during this dramatic moment that little Eva describes heaven in the familiar, "I see the beautiful gates ajar and behind them it is all mother-of-pearl." I would never recite those lines without remembering my old friend, Pearl Allen, and the mental block his name had created during the George W. Lowe Roadshow.

When a short time after little Eva's death her father dies, too, the unconscionable widow sells all the slaves. Uncle Tom becomes the property of the cruel Simon Legree, whose bestiality toward him prompts Uncle Tom's dying utterance, "Massa, my body may belong to you, but my soul belongs to God." In this third and best remembered scene of all, the Transformation Scene, Uncle Tom is dying and, in a vision, sees little Eva with extended arms, beckoning him to heaven. It was an impossible scene in which I again ascended an incline, by means of ropes and wires. Again, I was clad in a long trailing robe with wings, my long curls undulating as I floated away toward heaven, and my arms extended toward Uncle Tom. He watches me ascend, gradually drops his outstretched arm, and the curtain falls. Alas, this time my trip to heaven was not so elegant as in the more impressive surroundings of the Central.

Perhaps the most exciting experience with Harry Connors' Mammoth Pavilion Show was the parade. Although UNCLE TOM'S CABIN was considered a "theatrical sensation," it had much of the trappings of a circus—all but the elephants. When we arrived in a town and the men put up the tent, everyone "doubled in brass," as the expression went.Every worker had more than one job to perform. In fact, his proficiency at several jobs was the most important criterion for engaging him. All played a musical instrument or two, and these talents were used in the parade.

Ah, the parade—the joyous, noisy "umpah" of the band as I sat in the beautiful little wicker pony cart, pulled by the delightful white pony with the large irregular brown markings. To protect me from sunburn, I wore a wide-brimmed, white Leghorn hat. It had a wreath of flowers around its crown and long ribbon streamers down the back; and, to keep the capricious breezes from making off with the hat, there was an elastic band that slipped under the chin. The mama insisted on the hat—no sun must mar her little fair-haired beauty. And besides, who ever heard of a healthy, sun-tanned little Eva! So, dressed in my costume, I rode my beautiful chariot and was the main attraction of the parade. Before me were the drum major and band, followed by the two Great Danes on a chain. Behind me, marched the cast and chorus; and on both sides of the street were lined the cheering, clapping, and happy townsfolk. What little girl could resist the exultation of being the cynosure of it all?

Yet, the high point of the parades came on the occasions when I was able to bribe the boy who led the pony pulling the cart. I deliberately saved my small change to "persuade" him to relinquish his hold and allow me to handle the reins—a feat which seemed to me to really prove my capabilities. I regarded this my counter-stratagem to the mama's insistence that someone hold the bridle, lest the pony run off with me. Any child would understand the challenge had to be met.

The arrival of a show of the magnitude of Harry Connors' was an event of great importance to the towns and cities we visited. The schools considered UNCLE TOM'S CABIN a play of such historical significance that they made every effort to encourage the children to see it. When the teachers brought their classes to the train to meet little Eva, I would go to the observation platform for a personal appearance.

With their teachers hovering in the background, these lovely children came forward with handfuls of flowers—no doubt from their mothers' gardens—tied with strings or ribbons, and with that unmistakable home-grown touch. Very soon the platform loaded with flowers resembled a first class mortuary; still, I loved the flowers and the children's shiny faces. Both reminded me of the floral settings of the cherubs, frescoed on the ceilings of our earlier home. The children's enthusiasm was very real, and I can still see their precious little faces as I greeted them and answered their many questions. How I wished I could have played with them, but that was never part of the "script."

Once the children left, the question was what to do with the mounds of flowers. Fortunately, the cast, always ready to help me out of my glorious multiflorous predicaments, were willing recipients. In time the cars were festooned with flowers, up and down the aisles, on brackets overhead, and in some of the most unexpected places. To some, the cars resembled a garden show or a florist shop, but to me, they became the beautiful gardens the mama and papa were unable to provide because of our travels. It would be many years before I would sate my longings for a garden of my own.

Before taking leave of UNCLE TOM'S CABIN, I am impelled to present little four-year-old Cordelia Howard, the first little Eva. I'm sure she must have loved her dogs, pony, and ponycart, as I did. Her father, George C. Howard, manager of the Troy Museum in Troy, New York, was so impressed with Harriet Beecher Stowe's phenomenal book, published March 20, 1852, that he engaged his cousin, George L. Aiken, the Troy's resident playwright, to write a dramatized version of it. The purpose of the play would be to star his little Cordelia, whose acting skills the proud father was determined to proclaim. Aiken's play turned out to be a family venture, with Howard playing St. Clair until his death in 1887. Mrs. Howard played Topsy; her mother, Mrs. Fox, played Aunt Ophelia; the twenty-two-year-old Aiken was George Harris; and Charles Fox, Cordelia's uncle, played Fletcher and Cute. The only "non-family" lead was given to a close friend of the family, Green Germon, who was persuaded, against his initial repugnance, to being blackened with burned cork for the character role of the original Uncle Tom—a distinction he was later to cherish, as the play achieved undreamed of success.

Aiken's dramatization of UNCLE TOM'S CABIN had its debut at the Troy Museum on Septembr 27, 1852, barely six months after the book was published. After a hundred performances, the Howard Company moved to the National Theatre in New York City, where it played three hundred fifty performances. Captain Purdy, manager of the theatre, paid one hundred dollars a week for the Mrs. Howard-daughter combination. He was to question his original burst of "generosity," especially when in order to meet the public's demand, he was forced to present more than a dozen performances a week, necessitating salary adjustments.

Competition from four other companies of UNCLE TOM'S CABIN in New York City would lead to extremes in promotional gimmicks and dramatic license. The original, fairly straight rendition, was to undergo all manner of embellishments in acting, scenery, and music. Each company that was born tried to outdo the others, with sometimes garish results. Captain Purdy himself, in response to the heavy competition from Barnum's American Museum, came up with a "Grand Jubilee Festival," replete with a thirty-piece brass band, fireworks, and special lighting on the theater's rooftop, to mark the National Theatre's hundreth performance of UNCLE TOM'S CABIN, with little Cordelia.

Responding to another challenge, from the Bowery Theatre in January 1854, Captain Purdy repeated the same spectacular, to honor the National's two-hundreth performance of the play.

The instant success of the play spread in the United States and abroad, with numerous versions of unbelievable taste — from the impeccable, to minstrels, burlesques, and satiric burlesques. Dogs, horses, parades, Jubilee choruses, hymns, breakdowns, plantation festivals, steamboat races, cakes of ice, and "transformation scenes" became some of the stocks in trade of UNCLE TOM'S CABIN productions.

Our UNCLE TOM'S CABIN, under canvas, was hardly the original, for the first one was established in Dayton, Ohio, under the aegis of "Yankee Robinson" in 1854, followed by many, among them companies from Pennsylvania, Michigan,

New York, and Ohio. But our Connors' Mammoth Pavilion Show under canvas was a West Coast production of great sophistication for the times, and deserves its own niche in the history of "Tomming."

Returning briefly to little Cordelia Howard, records show that the Howard trio—father, mother, and daughter—played in UNCLE TOM'S CABIN for thirty-five years, until Mr. Howard's death in 1887. Cordelia's interest in this classic accompanied her all her life, for at the age of eighty-five, she was to see a revival of the play in Boston. In this Player's Club Show, Otis Skinner played Uncle Tom and Fay Bainter, Topsy.

Finally, since Cordelia Howard made her debut as the original little Eva at the tender age of four, I feel a very deep and close kinship with her, for I was only five when I first played the role in afterpieces at the Cineograph Parlors. While I must take leave of her now, it is fondly hoped that she and I will one day meet in a very special "transformation scene" of our own.

For reasons best known to the mama at that time, she summarily withdrew me from the Connors' Mammoth Pavilion Show's production of UNCLE TOM'S CABIN. Of course, I never thought to question her decision, for at the tender age of seven I accepted her guidance happily; however, my intuitive feelings that the mama was dissatisfied with both the food and finances involved, have been reinforced as a result of a little sleuthing. From the May 11, 1901 issue of the San Francisco Dramatic Revue, came the following notice:

> *"Baby Dody The Child Actress has severed her connection with Harry Connors' Mammoth Pavilion Uncle Tom Combination and is now at liberty and open for engagement—address this office."*

From the same publication, dated two weeks later, came the real answer:

> *"The rosy prospects of Harry Connors' Mammoth UNCLE TOM'S CABIN show has dwindled to nothing, and the owners of the outfit, Mssrs. Bloch and Wise, have called the show back to town, after clearing it from the tentacles of the law at Rocklin* (near Sacramento, California), *where*

it had been attached for salary due the forty or fifty members of the company. The salary is still forthcoming. (When the "ghost didn't walk" for me, the mama had to make her move.)

"As to just why this show was called in there are conflicting stories. There seems to be no denial that it made money, but there seems to have been too many people and a lack of management somewhere, so the owners of the outfit who had leased the show to Harry Connors, called things off . . . ."

Our great show had succumbed under its own weight—"mammothitis."

After a short time "at liberty," that lovely theatrical euphemism for "unemployed," there came a very exciting adventure that left many fond memories. The Alcazar Theatre was to present Francis J. Power's one-act play, THE FIRST BORN, which it had the honor of debuting in May, 1897 and presenting several times, since. This in itself, was a rarity for San Francisco. Plays appearing in our city usually originated in New York and then, either proceeded westward through the country to San Francisco, or came directly here. THE FIRST BORN was to reverse this pattern. After it played in San Francisco for nine weeks, David Belasco acquired the rights to the play and presented it in New York City to enthusiastic audiences.

During the first run of THE FIRST BORN, four years earlier, the author and his wife had played the two adult leads, Chan Wang and Chan Lee; and the "first-born," Chan Toy, was played by Little May Sawyer. A month later, the latter was replaced by Little Venie who portrayed the role for the remainder of the run and in subsequent replays at the Alcazar, until I had the singular fortune of playing it in 1901.

To better familiarize myself with life and atmosphere in our Chinese community, my parents took me on an extended tour of its streets and shops. We were escorted by a policeman in plainclothes, since it was considered imprudent for white women and children to venture into Chinatown unaccom-

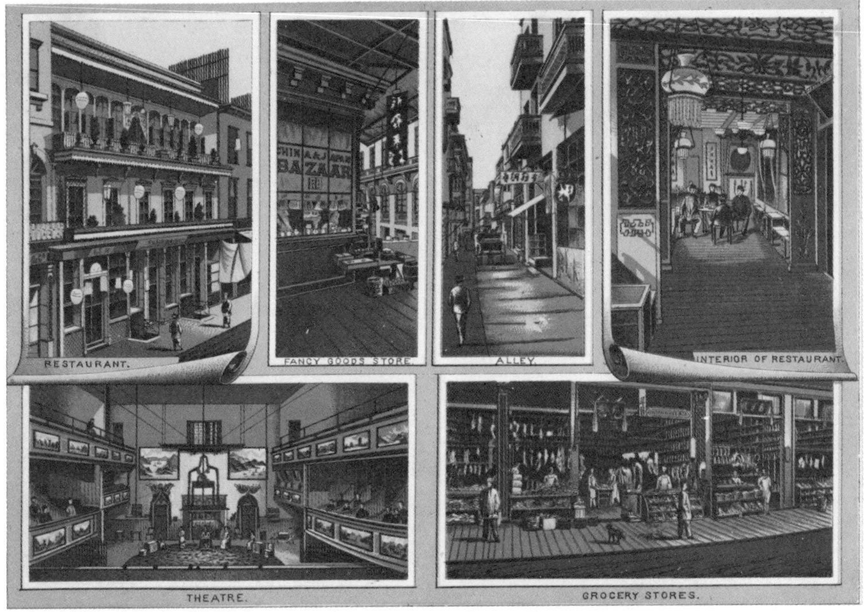

The Chinese Quarters, San Francisco Chinatown c. 1900
Credit: C.P. Heininger — Barrett-Miller Collection

panied by a man in authority. These were the days of opium
dens and attendant vices, and of Tong wars when "hatchetmen"
were known to stand in doorways, ready to cut down their foes.

Happily, what I remember seeing in the doorways of
Chinatown were Chinese men taking advantage of the better
lighting, as they sat at treadle sewing-machines, ruffling yards
and yards of lace onto beautiful China silk garments. These
creations were intended for the ladies of the adjoining neighborhood, a somewhat questionable part of San Francisco, then.
It was in one of these garment factories, I was measured for the
lovely Chinese costume I wore as Chan Toy. It consisted of: the
children's version of the black hat with the red topknot, worn by
most Chinese merchants; a tunic of lavender brocade, with a
pale green band around the bottom; lavender pants, also edged
in pale green; and lovely black, quilted satin slippers. The
costume was typical of the elaborate clothing styles Chinese
children wore. Theirs were the brightest shades of pinks,

greens, and lavender brocades; and for them, too, were re-served the most beautiful combinations of colors and trimmings. The cut of the garment, however, did not vary from the adult's.

Though these charming children were always indulged by doting parents, relatives, and other adults, it is worthy of note that Chinese children's comportment was beyond reproach.

Contrasted with the men's black pants that narrowed tight-ly around the ankles, the women's were of "stovepipe" lines—straight, smooth, and always neatly pressed. Like the men, women wore fingertip-length tunics, buttoned down the side with frogs of braid, or other material, that caught the buttons and held them secure. Some tunics were enhanced around the bottom with a border of contrasting brocade. On their feet, the women wore the familiar delicate slippers.

Many women hobbled about in bound feet, a practice that made for the tiny feet that were the mark of a lady. Every girl knew that if she were to reach this much sought-after status, she must submit, from childhood, to the torturous fashion of bound feet. This was not the fad for the menial classes who performed the arduous chores of their society. Alas, for the child or young girl with bound feet there would never be the freedom of boisterous movement or the romping in inviting fields. She was a "lady" and, consequently, had no choice: She must always be waited upon by others.

Chinese women's coiffures, I observed, varied little. For the most part, their hair was done up quite slick, with never a hair out of place; and very ornate pins were inserted across the back, through the glossy bun.

The more elaborate costumes worn by the men and women of Chinatown were confined to religious and social events, and were not what the average sightseer to that community saw. Of special interest were the ornate robes the mandarins wore. These scholars and intellectuals were highly revered and re-spected, and some became the political leaders of the com-munity. Their robes, brought from their homeland, were magnificent works of art. As the robes became scarce, they became, more and more, collectors' items until, in time, even pieces of them were in great demand. I have a very beautiful panel from a mandarin robe, among my "treasures." The strip is in a pale blue silk, hand embroidered with the finest of stitching, in delicate multicolored designs of birds, bees, butterflies, and flowers. The colors in my "swatch" are still vivid after more than eighty-five years.

Another, but less elaborate costume, was that often worn by the Chinese merchant. His was a very loose, colored robe, with sleeves that flared at the wrists and, at times, covered the hands, with the slightest movement of the wrist. On his feet, he wore black cloth slippers.

Most Chinese men, however, wore the tapered black pants, and matching tunic secured by the "frogs."

Scenes of San Francisco Chinatown c. 1900
(l. to r. Joss House   Ladies   Merchants   Interior Joss House)
Credit: C.P. Heininger − Barrett-Miller Collection

Men's heads were shaved, except for the center-back, from which hung a long braid, or queue, down their backs to their ankles. Those with naturally shorter hair or whose age began to take its toll by shortening it, interwove black silk floss into their braids. It was difficult to discern where the hair ended and the silk began. The queue was usually quite thin by the time it reached ankle-length, where, tied with a red ribbon, it bobbed about at the heels.

Since the custom of the queue held political implications, identifying their loyalty to the Manchus in China, Chinese men dared not shave their queues if they expected one day to return to their homeland.

In 1894, Dr. Sun Yat-sen had dared challenge the Manchu Dynasty's survival. He and his followers, mostly students, cut off their queues, in protest against what they considered the corrupt, prevailing order. In America, such daring was longer in coming, but gained much impetus as a remonstrance against the U.S. Exclusion Act of 1904, the act that precipitated anti-American boycotts in China. But the Chinese men I remember in my youth, in my trips to Chinatown, wore the long queues that bobbed rythmically with each step.

Hats worn by the Chinese men I saw were of two styles: the little, round, brimless skullcap, with a red topknot made of brightly woven braid into about half the size of a golf ball; and the large, black fedora-type, with the floppy brim, such as our laundry man wore.

Among the men with the floppy, brimmed hats seen throughout our city, might be the chair-mender, deftly balancing on his shoulders a long pole with three or four chairs at each end. Using split cane strips for reweaving, this craftsman re-caned the chairs in his shop, strung the mended chairs on his pole, and started his intricate feat of threading in and out of traffic, to the point of delivery. He bobbed as he wended his way, a condition created by the type of slipper he wore. It was a very thick three-part soled shoe—the usual dark sole that met the pavement; a very thick, white middle one; and a thinner dark one on which the foot rested. Altogether, these soles averaged two to three inches in thickness. Boat-fashion, the front end of the thick sole was tipped upward, so when the vendor or craftsman ran or walked on its surface, the result was a bouncy sort of gait that helped him balance the weight of the objects at each end of the pole.

In similar fashion, others I observed carried at the ends of their poles large cane baskets with vegetables or fruits or fish — whatever their craft or occupation might be. These pole-bearing artisans and workers would be hard put to maneuver today's more frenetic sidewalk traffic, but they were a picturesque part of the canvas that was San Francisco during my childhood. My admiration for their feats of poise, rhythm, and balance remains to this day — theirs was a remarkable "tradesman's ballet."

These lovely people of Chinatown influenced our daily lives with their stability and graciousness. San Francisco boasted that theirs was the largest Chinatown this side of China. We were scarcely aware that New York had its own, as did other cities eastward. We were only conscious that our ships returned with Chinese and products from China. The Chinese were very important to us, and they offered much of what we needed and admired in services and goods.

Among my childhood recollections of their products were: baskets; teakwood furniture, inlaid with mother-of-pearl; hand-embroidered pictures of dragons, geese, reeds, and flowers; ivory carvings, jades, Chinese green-gold jewelry; brocade and satin screens, soft brocades and shiny satins; and art offerings too numerous to list. These, and many more, were all part of their culture's contributions to our cosmopolitan city. While many of our imports are now marked "Made In Japan," in my childhood they were stamped "China," and came from what is now referred to as "Mainland China."

My escorted trip through Chinatown opened new horizons in my comprehension of how its people lived, worked, worshipped, and played: their dress, according to their general status in the community; their religious and cultural environments, as witness the Joss Houses with ornate incense-burning altars, and the Chinese theaters with brilliantly costumed actors; and finally, their numerous and varied social classes, from the lowly laborer on through the vendor, craftsman, merchant, scholar, priest, and politician.

But I had already learned much about the Chinese from a very dear friend, and parting recollections must include him. He was our Chinese laundry man who picked up the laundry each week in his horse-drawn, black, covered wagon. We called him "John." I know not why, unless it was an alliterative version of his real name. He accepted our name for him and we, in turn, relied on his services, with confidence.

Like others, John's laundry dried the clothes on the roof-top. Rows upon rows of clotheslines could be seen, with their assortments of colored articles flapping with the breezes. Their ingenious way of securing the hanging garments is worthy of mention. Each clothesline consisted of two cords, tightly twisted. At the proper place, the worker hanging out the laundry would spring apart a section just wide enough to insert a tuck of the garment, twist the cords again and, voilà, the garment was made fast, without benefit of a clothespin.

Unabashedly, I admit John was one of my admirers. He would pat me on the head, finger my golden hair in wonderment, and, in Chinese, make a sort of mumbling sound of admiration. When spring came, he always brought me narcissus bulbs imbedded in pebbles, in an elongated bowl. Soon the narcissus would bloom, their pungent, sweet fragrance finding its way throughout our home at the St. Ann's.

In the fall, John brought me melon-seed cookies—fat, large biscuits, with postage-size stamps of red Chinese characters on them, sheer delights to tickle the palate of any child. His thoughtfulness manifested itself in the numerous and unusual little gifts with which he regaled me. And how I looked forward to the litchi nuts and the strips of white-sugared coconut. It was a beautiful relationship, John's and mine, and so I was always eager for his visits; and he seemed genuinely pleased to have me for a friend.

Now, fortified by personal contacts with the Chinese and the enhanced knowledge of Chinatown as a result of the concentrated tour, I was to portray one of their children, little Chan

Toy, in THE FIRST BORN. Because the play was a short one, a so-called "curtain-raiser" would be presented first. It was a time filler, and it preceded the main feature, as the term implies. These curtain raisers were usually humorous skits, with titles like, THE THREE HATS, ENGAGED, BLACK EYED SUSAN, ANDY BLAKE, A SERIOUS TANGLE, or, as on our bill, GLORIANA.

Since costuming for THE FIRST BORN was as authentic as its theme, there developed the challenge of what to do about my long golden curls. From Goldstein's, San Francisco's leading costumers, on Market Street, the mama purchased a wig that simulated the bare shaven-head, with the long queue hanging down the back. To hide my hair, she rolled the curls tightly and pinned them as flat as possible. Around the hairline, she put a tight "wigband" that covered any trace of the telltale blonde hair. Over the "wigband" went the wig itself, covering curls and wigband. Then, down over my forehead the mama pulled my wig, inserting into it hairpins which she slid under the wigband to keep the wig from moving. Finally, with tawny-colored grease paint, she changed the tone of my complexion. The mama always made it impossible for the wig to wiggle, slide, or slip during any exuberant childish move that might reveal the occidental tresses underneath. Her thoroughness would later be tested in a disturbing incident. Needless to say, the wig was none too comfortable, but it was all in a day's work and I did not really mind.

When I played Chan Toy in this eminently popular play, the part of the father, Chan Wang, was enacted by the very capable artist, Howard Scott. In the story, father and son lived on one side of Bartlett Alley in San Francisco's Chinatown. The wife, played by Georgie Cooper, was in her husband's disfavor and, consequently, lived by herself, on the opposite side of the alley.

While playing in the street, Chan Toy is watched adoringly by his banished mother, from her screened balcony. She calls to me softly; I look up and she throws a rose, a token of her love. She beckons and entreats me to come up to her. I pick up her

Baby Dody as Chan Toy in "The First Born"   *Alcazar Theatre 1901*
Credit: Barrett-Miller Collection

offering and ascend the stairway, disappeaing from view. The time-lapse, representing the period I visited with Chan Lee, was a long one, spent on a platform behind the scenes.

Actually, I truly looked forward to these lengthy intervals on the platform because of the friendly stage hand, Jack Snell, a grip with crispy black curls. Jack Snell had a fascinating watch chain of alternating gold links and gold nuggets. He had brought the nuggets from the Klondike during that short-lived bonanza of 1896–1900, and had the unusual watch chain made as an everlasting memento of his days there. Jack was very proud of the watch chain and prized it highly; so it was, indeed, a privilege to be allowed to play with his treasure, during the seemingly interminable wait on the platform. He gave me three nuggets which I cherished until they, too, disappeared, along with many other possessions, during the earthquake and fire of 1906. I grew fond of the kindly man who did so much to mitigate the boredom of waiting backstage for my cue.

In due time, my cue was sounded and, with a piercing scream, I came hurtling down the stairs, to lie limp at the foot of the stairway. At the sound of my scream, my father would run out of his house, pick me up in his arms and discover I was dead. Carrying his limp, dead child to the curtain line, near the footlights, he laid me on the floor, knelt over me, and mourned, "Chan Toy, Chan Toy, my beautiful boy, my first born." I had to lie perfectly still, without so much as a visible breath to heave my chest, or a twitch of an eye to betray my demise; but I was often tempted to open the upstage eye (away from the audience) to make sure my father had not placed me directly under the dreaded heavy and enormous curtain roller. Thanks to Howard Scott's great precision and concern, however, the scene was always executed on a stage well marked to preclude just such a tragedy.

After what seemed an unusually long wait, the curtain came down on this very moving scene. At last I was able to take a deep breath. The audience applauded; the curtain went up again; and, once more, I held my breath—a procedure called "holding the picture." If the stage manager decided the applause warranted it, there might be several "holdings of the picture"—in this scene, the tabloid of the grieving father, Chan Wang, cradling his dead "first-born" in his arms.

When this holding scene had at last served its purpose, the stage manager commanded, "curtain call," and the main characters joined hands and bowed in unison, to the audience and each other, several times. The curtain calls were always the sugar on the cookie, with all actors. Every performer measured his worth by the number of curtain calls demanded by his audience. Finally, when the manager called, "strike," the order was clearly to strike the set—i.e. take it down, change the set. The command was irrevocable; there were no more curtain calls, and we repaired to our dressing rooms.

Besides Mr. Scott, there were others by now well known to me. Georgie Cooper, playing the female lead, was the daughter of Miss Georgie Woodthorpe (Cho Pow, the Chinese nurse) and Fred Cooper, noted dramatist. Miss Cooper's younger sister, Ollie, was the very same whose ulcerated tooth led to my being engaged to play her part in SAPHO. By such happpenstances is the direction of our lives sometimes set.

Walter Belasco, as the Ragpicker (actually titled "the Jewish Peddler," when the play opened in 1897) received special accolades for his make-up, his costume, and his characterization of the poor ragpicker who went about Chinatown, picking up rags and bottles for a living. He was an outstanding actor, markedly influenced by his talented brothers: David, the famous New York producer and playwright who got his start at the old Baldwin Theatre in San Francisco, and Fred, co-partner with Mark Thall at both the Alcazar and Central theaters.

To better establish the setting for an incident that occurred at an evening performance of THE FIRST BORN, it might be well to describe the rudiments of the stage. The wing that juts out onto the stage matches the valance, or Grand Drapery, which runs across the top of the stage, just back of the Proscenium Arch. More importantly, the front curtain dropped in front of the first wing, better known to us as "the tormentor." This particular incident started when Georgie Cooper said to me, after the curtain came down on the performance, "Come Baby," and took my hand. We were now with our backs to the curtain and sidling out between it and the "tormentor" when there came a mistaken signal. In response to renewed applause, the curtain began to rise, and the long queue down my back caught in the dreaded roller and was being rolled up with the curtain. The roller went high enough to lift me off my feet. Another half-turn would have broken my neck.

Quickly, Jack Snell, Harry Glendinning, and several stage-hands grabbed the ropes on both sides of the stage and, with their full weight, hung on to keep the curtain from rising higher. Their efforts acted as counter-weights and averted a tragedy, for the timely resistance alerted one of the men in the flies, who promptly lowered the curtain. I was picked up, carried to my room, and ministered by the doctor. Backstage, all were in a state of agitation, a feeling quickly sensed by the audience, whose concern for Baby Dody's welfare manifested itself in their refusal to leave. Their applause continued until I was forced to appear on stage for one more bow—more to reassure the audience than myself. It had been a very traumatic experience, but to be importuned, at all cost, to "go out and bow, Baby" was an embarrassment as well because, in stage parlance, "I was not prepared to meet my public." I was shaken and in a state of disarray, albeit the mama's wig operations had certainly stood their test. Of course, I did as I was told. Having satisfied my audience, I bowed and smiled, and left the stage for my dressing room, with the poor distraught little mama at my heels. Assured that little Chan Toy was uninjured, the audience left at last.

Upon returning the next night, I was shocked and irate to find they had hired a real Chinese boy to *walk* through my part. After all my protestations, however, the boy was dismissed, and I continued my role. But the ignominy of the entire incident was climaxed when the city's newspapers carried the Chinese boy's picture in *my* costume and with *my* name on the caption.

Mark Thall, Business Manager Alcazar Theatre c. 1900
Credit: Marston Thall Collection

The annoyance over my short-lived replacement in THE FIRST BORN was, of course, quickly dismissed, for it was really of little import. Before the year ended, there had occurred a sad event that made my appearance at the Alcazar in THE FIRST BORN a more cherished one than I realized at the time. I was to look back, ever so fondly and with greater appreciation, to the significant part Mark Thall had played in my life.

As with most people's, a retrospect of my career calls forth an outstanding event and person. The event was replacing Ollie Cooper in SAPHO, while the person was my beloved Mark Thall. Memories of this man are not solely based on childish awe and adulation, as poignant as that may be, for my regards were shared by his large circle of devoted friends and by his admiring public.

And so, when the shocking news spread throughout the San Francisco theater community that Mark Thall had died quite unexpectedly, I was bewildered by the expressions of sorrow all about me. This was my first encounter with the subject of real death. I was unprepared to understand its finality, as I found myself attending the first funeral in my short span of seven years. The dynamic Mr. Thall had led a very active and fulfilling life that merits some reflection.

Let us start with the Thall family background. His ancestors were from Bohemia in North Germany, whence the name Thall had an unusual origin that explains both the etymology of the word "dollar" and the genesis of the family name, "Thal," spelled with one "l."

In 1516, a silver mine was discovered at Joachim's Thal (St. Joachim's *Dale*) in Bohemia, and the proprietors, the following year, struck a great number of silver pieces. These bore the name of "Joachimsthaler," subsequently abbreviated to "thaler," from which the English word "dollar" evolved. Our word, "dollar," then, may be termed a corruption of the word for the type of site (Dale) of the Bohemian silver mine which supplied the first "thalers." The Bohemian Joachimsthaler was replaced by the mark in 1891, but the surnames Thaler (the coin) and Thal (the dale) persisted.

When Mark's family name first appears in the 1868 San Francisco Directory, it is spelled "Thal," but within ten years Mark added another "l" to his surname, and the rest of the family adopted the new spelling.

Born in Montgomery, Alabama in 1857, Mark Thall came to California with his parents, Henry H. and Elise Thal, his two brothers, Frederick and Sigmund (later known as Sam), and a sister, Rebecca. The family settled in Placerville, and after attending school for less than four years, Mark did the most exciting thing a young boy could do then: He joined the circus. This was his introduction into the amusement world, a world he was to leave only upon his premature death, October 12, 1901.

When the family moved to San Francisco in 1868, the father became a policeman assigned to the City Hall, a position he held for the next four years. During these years, Frederick worked, variously, as tinsmith, clerk, and collector; and Sigmund, as a harnessmaker with the Main and Winchester Company. Young Mark had had a thorough indoctrination into the challenges of the circus, "marked by various vicissitudes," when he joined his family in San Francisco and became an usher at the old California Theatre, 1875—1876.

Thall's stint at the old California Theatre, 444 Bush Street, could not have come at a more fortuitous period, for the famous playhouse, under John McCullough, was enjoying a surge of popularity. The noted thespian-manager selected the very best entertainment available, often booking the same shows appearing at the famous Maguire houses: The Opera House, Maguire's New Theatre, and Baldwin's Academy of Music. McCullough's preoccupations with the business side of the theater left him precious little time for acting. But with his partner, Barton Hill, he guided the artistic destinies of the old California Theatre. Great Shakespearean plays, like HAMLET, JULIUS

Performance At The California Theatre 1901
Credit: California Historical Society, San Francisco

CAESAR, and MACBETH were quite regularly booked there. When the renowned Edwin Booth appeared in his repertoire of Shakespearean plays, he was supported by Barton Hill. Other well-known artists of the day like Charles Fechter, Miss Mary Anderson, Emma Waller, and the idolized Miss Adelaide Neilsen appeared in various vehicles at the California—no doubt leaving their influence on the impressionable and enterprising young Mark Thall. More importantly, McCullough himself could have set a pattern, molding Thall's predilection toward the business end of the theater.

When Thall ushered at the California, the theater was but six years old. Built in 1868 by William Chapman Ralston of the Bank of California, at a cost of $125,000, it was to be a temple for the two famous artists, John McCullough and Lawrence Barrett. Both Barrett and McCullough had played the boards in San Francisco for years. McCullough was a noted tragedian and Shakespearean actor. Barrett, too, had achieved notice, but with less personal impact on the San Francisco theater-goers because, of the two, McCullough was the more colorful. Ralston hoped that with the new theater as an incentive, he might dissuade two of San Francisco's most popular actors from leaving for the East Coast. In the face of such a flattering offer, the two artists could hardly demur. So, with "the approval and cooperation of the bemused actors," Ralston built the "most magnificent playhouse the West had ever seen." It opened the evening of January 18, 1869, with Messrs. Barrett and McCullough as lessees. The play presented was Bulwer-Lytton's comedy, MONEY, in which John McCullough played the lead, Alfred Evelyn; Mrs. Judah was Lady Franklin; and Miss Marie E. Gordon of the Haymarket Theater of London, Clara Douglas. The dedicatory program featured an opening address in verse, written by the noted F. Bret Harte and delivered by Lawrence Barrett.

Reviews of the California Theatre's opening night gave detailed accounts of its audience of "full silk gowns sweeping across tessellated marble floors," of "ladies romantically coiffured in long 'follow-me-curls' over one shoulder," and carriages discharging and picking up San Francisco's elite theater patrons.

Of the physical aspects of the house itself, descriptions told of its immense size and elegance, and of the beautiful drop curtain designed by the painter G.J. Denny, representing, according to the original program, a "view of The Golden Gate." Denny also did the impressive panels of California views that were seen on the facades of the upper and gallery circles, and boxes. The first three rows of the dress circle had an unheard of innovation: legless chairs with "high backs fixed with hinges and springs, like rocking chairs."

The magnificence of the California Theatre was enhanced by "Argand burners with glass chimneys." These burners, with tubular-shaped wicks set between two metal cylinders, produced a bright circular flame. They were named after their Eighteenth Century inventor, the Swiss chemist Aime Argand. The glass chimneys of these kerosene lamps intensified the flame and reduced the smoke factor.

This, then, was the atmosphere of the first theater in which the young Mark Thall worked. It was a milieu well calculated to stimulate and develop his career in the entertainment world, and he soon took another step forward. He became advance agent for the McDonough and Earnshaw Royal Marionettes, at the age of nineteen. Among the many bookings of the show, was a July, 1876 presentation at Maguire's Opera House. After that, the Royal Marionettes went on the road, with young Mark Thall as their manager—his first managerial undertaking. I have often wondered if these were the same marionettes that came to rest in the basement of the theater in Crockett, California—the incident already referred to during the George W. Lowe Show.

When Charles E. Locke assumed management of the Bush Street Theatre in 1877, Mark Thall was drawn back to familiar surroundings. Locke engaged him as office boy, and young Thall was once again enveloped in a climate disposed to further and encourage his interests in the business side of the theater. It was said that "by sheer hard work and close attention to business and a genial manner he made his way up the ladder of success until be became treasurer." Records show that from office boy, he became the Agent for the Bush Street Theatre, its Assistant Treasurer, and finally, Treasurer.

It was during Thall's first year there that the famous Buffalo Bill Dramatic Company played a month's engagement at the Bush. The seventeen members of the company were billed as, "The Celebrated Scouts." Their repertoire consisted of three plays: LIFE ON THE BORDER, THE RED RIGHT HAND (or Buffalo Bill's first scalp for Custer), and SCOUTS OF THE PLAINS. William F. Cody and J.W. Crawford (Captain Jack) played themselves. The plays drew enormous crowds, for these Western dramas depicted historical events still fresh in their memories—life on the Plains, and the Indian Wars.

After some three years at the Bush Street Theatre, Mark Thall became a theatrical agent on his own and was once again "on the road," meeting, at times, with unusual challenges.

It was said that he reminisced gleefully over one of these—an episode when he and Al Hayman, a friendly competitor, were advance agents for "two of the worst shows that ever happened." Hayman's assignment was doing advance promotion work for M.B. Leavitt's SPIDER AND FLY, while Mark Thall's, was piloting a show he considered hardly better, so he never deigned to identify it in the recounting. It was an accepted fact that the first show to hit a town made all the money, especially if both were hopeless, for the town's victimized audience was not about to be "taken," for months after.

Thinking to get a start on Hayman, Mark Thall went from Sacramento to Stockton, California by freight train one night. Upon arriving in Stockton in the early morning hours, he proceeded to wake every bill poster, in hopes of getting his bills up before Hayman arrived, only to learn, to his dismay, that they had already been hired by Hayman, by telegram. But he knew of a former bill poster, a Mexican War veteran who lived about ten miles out of town. Thall hired a horse and buggy, drove there in the dawn hours, and offered the man double wages for the job. The veteran, who could hardly reject the offer, agreed to return to town with him.

With haste and resolve, the bill poster and Thall began plastering a large barn on Stockton's Main Street, when Hayman appeared. Looking up to Thall who stood atop the ladder, posting as if his life depended on it, Hayman shouted excitedly, "Come down from there! That barn belongs to me."

"Well, come and get it then," taunted Thall.

"If you don't come down, I'll shake you down," threatened Hayman as he gave the ladder a jerk.

"Look out, you'll spill my paste," warned Thall, his hand on the paste bucket.

But the dauntless and determined Hayman, ignoring the forewarnings, gave the ladder a violent shake. The bucket fell on its side, and the paste splattered the immaculately attired Hayman. Thall always revelled in his description of his worthy opponent, "He looked like a statue in batter!"

These two adversaries were to leave their mark in the annals of San Francisco theater history. Among his many accomplishmets, Al Hayman, from 1884 to 1897, became lessee and manager of the Baldwin, the California, and the Bush Street theaters almost concurrently, and he formed the Al Hayman Company in 1892. So, while Thall and Hayman each went his separate way, their paths crossed many times.

Notwithstanding Thall's many successes away from San Francisco, there seemed to be a sort of magnet that drew him to the city of his choice. We find that his travels were interrupted in 1887 when he joined the Alcazar Theatre as its manager. At that time, the lessees and proprietors of the Alcazar were George Wallenrod (original lessee when the Alcazar opened in 1885), George Osbourne, and L.R. Stockwell. Mr. Thall's genius for theater management was to play an important part in leading this lovely San Francisco theater into a prosperous era during his next five years there.

Wallenrod's two associates had formed the Osbourne-Stockwell Comedy Company, in which they also participated as actors. Among other well-known members of their company were Frank Mordaunt, Harry Davenport, and Hobart Bosworth. Early Alcazar programs, after Thall joined the theater, show the Osbourne-Stockwell Comedy Company still extant in the comedy, SHADOWS OF A GREAT CITY. But under Thall's management, the company became known simply as, "The Alcazar Company." A more diversified format appeared, with all manner of drama, including an occasional comedy-drama. The new company's complement expanded to include other increasingly familiar names like: Leo Cooper, Nick Long, George Hermance, Julius Kahn (later a Congressman), James E. Wilson, Mrs. F.M. Bates, and the Misses Idalene Cotton, Ethel Brandon, Eleanor Barry, and Fanny Young.

To vary the fare in which only the local talent was used, Thall booked nationally known shows with prominent actors and actresses. Among them was Miss Effie Ellsler, billed: "America's Greatest Actress In D'Ennery's Emotional Play, THE TWO ORPHANS—All Original Music." In this play, Miss Ellsler played the lead orphan. The Alcazar Theatre Stock Company took the supportive roles, with their Ethel Brandon the second orphan, and L.R. Stockwell, James Carden, and Frank Weston, male leads.

Another importation was the eminent actor, Lewis Morrison, in THE DUKE'S MOTTO. This play, too, was supported by the theater's stock company. Mr. Morrison's wife, Florence Roberts, had a minor role. This was in August 1891—two years before I was born. Her star would rise in a few years, but, for the time, Lewis Morrison's was at its zenith. He played a five weeks' run at the Alcazar; and since he was always a good drawing card, his booking by Thall proved another financial success.

Occasionally Mark Thall engaged a self-contained company, such as in THE WAIFS OF NEW YORK, starring Miss Katie Emmett, "the sparkling soubrette, a success from the Pacific Coast to the Atlantic."

Another, A TIN SOLDIER by Charles Hoyt, appeared under the management of Mr. Frank McKee. Its droll interest stemmed from the written program, *a jeu de mots* that read as follows:

The Players And What They Attempt
Vilas Canby, the "Professor," a practical plumber

Brooklyn Bridge, a gentleman of high position
Col. I.B. Boosey, a hero of Gettysburg
Wright Handy, Bridge's partner
Col. Wood B. Fuller, hero of Gettysburg
Steele Coffin, secretary of Tar and Feathering Committee
Rob Graves, business man
Mrs. Fulton Ferry, mother-in-law of Brooklyn Bridge

If the cast of characters sounded more like those to be found in an afterpiece, the play, if nothing else, had a printed program that was quite a topic of conversation.

In 1892, Mark Thall again left San Francisco to go on the road. During the next four years, he spent most of his time away from our city, traveling throughout the country. He spent considerable time in New York, where his contacts with David Belasco were to lead, later, to his association with the latter's brother, Fred Belasco.

Upon returning in 1896, Thall became Resident Manager of the new MacDonough Theatre, 14th and Broadway, Oakland, California. The MacDonough was to Oakland what the Alcazar was to San Francisco. With its plush appointments, it was the most luxurious theater Oakland had ever known. Competing for superlatives, its Lessees and Managers, The Friedlander, Gottlob Company, billed it as, "The Most Modern Theatre in America." At the MacDonough, the elite "carriage trade" would enjoy only the best Mark Thall could book: traveling shows of renown, concerts, recitals, ballets, and symphonies—all featuring outstanding artists.

The MacDonough's spacious, uncluttered interior was tastefully relieved by a frescoed vaulted arch that extended from the proscenium, encompassed the lavish, ornate double-tiered boxes on each side and rested on handsome pilasters. Above, bordering high on the rim of the auditorium's walls, was an arabesque frieze that set off the formation of a beautiful central dome, from which hung a magnificent chandelier. In general, the impression was one of rounded arches, vaults, and curvilinear boxes, balconies, and galleries. The main floor's seating arrangement consisted of the modern center row, flanked by aisles separating it from the rows on each side.

MacDonough Theatre—Oakland, California 1892-1945
Credit: The Archives For The Performing Arts, S.F.

Personal, vivid recollections of the MacDonough include its very fashionable, basement restaurant, where the mama and I ate at times, and enjoyed watching what would now be referred to as "the beautiful people" of that day partake of sumptuous meals.

Built in 1892 by Joseph MacDonough, the MacDonough Theatre was first leased and managed by George Mothersole. It opened November 14, 1892, with COX AND BOX by Burnard and Arthur Sullivan, and CAVALLERIA RUSTICANA of Mascagni, presented by the J.C. Duff Company. Artists in this opener were: Helen Bertram, Villa Knox, Charles Bassett, J.B. Dupuis, and Helen vonDoenhoff.

From its inception, the MacDonough thrived as Oakland's leading theatre of stage plays for many years, while still booking classical ballet, concerts, operas, and symphonies. The best attractions of San Francisco theaters also came to this fine house:

SAPHO, GISMONDA, A VIRGINIA COURTSHIP, THE HEART OF MARYLAND, A FOOL OF FORTUNE, BURIED AT SEA, THE SENATOR, EAST LYNNE, DON'T TELL HER HUSBAND, and the Shakespearean plays were typical fare at this lovely theater.

In 1915, Mr. George Ebey leased the MacDonough and renamed it The Crane Wilbur Playhouse, after Oakland's handsome and adored dramatic idol. Soon after, however, the new playhouse proved a financial failure and was bought by Irving C. Ackerman, who named it the State Theatre and introduced vaudeville to its stage.

In the mid-twenties, Warner Brothers bought the State, named it the Vitaphone, and converted it to a motion picture house. Like other movie houses of that time, it showed the first sound picture, Al Jolson's THE JAZZ SINGER, March 1928.

In time, the name "State Theatre" was returned to this venerable establishment, and it continued as a house of movies until its closing in 1945.

More than a decade later, the State Theatre building was razed; and in 1957, it became the locus of the present United California Bank Building. Thus was obliterated all physical traces of the once magnificent old MacDonough Theatre which Mark Thall had managed for a year; where I had played at times—most notable of which, in BURIED AT SEA in 1903— and which was so very dear a part of my early memories.

Although Mark Thall's association with the MacDonough Theatre lasted only a year, his influence would be felt for many years to come, in the format he helped perpetuate.

After the year with the MacDonough, Thall again returned to the Alcazar Theatre, this time in a partnership with Fred Belasco, launching the famous San Francisco theater on its most notable period of success, according to the critics. Mark Thall was now at the peak of his career and barely forty years old. His return to the Alcazar, replacing Arthur A. Lotto, occurred in June 1897; and the play there, at that time, was none other than the newly premiered, THE FIRST BORN, in which I played four years later, as already detailed. It is noteworthy that from its inception, THE FIRST BORN was so popular it ran for nine consecutive weeks, and went down in San Francisco theatrical history as one of its few long-run plays.

The new partnership of Belasco and Thall was to resurrect the theater from the doldrums when it was known as "Grover's Alcazar" for about the year, September 1895–1896. Belasco and Thall adopted bold innovations, tempered by good taste and excellent judgement; and together they shaped the general tenor and high principles for which the Alcazar became known. The needs of the San Francisco theater public for good shows at popular prices were met, in the main, through Thall's astute business acumen. To the end of encouraging more and more attendance, prices at the Alcazar were set as follows:

EVENING

Orchestra	.50¢
Dress Circle (First Two Rows)	.50¢
Dress Circle (Other Rows)	.25¢ and 35¢
Balcony (First Two Rows)	.35¢
Balcony (Other Rows)	15¢ and 25¢
Box Seats	.75¢

MATINEE

Orchestra	.35¢
Dress Circle	.25¢
Balcony (First Two Rows)	.25¢
Balcony (Other Rows)	.15¢
Box Seats	.50¢

With Thall capably handling his bailiwick, the business management, and Fred Belasco replicating techniques used by his famous brother, David Belasco, the Alcazar became one of San Francisco's finest and most successful theaters.

Testimony to this fact occurred often in the local periodicals. Typical, was the "First Nighter," critic of the Wasp, writing on the Alcazar, as he offered a commendation and an exhortation:

> *I have both personal and public hope that Messrs. Belasco and Thall, after having elevated the Alcazar Com-*

pany to a plane where it had commanded serious and interested attention, are not about to allow a change which is not for the best. We have had a most excellent season at the house....The list of plays in the past...has been the best that I have ever seen in any stock house in America. How much the public appreciates the use of royalty plays...has been evidenced by the patronage extended to the Alcazar. But royalty plays are expensive, and the risk of presenting them without the best company of players that can be gathered is considerable. I trust the Alcazar will not weaken its fortifications in this last respect.

The First Nighter's concern proved unwarranted, for as long as the Messrs. Belasco and Thall headed the Alcazar, there was only the best possible fare offered. The list is as long as it is prestigious, and one can only present typical examples. Alcazar audiences were to see successes like David Belasco and Henry C. DeMille's, MEN AND WOMEN and THE GIRL I LEFT BEHIND ME; Henry G. Carlton's, THE BUTTERFLIES, a John Drew production; and Shakespearean plays starring Lewis Morrison and his wife, Florence Roberts. Later, Florence Roberts, supported by White Whittlesey, was to star on her own in, THE NEW MAGDALENE, UNDER TWO FLAGS, THE COUNTRY GIRL, and A SUIT OF SABLE. Later still, she would draw tremendous audiences in a long repertoire that included the three plays in which I had the honor af appearing—SAPHO, FROU FROU, and THE ADVENTURES OF NELL GWYNNE.

Worthy of mention in the glorious era of Mark Thall's second stay at the Alcazar Theatre, were the growth and prestige of the new Alcazar Stock Company. Organized August 1896, just before Thall's return, the company was well acclaimed, and justly so, not only in San Francisco but throughout the country. I have already noted many who touched my life and left their influence, but there were others: Barton Hill, who had previously worked with the great John McCullough at the California; Herbert Farjeon, who had run the gamut of "call boy," prompter, and Assistant Stage Manager; Grant Wagner,

Paul Gerson, Frank Clayton, Charles Smily, and Eugene Ormonde. Further, on the distaff side, were Juliet Crosby (Fred Belasco's wife), Mae Keene, Laura Hope Crews, Anita Fallon, Lila Convere, and Agnes Ranken. While the lists are not complete, they are truly representative of the type of first class artists Mark Thall engaged.

As preoccupied as Thall was with the Alcazar's business, he still gave generously of his time, energy, and money to worthwhile causes. His generosity to those less fortunate than he, was familiar to those who knew him. In those days when actors and actresses did not share the benefits of organized labor as they do now, the burden of helping their own during leaner times rested on the gainfully occupied. An observation made after Mark Thall's death summarizes his compassion: "Dollars and enemies were hard for him to keep. His riches were his friends and he leaves many."

His tenderness toward others was matched by his civic-mindedness and patriotism. When San Francisco was caught up in efforts to show its appreciation for the returning volunteers of the Spanish-American War, Thall was among the leaders of the theater community actively involved. Through his aegis, the Alcazar, concurrently with other San Francisco theaters, opened its doors to these service men. Until the last one, each ship-arrival prompted a "theater party" at the Alcazar, as at most of the city's theaters.

So successful was the partnership of Belasco and Thall that in December, 1900, with Morris E. Mayer, they opened the Central Theater on Market Street near Eighth, San Francisco. In this venture, these three gentlemen were proprietors, and Charles E. Cook, business manager. Belasco and Thall retained their interests in the Alcazar, however; and they continued its operation as before. Always aiming to keep both theaters the top attractions they were, Thall made a business trip to the East Coast in July, 1901. His great plans for the Alcazar and the Central are well delineated in the following, in the July 27, 1901 San Francisco Dramatic Revue:

> *"I engaged a number of people for the Alcazar and Central theatres. M.L. Alsop, who for many years was with (William) Gillette and who played all Gillette's parts in Europe, will soon be here as leading man at the Alcazar. Alberta Converse, a clever and versatile actress, will play leads at the same theatre. She has been starring and is extremely popular with play-goers. I secured several of Frohman's successes for the Alcazar, and a dozen fine melodramas for the Central. Ernest Hastings is doing well and will be at the Alcazar next year. FLORADORA is the reigning success of the East. It is the property of John Fisher of San Diego, and will be produced in this city within the next year. All of William A. Brady's successes will be produced at our playhouses. Our plan to have a chain of theaters on this coast is meeting with the greatest success, and within the year we will be in a position to give the play-goers excellent productions of the latest plays now before the public. While away I took a trip to Buffalo, and found California very slightly represented. But, I tell you, I am glad to get back. **No more East for me.**"*

How prophetic that last short sentence would turn out, even Thall himself had no idea. Barely three months after that trip, and ten months after his second success, as co-proprietor of the Central, his brilliant career as "one of the best theatrical men in the United States" came to an end. He had been nursing a severe cold for several weeks. His partner, Fred Belasco, was in New York on business, and Thall was doubly burdened with work, precluding the complete rest he so desperately needed. By the time he was rushed to Mt. Zion Hospital, all efforts to save his life failed; and on October 12, 1901, he succumbed to pneumonia.

His death came on a Saturday afternoon, at one o'clock, just before the matinee crowds arrived at both the Alcazar and Central Theatres. Accounts told of the makeshift notices hastily tacked on their doors; and that, "no greater tribute to the popularity of Mark Thall could possibly have been paid than the manner with which his patrons received the sad intelligence." Playing at the Alcazar, was the popular, TOO MUCH

JOHNSON, a William Gillette comedy; while BEACON LIGHTS was the Central's bill. When the mama and I approached the Central Theatre for the matinee, we were to learn, for the first time, of the tragic news of our dear friend's death. The notices indicated that both the Alcazar and the Central Theatres would remain closed until after Mark Thall's funeral.

Shock and disbelief intensified the sorrow all of us, in both his Alcazar and Central stock companies, felt at his sudden passing. I had never known real grief before, but it was all about me now, and I could not escape it. This very kindly and charismatic man would never again carry me to his elegant office off the lobby of our "Moorish Gem" and watch, mischieviously yet indulgently, as he observed me "sign" my paycheck. I was supposed to print my name, but I always managed to print most of the letters backwards. This never failed to amuse him.

Arrangements for his funeral were delayed until the following Tuesday to accommodate his brother Sam who was in Seattle. Sam's telegram, dated October 12, 1901, read, "Leave tonight, arrive Monday night; try postpone funeral til Tuesday"—a commentary on the fastest mode of travel in those days, the train. Sam, too, was in the business of theater management, and would replace his dead brother, at both the Alcazar and Central Theatres, for the next two years.

Expressions of sorrow poured in from throughout the country. From near and far, friends came to attend Thall's funeral. After brief services by Rabbi Nieto at the home of Thall's partners, M.E. Mayer and Fred Belasco, the cortege proceeded to the Elk's Hall on Sutter Street where the main services took place. When the Exalted Ruler, Thomas E. Dune, had completed the lodge's ritual, Mark Thall's old friend, Congressman Julius Kahn (a member of the first Alcazar Theatre Company, 1887–1892) delivered the eulogy. I remember that the great crowd about me concealed all the activities, but not the profusion of floral displays that lined the walls of the hall. Accounts recorded that the flowers filled five big express wagons, and when transferred to the steam train, occupied a full baggage car.

From the Elk's Hall, a procession, headed by a sixty piece band, included the Theatrical Mechanic's Association, Unity Lodge of B'nai Brith, and the Theatrical Managers Association represented by: Morris Meyerfeld Jr. of the Orpheum; Melville Marx and J.J. Gottlieb, the Columbia; M.E. Mayer, the Central; V.H. Leahy and Mrs. Ernestine Kreling, Tivoli; Lewis Bishop, Grand Opera House; Selby C. Oppenheimer, California Theatre; Edward P. Levy and Albert Wallerstein, the Chutes; and Phillip Hastings—all greats in San Francisco theater history. Other friends and associates of the mourned Thall followed, lengthening the funeral cortege as it proceeded to the Third and Townsend Depot where it entrained for the Hills of Eternity Cemetery in Colma, just south of San Francisco.

Again, I found myself amidst a sea of giants engulfing me. I never caught even a fleeting glimpse of the casket, described as "draped with a blanket of blue violets and red rosebuds." The graveside services were also obscured from my vision—a maneuver, no doubt, initiated by the mama to spare me its sadness. But she could not stop the flow of music that resonated over the crowd. I had heard the strains of Chopin's Funeral Music over and over by now, and I thought it was lovely; so I began to hum the melody. The poor mama was shocked and horrified over what she considered my unpardonable breach of decorum, and she promptly put an end to my humming.

But I prefer to think that my dear and indulgent friend, Mr. Thall, understood and, moreover, was bemused that while all about me was sadness, I had found a ray of joy. Never, had I seen the kindly, cheerful Mr. Thall without a smile on his face. The sorrow about me, therefore, was inconsistent with the man I knew. In childish simplicity, I could not comprehend the depth of the anguish suffered by his family and friends. It would be a few more years before I would understand the finality of corporeal death and the loss of a loved one. This insight, for me, marked a benchmark in my life.

Mark Thall left a daughter Ella, 19, and a son Charles, 18, as well as an aged father, Henry H. Thall, two brothers, Frederick M. and Samuel Thall, and a sister, Mrs. Rebecca Herman who published the family's sorrow in a poem in the local press.

A TRIBUTE OF REMEMBRANCE
TO
MY DEAR BROTHER MARK THALL
There came no gentle warning
To remind him death was near
No time in which to say farewell
To those he loved most dear

Our hearts are wrung with sorrow
For the form we shall see no more
For death did strike a cruel blow
In that sad, fatal hour

Mark Thall left his legacy of superb theater management to both his brother Sam, who very ably managed both theaters until 1903, and to his son Charles Mark Thall. The latter started as a press representative for the Alcazar, after his father's death; and following the example set by him, pursued a brilliant career that led, eventually, to his position as Assistant Booking Manager for Fox-West Coast Theaters.

Perpetuation of the Thall name continues in the persons of Charles' son, Marston, and the latter's two sons, William Mark and Mark Charles Thall.

During the twenty-one year life span of the first Alcazar, Mark Thall had played a very important part in two scintillating periods, 1887–1892 and from 1897 until his death in 1901. But the story of the first Alcazar (There were three.) starts two years before Thall became its business manager. It was then being built by Mr. M.H. De Young, publisher of the San Francisco Chronicle. Announcements in the local media were setting the scene for the grand opening of the theater that was hoped would "give all the conveniences of a concert hall, a theater and a lecture room, where performances can be given even of an ambitious kind." It was to be the handsomest hall in the city, for Mr. De Young had spent over $30,000 in decorations alone. His own newspaper announced proudly:

*It is pure Moorish in style, and the very latest im-
provements in every department have been lavishly introduced. While it will be possible to put even a spectacular
play on the stage, it has been specially arranged so that a
lecturer, a singer or an orchestra can be equally comfortably
and satisfactorily placed on it. Indeed, the intention has
been to make a building suitable for the production of
special entertainments, which the regular theaters offer no
opportunity for. The house itself will be a sight (!) and it
will enhance the enjoyment of the audience in every way.*

The last three weeks saw completion of final details, including the painting of the scenes and the magnificent front drop
curtain. Advance notices of the sale of season tickets at San
Francisco's venerable music house, Sherman and Clay, offered
prices for Monday, Wednesday, Friday, and Saturday matinee
concerts at nine dollars for Dress Circle and seven dollars for
Parquet. Single tickets would be sold on opening day; no single
tickets would be sold in advance; and, finally, no more than six
would be available to anyone, the only exception being the
theater party. Regular prices would range from $2.50, Dress
Circle; $2, Parquet; and $1, General Admission—high prices
for the times, to be reduced later, as we have already seen.

Bold advertisements for the gala night appeared in all the
newspapers and magazines. What theater devotee could resist:

A DOUBLE MEMORABLE EVENT
Grand Inaugural Night—Monday November 16, 1885
at 8 p.m.

AND

*Triumphant Re-entry of Emma Nevada, the World
Renowned American Prima Donna, Who Will Return To
San Francisco For Only Four Grand Opera Concerts*

Much was made of the fact that Miss Nevada had arrived by
train in her own private car, previously owned by Miss Lillie
Langtry; and that she was accompanied by her own company
which included her director, C.A. Chizzola, her manager, D. De
Vivo, and a tenor, baritone, violinist, and pianist.

Emma Nevada, Opening of Alcazar Theatre 1885
Credit: Barrett-Miller Collection

When the great evening arrived, the grand affair started at precisely 8 p.m. to a packed house. Mayor Washington Bartlett, in his dedicatory speech, called the Alcazar, "The Moorish Gem, a palace of beauty"; and congratulated the architects, Frederick Hyde and William Patton, for designing the prettiest theater in America and one which San Francisco could justly admire.

Box holders were San Francisco renowns, all: Colonel R.J. Tobin, Mr. and Mrs. H.S. Crocker, William Talbot, James D. Phelan, Mr. and Mrs. M.H. De Young, James Fair, Loring Pickering, Judge and Mrs. Hunt, Mr. and Mrs. James Denman, Colonel A.A. Andrews, and Andrew S. Hallidie, the inventor of San Francisco's cable cars.

So, the Alcazar, under the management of George Wallenrod, was born into a city that boasted such famous name theaters as the Baldwin, the California, the Bush Street Theatre, the Standard, the Tivoli, and the Grand Opera House. Wallenrod, with the aid of various assistants as business managers, remained as general manager of the Alcazar until 1894. Among his business managers were L.R. Stockwell, George Osbourne, and, as already noted, Mark Thall (1887—1892).

In 1895, J.P. Howe and R.H. Devereaux managed it for about six months; after which time, it became known as "Grover's Alcazar, the Palais Royal of America." As such, it was managed by Leonard E. Grover for about a year, with the lessees listed as San Francisco Amusement Company Incorporated. During this year, Mr. Grover wrote and presented several plays starring his son Leonard Grover Jr. For opening night the father wrote A RINGER, a farce comedy, "with singing, merry making, and one continual laugh from start to finish." Other works of Grover Sr. included: MY SON IN LAW, THE WOLVES OF NEW YORK, and CAD THE TOMBOY. Besides Grover Jr. and Gracie Plaisted, his leading lady, other names prominent in the stock company included: Hereward Hoyte, who doubled as stage manager; his wife, Mrs. Auzerais Hoyte, Miss May Noble, Agnes Ranken, Josephine Gassman, Baby Lewis, and Francis Powers. The latter would come into his own when he wrote THE FIRST BORN, the following year.

In August of 1896, the theater's management again underwent a change. Fred Belasco, Frank Doane, and J.B. Jordan became its lessees and managers, and restored its original name, The Alcazar Theatre, a more acceptable identification with San Francisco theatergoers. Less than a year later, Mark Thall joined Fred Belasco, replacing Doane and Jordan; and as already detailed, was the Alcazar's business manager until death severed the partnership.

After Mark Thall's brother Sam left as business manager in 1903, the Alcazar was operated by the new partnership of Fred Belasco and his brother-in-law, Morris E. Mayer, until 1907. Of course, it was during this period that the Alcazar Theatre I

Juliet Crosby (Mrs. Fred Belasco) Alcazar Theatre
Credit: Barrett-Miller Collection

loved and remember so well, became a casualty of the San Francisco earthquake and fire of 1906.

Belasco and Mayer immediately built another Alcazar, this time at Sutter and Steiner Streets. It was nothing like its predecessor, but it received the distinction of being the first "Class A" building to be built in the city when it opened March 16, 1907, just eleven months after the fire.

A week later, double tragedy hit the team of Fred Belasco and Morris E. Mayer; and, again, great sadness enveloped the Alcazar. Juliet Crosby, married to Fred Belasco for nine years, gave birth to their first child, who died shortly after birth. Three days later, Juliet Crosby Belasco herself died of complications of childbirth. Her death terminated a career in which she had been acclaimed one of California's best contributions to the American stage. San Franciscans were proud of her "beauty, of her ability, and of the charm of manner and personality that (made) friends of all whom she (met)." She was particularly noted for her role as Madame Butterfly in David Belasco's play of the same name. When she had played Trilby earlier, she was hailed as, "showing what a fine actress" she was, one who nightly received "expressions of popularity and affection that might be proudly claimed by any of San Francisco's great artists."

Upon hearing the tragic news of Miss Crosby's death, Mayer, who suffered from a heart condition, fell to the floor and was dead within a half hour.

Mrs. Mayer succeeded her husband as Belasco's partner. Together they built a third Alcazar, this time at 260 O'Farrell Street, near the site of the original "Moorish Gem." This third and last Alcazar opened December 23, 1912, and after a checkered history, closed in 1962.

Since Alcazars numbers two and three hold no place in my early memories, they have been researched and treated with great dispatch. It is the original Alcazar to which I wish to return now for the purpose of describing, more fully, details of its interior. According to modern-day connotations of the word "sight," its description as such, in the pre-opening promotional, hardly seems a suitable term for describing the magnificence and opulence of the Alcazar Theatre I remember.

Drawing from the Mauresque art form best expressed by an Alcazar (a temple, a palace, or a pleasure house), the artist who did the interior of the theater, Mr. John Borden of New York, undertook a work of formidable artistic challenge. Using plaster of Paris casts taken directly from the originals in the Alhambra of Spain, reproductions of plates from the palace of Hassen Pasha at Bagdad and the Alcazar at Seville, and his own original designs, Borden was to conceptualize and create a masterpiece of Moorish art never attempted in San Francisco or, perhaps, even in the United States.

In an especially set-up workshop on Mission Street, this genius, using a simple chisel, carved in plastic (malleable) clay some of the beautiful panels that were used in the auditorium. While these were done without benefit of previous design or pattern, reproduction of the thirty-two plates he purchased abroad was a more complicated process. He had carefully selected only the small sections of the originals that truly represented the whole concept. Using a mold, Borden cast each of these sections six times. Every resultant set of six, fitted and fastened together, made a working model for one of the thirty-two finished plates. From each plate, he made the larger molds used to form the final thirty-two stucco casts.

Accounts of the very sensitive John Borden's repugnance over the placing of gas reflectors in the beautiful ceiling he had designed, can be appreciated in light of the sometime-struggle between art and utilitarian-functional demands:

> *Judged by the strict standard of Moorish art which flourished before the hideous gas tank, which defaces and poisons all of our cities, was yet dreamed of, even in a nightmare, they* (gas reflectors) *present, of course, a palpable incongruity which cannot be obviated. The aim of the present day architect is to establish harmony between old ideas of beauty. . . .and the new practical needs which we have ourselves created. The solution of this problem is one of the marked triumphs in the construction of the Alcazar. The modern means of lighting it have been happily adapted to the ancient style of decoration and are, in fine, an important additional embellishment.*

(San Francisco Chronicle, November 15, 1885)

Mr. Borden's embellishments were perforated reflectors that not only added to the beauty of the ceiling, but served to hide the elaborate system of vents that acted as air-pumps, located above each reflector.

A similar challenge, the need for ventilating-openings in the walls of the parquet, he solved by camouflaging the holes with very ornate screens. Indeed, these were considered, "one of the most graceful details of the interior."

But before entering this "Moorish Gem," one was struck by what could have seemed an incongruity: the Tudoresque facade, the many Saracenic minarets on the roof of the Alcazar, and the lower front of stained glass in Oriental designs, had not all modes been so harmoniously executed by the famous architect, William Patton. An integral part of the lower facade of stained glass, were the Alcazar Cafe on the left and Norman's Retreat (saloon) on the right. Both opened out onto the street, as well as into the lobby and auditorium. Their interiors carried out the Mauresque theme of the theater.

Above the very impressive bronze entrance gates, the word "Alcazar" was inscribed in large letters, "with rundels, disks, crystalline fragments and stones, with facettes" that shown brilliantly at night, reflecting the lighting of the interior behind them.

Just past the bronze gates, one beheld the scalloped Byzantine arch that spanned the main doors of carved wood and glass, and the striking transom done in rare stained glass with "designs composed of cut gems in various forms and colors."

Through the glass doors one came into the elegant lobby with polished marble floors. The over-all effect was that of "a general shimmer of gold and bronze and silver." Above, a beautiful chandelier of antique bronze hung from a ceiling "broken with gracefully foliated arches supported by slender columns" that set off the grand stairway. A flight of wide, carpeted steps descended from the lobby to the parquet or main floor, over the doorway to which, was an enormous plate glass mirror set into the wall. Above the mirror, was the famous hemisphere-shaped rose-window, considered "a masterpiece of the painter's and glassworker's art." It held in its center a musical muse represented by a lovely lady, robed in "loosely flowing purple" and holding a three-stringed lyre. Her beautiful face was clearly visible from either the lobby or parquet sides.

Once inside the auditorium, I can only remind the reader of my feelings of being in a cathedral.

The two great gilded pillars on each side of the proscenium arch, matched the two in the lobby. High on their smooth, cylindrical, silver shafts, appeared entablatures with "coarse arabesques on their sides"; and from the entablatures sprang groins, or radiating arches, that rose to the ceiling. In Moorish architecture the groins were interpreted as "the stately spreading of the palm"; the ceiling, with its intricate tracery, was regarded as the foliage; and, the palace or temple itself, represented the sacred groves "which probably witnessed the first rites of worship."

So subtle was the lighting of the ceiling, that I can never forget the delicate blue glow over the silvers, golds, and bronzes. It was my very own Fairyland, the only one I really knew.

Supported by slender pillars, the front of the balcony was a magnificent semi-circle, ornamented with a very striking balustrade, each panel representing "the portal of a shrine." On this upper level were the dress circle, and the stage boxes on each side of the stage. The elegant Boxes had no cover, and were separated from the dress circle by heavy railings of carved woods.

Seats in the Boxes were luxurious arm-chairs covered in a heavy plush, "figured in Turkish style." Those of the dress circle and parquet, were "plainly, but (richly) upholstered in dark crimson plush." The parquet seats had bottoms that tilted back automatically when the spectator rose and, "by merely laying a hand on the back, they dropped into position again." Altogether, the Alcazar seated twelve hundred people.

Woodwork throughout the Alcazar further conveyed the feeling of warmth and majesty that prevailed in my "Moorish Gem." The woods used, it was said, were of the finest: mountain pine, stained a deep red, and mahogany. The beautiful designs, carvings, and scrollwork on the dadoes, balustrades, and rails were expertly executed under the supervision of F. Cahto.

When first built, the Alcazar had a lighting system that included, on the walls of the balcony and parquet, gas brackets in antique bronze, with burners representing wax candles. Their shiny metal was spangled with "disks and rundels of the finest cut and stained glass." By the time I played there fifteen years later, these gas lights had been converted to electricity.

In the prompter's nook, stage right, was a marble-topped console with labeled levers protruding. It enclosed an electric box from which wires led to the main lights in the house. Using ten valves, it was possible to turn on the seven-hundred gas jets all at once, or selectively, any one section, or combination of sections:

> Valve #1 turned the gas on at the footlights;
> Valve #2—the main border lights;
> Valves #3, 4, 5, and 6—the minor border lights;
> Valve #7—the huge chandelier in the main dome, the
>   center of which was a great silver ball;
> Valve #8—the two reflectors in the ceiling;
> Valve #9—the candelabra around the walls; and
> Valve #10—the bunch lights on the stage.

A powerful electric battery provided the means of instant illumination, creating the "strikingly beautiful spectacle" so raved about in all the reviews. First-nighters' "ohs" and "a-a-a-hs" when the innovative lighting system revealed dazzling chandeliers, graceful Moorish arches, subtle colorings, sparkling gems, and the aura of magnificence throughout the beautiful theater, were testimony to the architectural and artistic successes of Mr. De Young's new business venture.

Besides the conversion from gas to electricity, another change had taken place in the Alcazar before I played there. The main floor, originally a level surface, was easily and quickly converted into a dance floor. On its broad middle aisle, near the main door, was a trap with a slide that lead to the storeroom below. When a ball was to take place immediately after a performance, the seats, fastened together in fours, were quickly folded and sent down the slide to where waiting attendants below could stack them in fifteen minutes. The entire operation took only three or four men. Apparently, the need for this "metamorphosing," so highly advertised in notices, did not warrant its continuance, for the following year (1886) the Alcazar underwent a remodeling that eliminated the center aisle and replaced the level floor with the traditional inclined one with which all are familiar. To accommodate the conversion, the enormous storeroom that had originally reached from under mid-stage to under parquet entrance, was virtually usurped, as was the Green Room. The latter probably became the prop room I remember and have already described. The original "spacious dressing rooms," located off the enormous storeroom, were now located *under* the stage, and were not all that spacious. The originals were also said to be "comfortably furnished with chairs and settees, and in each a marble lavatory with running water and a mirror"—descriptions that do not agree with my recollections of our quarters below. The remodeling had, apparently, been achieved by some radical surgery.

In spite of the changes to some parts of the Alcazar, the stage, spanned by its beautiful proscenium arch flanked by the massive, ornate pillars, was still the same. While not very deep, the stage was wide and sufficient to its needs. It measured thirty feet from the footlights to the rear wall, and the proscenium arch spanned some thirty-six feet. Of course, the wings on each side added more space for scenery and properties.

The orchestra pit, too, was still the same when I entered the magic portals of the lovely Alcazar. It was large enough to accommodate thirty musicians, and had its little "secret door" that led into their practice room below. Around the pit was a lovely iron rail, heavily bronzed. It was there, at this "altar rail," I made my first stop with Mr. Thall, that momentous day that I became a member of the beautiful temple.

Always an attraction for me, were the fly galleries on each side. In the right gallery were over sixty pulleys on which the myriad ropes traveled up and down in a purposeful rhythm, fathomable only to the fly men. Above the stage, were six sky borders and four sky reflectors. There were, according to early descriptions, "twelve complete scenes representing forest, glade, chateau, vale, city, streets and interiors" when the Alcazar opened, but many changes and additions had taken place to meet interim needs by the time I arrived there.

The changing of a drop scene was an operation I truly enjoyed. It was started by a man in the right fly gallery who lowered the properly "trimmed" drop to the stage, where "scene-shifters" eased it to just the right spot, always careful no distortion of the scene occurred in the process. The appropriate wing was then moved in, at the proper angle, to mask the backstage from the audience's view.

"Trimming" the drop was an art I watched with much admiration and understanding, considering my tender years while at the Alcazar. The term referred to readying the drop and making it hang smoothly—a process familiar to anyone who has made ready sails and yards for sailing. The painted canvas drop-scene was secured top and bottom to "battings," or wooden slats. To the top slat, lines were attached through three holes—one on each side, and one in the center. The line on the far end (stage left) was the "long line." It was looped over a pulley above and spanned the width of the stage, coming to hang on the near side of the drop, stage right. The "center line" started at the center of the batting and, after looping its own pulley above, also traveled in the same direction until it came to an end alongside the "long line." The third or "short line," starting at stage right on the batting, hung a very short length as it joined the other two. Wrinkles were deftly removed from the drop by adjusting the pull each line exerted on its section. When the stress was equalized, the smooth drop was considered properly "trimmed," and the three lines could then be fastened together and pulled in unison—a convenience when the used drop had to be hurriedly removed up into the flies at the command, "take it away." After the drop reached the flies, a flyman took the slack rope and secured it to the "pin-rail"—a bar with large pegs, in and around which the lines were wound. If the pin-rail was at stage level (running the depth of backstage right), a grip performed this same operation.

A stage scene, usually an interior, was often made up of "flats" representing walls, doorways, windows, archways, or fireplaces. "Lashing the flats" was a skilled art employed to hold them together. This was achieved by lacing rope around large-headed screws inserted on the frames along the back margins that were to be joined. After the flats were properly lashed, stage braces were used to support them.

A look at the back of the flat revealed that, set into a cross-piece along the middle of the frame, was a screw-eye into which the stage brace was hooked. The brace consisted of a wooden two-piece adjustable bar, the top section of which, slid along the lower one. When the desired angle of uprightness had been achieved by this sliding of one over the other, the two sections were made firm with a "butterfly screw," or wing nut, and then anchored to the floor, with a stage screw. The lower section of the adjustable bar was fitted with a curved metal plate with a hole through which the stage screw was inserted. The stage screw, a three-holed device through which three fingers were inserted by the stage hand, facilitated the operation of securing the set to the stage floor. Protecting the stage, was a heavy, brown canvas "floor cloth"; however, the screw holes on the wooden planks of the flooring would in time necessitate the replacement of the pocked one with a new floor, or a section thereof.

Of great importance to life backstage, was the Alcazar's fire fighting equipment, to which much publicity was given when the theater opened. The Alcazar emphasized the twenty-two fire hydrants: "each with a full length of the finest hose, with a patent reel. Water can be poured by means of the fire apparatus into every part of the building at a moment's notice. Each hose is capable, under full pressure from the water mains, of throwing to a distance of 100 ft." Of the twenty-two fire hydrants, six were located on the stage, two in the fly galleries, and the rest, in basement corridors and other locations considered most crucial. But, alas, like those in the other theaters, the efficacy of the Alcazar's fine fire equipment was predicated on water pressure—*the sine qua non* missing that fateful day, April 18, 1906.

The only impressions I carry of the Alcazar's great fire-fighting system backstage, are those of a few reels of white canvas hose, hung in various places; and of the required uniformed city fireman. Every night there was a new fireman. Apparently, the privilege of watching performances from the inner sanctum backstage, was one zealously shared among the city's intrepid fire fighters. But the fireman always seemed so absorbed in the performance, we wondered what he would have done in an emergency. In truth, he was always in the way, and everyone backstage shared a kindly resentment toward him.

Other fascinations backstage at the Alcazar were the paint-frame and car, located behind the backdrop. When a new set was needed, the scenic artist went to work perched on a seat on rollers, which he moved back and forth along a scaffolding in front of the canvas. Since the scaffolding was on pulleys, he could also move up and down the canvas, at will. I can never forget the many happy moments I spent watching works of art blossom above me, while the mama admonished me about getting my ever-present white dress paint splattered.

Before leaving the Alcazar's stage, I must "pull" the front drop-curtain—as it looked on opening night and then, as I remember it.

The original drop-curtain that drew so much admiration, and measured 28 x 36-1/2 feet, was painted by the very accomplished scenic artist, John Mazzanovich. It was depicted as "an oriental scene, a characteristic sketch of Palestine, with signs of Turkish domination of architectural forms in the middle ground"—a bit of a mind boggler! Its middle ground was a "group of low white buildings with Moorish or Arabic domes overshadowed by a stately tower from which a muezzin might be expected to sound his regulation Moslem prayer."

Of the right foreground, terms used to describe it could be summed up in, "clumps of palms; cool shadows; dusky waters of a pool; and a canopied spring with herbiage."

The left foreground was considered the most striking part of the scene, for it represented a "rich heavy Moorish curtain draped in magnificent folds and fringed with the golden, half unraveled threads of the precious texture. From the taut cord which supports the curtain, a Moorish lamp is suspended." On the upper portion of the curtain, "a gorgeous Arabic vase filled to overflowing with flowers, stands upon a Turkish stand . . . and behind the vase a rug of brilliant and rich colors hangs upon some invisible supports."

Of the background, Mazzanovich exclaimed that, "It is the most charming portion of the picture—purple mountains in the distance, purple vale below, and purple sky above."

None of these accounts match the curtain I remember so very well. By 1900, when I joined the Alcazar, the original curtain had been replaced by one with a very different theme. The scene was not the bold Moorish one, but an idyllic French lake whose far shore—with trees, shrubbery, and suggestions of flowers—was rendered, predominantly, in shades of soft, muted greens and blues. The lake's reflections presented a calm, serene picture for the middleground, and the narration un-furled in the peaceful fore-shore, nearer lower canvas. There, on the sandy beach, a blunt-nose rowboat, filled to overflowing with flowers that cascaded over its sides, still held the last of a happy foursome, a beautiful young peasant girl. She was par-tially immersed in the mounds of flowers of myriad bright colors, so that only her striking white blouse stood out. Drawing the bateau onto the beach, was one of the young men, dressed in French peasant attire. Standing close by on the sand, to his left, was the second girl. She wore a flowing scarf around her head and was dressed in a colorful costume—a white blouse with billowing puffed sleeves, black bodice, and a multicolored striped skirt. The fourth member of the group, another young man, looked appraisingly from a position on the beach, closer to the stern of the craft.

I wondered what story the lovely scene told and was in-formed that it showed French peasants arriving with a load of flowers, gathered for the country's foremost business, the per-fume industry.

On this poignant and "sweet" note, I think it fitting that I close *my* curtain of the Alcazar; for behind *my* curtain remains, forevermore, my fondest recollections of San Francisco's fabu-lous "Moorish Gem."

Left: Gutted First Central Theatre (1900-1906)
Right: The Second Central 1906-1909
Credit: The Archives For The Performing Arts, S.F.

Chapter Five

Gallery of the Gods

On December 22, 1900, Fred Belasco and Mark Thall's second theater, the Central, opened with David Belasco's THE HEART OF MARYLAND. The new house of melodrama was located on Market near Eighth Street, across from the old City Hall. Previously a part of San Francisco's Central Amusement Park, the building was used to display panoramas; but the vogue of panoramas was about over. The age-old melodrama form of the past two centuries, however, was still intact, albeit, at times, more refined and sophisticated. Belasco and Thall were intent on finding a suitable place dedicated, mostly, to this form of drama. Their Alcazar served the purposes of "legitimate drama," and their new house would answer those of, shall we say, "less legitimate" drama. In the Central Park building, they found what they sought—a large enough edifice whose interior lent itself to the changes required for the conversion to a theater of melodrama.

Special permission, in the nature of a building permit signed by each of the city's supervisors, was granted. Work proceeded at a fast pace for six months, though not fast enough to complete the job before opening night. Unexpected time delays occurred as a result of the city's new fire ordinance that made certain changes in the construction of the Central mandatory. The new regulations required that all structures had to be, "if not fireproof, at least slow burning." All buildings with a height exceeding eighty feet had to be made of fireproof materials, and the Central, of course, had to meet the requirement.

Although the conversion job had not been completed, license to conduct theatrical performances in this Central Park building was issued barely a week before opening night. On that gala night, a cold wintry one, Ashton Stevens of the San Francisco Examiner complained that the drafts coursed freely throughout the entire building, the entrance was unfinished, and "they need plugs and oil stoves out there in Central Park and until they get them it wouldn't be a bad idea to offer a box of cough lozenges with every ticket." I do not recall that conditions were as bad as Mr. Stevens described them, and other accounts of the Central's opening night seemed to have ignored them.

THE HEART OF MARYLAND by David Belasco, a Civil War melodrama, had played three years earlier at the Baldwin Theatre, with Mrs. Leslie Carter and Maurice Barrymore playing the leads. Belasco had written the play especially for Mrs. Carter. When it debuted at the Grand Opera House in Washington, D.C. (October, 1895), she and Barrymore played the romantic leads, Maryland Calvert and Colonel Alan Kendrick. When the play ran at the MacDonough Theatre (1897) in Oakland, she had shared star billing with the famous James E. Wilson. Fully aware that Mrs. Carter's fame would occasion comparisons, Belasco and Thall drew on the best talent their Alcazar had to offer: Effie Darling as Maryland; and Howard Hall, also very popular at the "Moorish Gem," as the male lead, Alan. Both Miss Darling and Mr. Hall were members of the newly formed Central Stock Company, as well.

Among others in the Central's new stock company, some of whom played both the Alcazar and Central theaters, were: Myron Leffingwell, Stanley Ross, Charles Arthur, Clarence Arper, Frank Opperman, Ernest Howell, Grant Wagner, Louis Belmour, George Nichols, Edward Greenleaf, Margaret Marshall, Lillian Bartlett, and Oza Waldrop.

In the Central's Opening Day offering of THE HEART OF MARYLAND, it was Effie Darling who drew the most accolades. She tried valiantly not to be outdone in the role Mrs. Carter had made famous; and, for the most part, critics agreed she had played Maryland admirably, with "great dramatic power." This was particularly so in the "sensation scene"— typical of latter-half Nineteenth Century melodrama—when she ascends the belfrey of the church and clings to the clapper of the bell because its ringing would have sounded the alarm of her beloved Colonel Alan Kendrick's escape. It was a very compelling scene—the distraught Maryland swinging determinedly in her desperate effort of devotion. This particular scene in Belasco's play was considered odious by many critics, but well received by audiences everywhere. San Franciscans welcomed it.

Though entranced by Maryland's feat, I was too young to appreciate its emotional implications. But, as with those about me, I would remember that particular scene, above all others.

As always, David Belasco's THE HEART OF MARYLAND was, again, a great hit with San Francisco theatergoers. It was reviewed, variously, as: "cleverly constructed melodrama," a "composite masterpiece," and the author as a "remarkable genius in handling dramatic and emotional situations." During its two weeks' run, Belasco's great success played to packed houses, and Fred Belasco and Mark Thall were lauded for their opening choice.

I had wanted very much to be in this gala opening play, but there was no speaking child-part. I would have to wait until three months later, when I had my chance at the Central in UNCLE TOM'S CABIN, as already described.

Definitely, the Central Theater had opened with a "splash," and I use the word advisedly, for in succeeding plays much use would be made of the large water tank hidden under its stage. The tank was only one of the many spectaculars the Central boasted, but it alone accounted for many a "splash" on the mammoth stage. Other "sensationals"—boats, buggies, horses, bridges, and trains—were also used to maximum advantage, as stage mechanics evolved. Deployment of large equipment and animals needed for some productions was possible through an alley from Seventh Street to the Central's stage door.

The two-story, brick-and-stone front Central, with its spacious lobby, wide aisles, interior tinted in cream and gold and hung with rich draperies, was refreshingly light and uncluttered. Starting from the stage, the ground floor included a large orchestra pit, a row of boxes on each side of a broad center aisle, the dress circle, separated from the boxes by a spacious walk-through; and an expansive passageway around the back of the auditorium. Upstairs, the balcony reached halfway to the stage, with the gallery taking up the back-most. The Central was proud of its twelve stage boxes and its twelve loge boxes, but it hastened to assure all that a superb view of the stage was possible from any part of the house. To offset any problem that could arise as a result of its shape, the Central, it was said, had "a good broad arch flung . . . to counter-balance the bad acoustics of a circular building." It had a seating capacity of some 2,200; its prices ranged from ten to fifty cents; and its intent, from the start, was to make it a "first class popular family theater."

Because its stage was so enormous, the Central required an entirely different technique of acting from that of other San Francisco theaters. While on the Alcazar's cozy stage one could take two or three steps toward the exit, turn, and deliver the exit speech and go out the door, the Central's stage dictated a quite different method of execution. There would have been an intolerable silence while one walked across the Central's stage to exit, then stopped to deliver the exit lines. So, one adjusted to the necessary timing by doing a marathon of sorts, all the while saying the lines and praying that, somehow, one would break even. To the actor, it seemed as though he was constantly in full gallop; to the beleaguered stage manager, all this "business" was leading him to premature grayness and an early grave. I shall always be thankful I was trained at the Alcazar, where the technique was fine and exquisite.

Other noticeable differences between the Alcazar and the Central theaters, besides size and stage techniques, were the types of plays presented and the kinds of audiences that attended. Plays for the charming "Moorish Gem" were definitely "higher class"—perhaps analagous to "better literature," as contrasted with the "ordinary literature" of the Central's melodramas.

Audiences at the Central were a special phenomenon. The actor felt he was always addressing himself to a friendly mob, for there were galleries to reach. The admission price of ten cents for gallery seats led, as in other theaters of melodrama, to the emergence of what we called the "gallery gods." If the gallery gods approved, they not only applauded, they stomped their feet, and shouted and whistled their approbation. They could get quite out of hand, so there were always house police-men about. If the gods became too raucous, the policeman would rap his stick on the edge of the balcony, and that was all it took to restore order. Of course, if the audiences did not like the villain or villainess, they resorted to the well-known responses of hissing and booing (always welcomed by the heavies)—a marked contrast with the genteel responses from Alcazar audiences.

Reactions of the Central's "gallery gods" differed from those of its main floor audiences, who were always more sub-dued; still, we all knew on stage that we had better please that gallery. We reached out to them; we played to them; and we sought their responses. In melodrama, we offered them clear-cut characterizations that boiled down to the good and the bad. There were no subtle nuances to confuse them, and so their responses were natural to the vehicles offered. Had more re-fined, heady drama been their choice, they would have been sitting at places like the Alcazar, the Tivoli, or the Grand Opera House. In defense of the denizens of the gallery, I would like to submit that they were not raucous for the sake of being rowdy; rather, they were intensely and personally involved with the show. They could identify with some of the characters por-trayed, and they could eschew the others, with equal fervor— tendencies shared by the main floor audiences.

Although my debut at the Central in UNCLE TOM'S CABIN, early in 1901, had been an exciting one, it was hardly a harbinger of what was to come as I ventured further into this house of melodrama. Adventures attendant to melodrama there, could be, in turn, exhilarating, repetitious, monotonous, and, sometimes, unpredictable. In spite of our sincere and diligent efforts to keep to the script, both the size of the Cen-tral's stage and the nature of melodrama could lead to surprises, from time to time. The theater was quite capable of spawning and nurturing the unexpected, as witness the following episode:

Rarely did the Central miss an opportunity to use its mon-strous water tank, which alone could precipitate its share of misadventures. When not in use, the tank was safely covered with flooring to disguise its presence. In one play in which it was utilized, the leading man, driving his horse and buggy, had to cross over a wooden, country bridge that spanned the "river." The villain, however, before the lead reaches the bridge, has been cutting its supports, in order to thwart our hero's progress.

The first night, the leading man drove over the "break-away-bridge" as far as the center when, as planned, the bridge gave way, hurtling man, horse, and buggy into the water. The gallery gods were ecstatic and exploded into thunderous applause. The curtain went down; the drenched victim was fished out of the water and dried; and the horse was led away.

The following night, our hero and his horse were in the wings, ready to repeat the "break-away-bridge" scene. The horse, however, had second thoughts. He dug his hooves right there and refused to budge an inch. The stage hands did everything conceivable to start the recalcitrant beast on his way; but he stood his ground, as if to say, "You fooled me once, that was your fault. You fool me twice, that is *my* fault." So, the curtain was dropped that night, without the spectacular "break-away-bridge" scene. Thereafter, a different horse from the livery stable was used for each performance, for the duration of the play's run.

This very tank was almost the undoing of our director, George P. Webster. He was a mild-mannered man whose versatility suited him to many different roles. He was also quite familiar with the tank and its deep pocket, marked off by four floats. In one play, during a very dramatic scene, he was to dive between these markers into the "lake." But he missed the deep pocket, hit his head against a more shallow section, and was rendered unconscious. Down came the curtain. He was hastily rescued and taken to his dressing room where, happily, he was soon revived.

George P. Webster was truly a "utility man." He directed all the plays in which I appeared at the Central, with the exception of DOWN YONDER. He had a special rapport with his fellow actors, eminently qualifying him for the type of directorship melodramas required. Perhaps "co-ordinator" was a more suitable title for him. He knew his colleagues well; they knew their art well; and since he was one of them, detailed instructions from him were superfluous. Indeed, the size of the Central's stage precluded finesse in the techniques used. Nuances there, were not perceptible. Only broad gestures fitted the setting of so vast a stage. Such gestures on a smaller stage, such as the Alcazar's, might have interferred with someone else's, or even landed on another's nose.

Besides his duties as director, Webster played all manner of bit parts, straight or character roles, even to the absurd, where others dared not tread—such as jumping into the formidable water tank. His willingness, good nature, and versatility conspired against his becoming "great." Had he been more reticent, eschewing all but special type roles, I'm convinced he could have achieved much fame. Perhaps his slight stature also militated against that. Whatever it was, this amiable, mustached

George Webster c. 1902   Central Theatre
Credit: Barrett-Miller Collection

friend was a success in his own way and a very important person to me.

George Webster once wrote of his start in 1881 at the Baldwin, where after "playing general utility . . . and getting a speaking acquaintance with the ups and downs of the business, I was seized with a desire to go on the road and make my everlasting fortune." He joined the Alf Wyman Company, traveling in notoriously uncomfortable coaches and playing saloons, hotels, churches, town halls, and even blacksmith shops. For all his efforts pitching in to, "string wires, hang curtains, put up, make shifts for scenery, etc.," he made this woeful confession, "I never received a cent the whole time I was out with the Wyman Company. The ghost persistently refused to walk." (No payday.)

Their itinerary took them to Sonora, then over the Sierras to Bodie. Since there was no money for hotel accommodations, the women slept in the wagon and the men, under it. Food consisted, mostly, of crackers and canned goods. On the way, they camped at Strawberry Pass and then, Hot Springs, where they arrived, "half dead from starvation, having divided a small piece of bread and a smaller piece of bacon." That night, the men were allowed to sleep in the hotel's barn, with the horses; while the ladies spent another night in the coach. After another twenty-four hours of continuous travel, they arrived, again starved, at Bridgeport at 9 a.m.; but the boarding-house manager refused to feed them until twelve, at which point, "It is all vivid to me, even now—that stampede for the dining room when the bell rang." That night, the company made sixty dollars and then proceeded to Bodie, where they opened on July 3, 1881, in an old dance hall.

Although they were the first theatrical organization to appear in Bodie in two years, they had the consummate bad luck to have been billed the same night a big ball took place. Webster spoke of his dejection upon looking through the curtain about 8 p.m. and, "discerning three men and a yellow dog. The men had come in on passes and the dog had sneaked in someway." They decided not to play that night. As Webster was about to go to bed, an old schoolmate of his, Billy Buckley, whose father was superintendent of the Bodie Tunnel Mine, stopped by for a visit. Buckley assured his dejected friend that all was not lost, yet. It was, indeed, too bad they hadn't played at the Miner's Union Hall, *following* the dance, but they could still rent the hall for an engagement. Wyman hired the hall for two weeks and charged $1.50 a seat—quite some "lettuce" in those days.

In his usual versatile way, Webster played three roles in UNCLE TOM'S CABIN—George Harris, St. Clair, and Legree. After two weeks of playing to packed houses, Wyman bought them "new store clothes," according to Webster. He noted that, "The clothes and grub we ate, was the nearest Wyman came to paying us." Besides UNCLE TOM'S CABIN, the company presented YACKE, KATHLEEN MAVOURNEEN, DORA, THE BLACK DIAMOND, and LADY AUDLEY'S SECRET. The plays were typical "domestic melodramas" in which the moral codes were quite explicit: even the heroine, Lady Audley, paid the supreme penalty for sin.

On their return to Sonora, the Wyman Company was accosted by an armed, masked bandit who asked them who they were. When Wyman shouted, "Actors, going to Sonora," the disdain and disappointment were evident in the reply, "Oh hell! You can pass."

At Sonora, Webster left the company and, "got home as fast as I could to my mother." He had been gone six months, and arrived home without so much as a penny in his pockets. But, in his usual good-humored way, he observed, "I probably got home just in time, for I was looking decidedly seedy, and there was urgent need for a mother's needle and thread and patches on the broad part of my trousers." Alas, he had not made his "everlasting fortune."

While still a very young man, Webster became a partner, with William Brady, of a company touring the Pacific Coast in such melodramas as ROSEDALE, STREETS OF NEW YORK, SHE, and UNDER THE GAS LIGHT. UNDER THE GAS LIGHT was another domestic melodrama, noted only because it introduced a "sensational scene" with a train "barrelling in" on a hapless, tied victim—a gimmick that proved very popular after this Augustin Daly play of 1867. Webster played the villains in these until he tired of them, and then changed to the hero roles.

William Brady, it seems, invested his proceeds, from this and other successful ventures, more wisely than did Webster. In due time, Brady went from one success to another and, finally, became one of a half dozen truly big men in the theater business. It was said that, "Brady won out, while Webster missed his chance."

If financial success was the criterion, perhaps the conclusion had some validity; but there was something very "rich" about the George Webster who, in spite of countless tribulations and disappointments, had the perseverance to stay in the business he loved, albeit on a less famous level. Those of us who worked for and with him marvelled at his equanimity, even during the many humorous but challenging mishaps that occurred at the Central.

Another incident involving a horse, comes to mind:

It happened during one of the wild Western plays familiar to Central Theater audiences. In this one, I was not a participant but a viewer, an advantage I shall always relish. Herschel Mayall, the picaresque leading man, dressed to the nines in cowboy grandeur, came riding into the saloon, on his horse. As if that were not enough to catch the attention of the patrons of the establishment, this swaggering pirate of the plains dismounted with a flourish, all the while holding the occupants of the saloon at gun point with one hand, and the horse's reins with the other. In so doing, he necessarily turned his back to the audience—a "no-no," excepting in a moment such as this one when a strong dramatic point had to be made. As he moved backwards, still leading his horse and "covering" his victims, the protagonist, in stage parlance, now "dominated the scene." This was the time to lower the curtain on the scene, for maximum dramatic effect. Down came the curtain, and then the unexpected occurred. Out on the large apron of the stage, the horse had swung around and gotten himself hindquarters first, to the audience. When the curtain had come down, it had come between the man and the horse, leaving the poor animal alone on the apron. Blocked by the curtain before him, the stunned bronco then swung half circle, to be met by the more bewildering dilemma of footlights in his eyes. As he thrust out his neck over the footlights to see what was out there in the dark, he perceived the sea of faces below him, and but one open space—the broad center aisle for which the Central was noted.

It was then the orchestra's moment of panic. The orchestra leader, Louis Homeier, finding himself uncomfortably close to the frightened horse, and mistrusting the latter's intentions, started waving his precious Stradivarius. Hurling choice invectives in a strong guttural German accent, Homeier gesticulated wildly as he tried to intimidate the noble steed with, "Go back, you damn horse, go back!" But the die was cast and the skittish stallion, in one burst, leaped over Maestro Homeier and his precious violin, and cleared the orchestra pit. Landing on all four feet in the center aisle, the terrified horse galloped full force onward to the front of the theater, where an usher finally caught him—much to the relief of the frozen spectators. Obviously, bedlam was very much a part of the Central, setting it apart from the more dignified atmosphere of San Francisco's other theaters.

Baby Dody as Little Jim "Lights O'London" 1901   Central Theatre
Credit: Barrett-Miller Collection

In some melodramas at the Central, pathos was the keynote. Pathos, especially when carried by a small child such as I was then, was a very effective tool of melodrama. In LIGHTS O'LONDON, I played little Jim, the young urchin in rags, found sleeping under a bridge abutment. (My introduction to the infamous water tank, as well as to George Webster whom I came to regard as "Mr. Theater.") When the Irish policeman, played by George Nicholls, finds me there, he drags me out and questions me on why I don't go home. When I inform him I have no home, he decides there is only one solution to the plight: he will arrest me and take me to the police station, where I will receive warm shelter and care. The pathos is summed up in little Jim's reply, "You have nothing to arrest me for. What must I do to be arrested? Shall I swipe your handkerchief, Sir?" It took six acts, eleven scenes, twenty-seven characters, plus detectives, police, co-stars, et al, however, to wind up the story.

Pathos also set the tone for my part of Cissy Denver in THE SILVER KING, Arthur Jones's melodrama, written in 1882. In this one, I was the very sad little girl, daughter of the silver king, Wilfred Denver. I was shunned by the other children because, "they say my father killed a man." THE SILVER KING was in five acts and boasted fifteen scenes that ran the gamut of: interiors, exteriors, gardens, lanes, inns, villas, Kensington Gardens, Coombe's Wharf, Coombe's Den, to The Grange where it all ends with, according to the printed program, "Peace and Happiness." Somehow, they managed to involve twenty-seven characters in the cast, supported by lesser ones like: railway officials, passengers, children, detectives, et al.

But large casts were not unusual. Indeed, they were necessary to most melodramas. This was especially so at the Central, where they served the purpose of dressing the vast stage. The usual cast of characters in these melodramas consisted of: leading man, leading lady; sometimes second leads; villain/villainess; character man, character woman; juvenile (man), soubrette or ingenue (depending on the story's need); a servant, Mary or Nora (with feather duster), or a butler with a soliloquy that set the theme of the plot. Countless lesser characters called "supernumeraries," abbreviated to "supers" and finally shortened simply to "sups," made up the full complement on stage.

Since most plays were English, the setting was usually London — London mansions, London hovels, London streets, London prisons — London, London, London. There was what I came to perceive as a certain sameness about all these English plays at the Central. It was so in THE WORLD AGAINST HER when I played little Annie, age seven, daughter of James Carlton, played by Edwin T. Emery. There was a similarity about the plots that reflected their common origin. The same performers were involved. The acting bordered on ranting, at times, and this heavy handedness, endemic to melodrama, was not in accordance with my early training. I, nevertheless, willingly accepted it, under the circumstances. I never fought any characterization I was called upon to play; rather, I entered wholeheartedly into the part, and lived it all the way.

Freneticism was another quality of the melodrama I remember. In LOST IN NEW YORK, by San Francisco's Leonard Grover, the ubiquitous water tank was again uncovered. In this play, one of the wildest and most uproarious, people chased each other pell-mell. It had a fire scene that could have driven the audience to cover, were it not that San Francisco theatergoers had become inured to the Central's insanity. I played little Susie to Georgie Cooper's Jennie Wilson, a New York waif. Together in a rowboat, we had to make an escape from the asylum on the East River (stage left to stage right). Regrettably, Georgie Cooper, the accomplished actress, was a pretty bad oarswoman. Everytime she pulled the oar, she sent water splashing over me; and every night I played in LOST IN NEW YORK, I had a thorough drenching. How the poor mama was discomfited and distressed by these unsolicited shower baths. But when Georgie and I had finally made our escape from the villain and landed safely on the other side of the river, the gallery gods broke into roars of approval — how they loved it, and how *we* waited for just such approbation. It is interesting to note that below the list of characters of LOST IN NEW YORK, is the following:

"CHARACTERS IN INSANE ASYLUM BY MEMBERS

OF THE COMPANY" (Touche!)

This freneticism was also characteristic of MASTER AND MAN, in which I played Little Johnny, Hester's child. While the play lacked the frenzied activity of the plot of LOST IN NEW YORK, it more than made up for it with the need for frequent scene changes. When the curtain dropped, the scenes seemed to be animated, for the flats ran back and forth at incredible speeds, with the grip at the helm. The main thing I quickly learned in this melodrama was to step lively and, above all else, to keep out of the way of the stage hands—my life depended on it.

Again it would be a play with a New York setting, THE PULSE OF NEW YORK, that was to epitomize frenzied, exaggerated action. The American authored vehicles I played in were usually hectic, compared to the subdued English ones; but, I confess, I preferred them to the doldrums of the latter. In THE PULSE OF NEW YORK, in which I played Edith Dennison, there was everything. It was the wildest melodrama of all. The famous or infamous water tank was used, for this one also had an East River setting. New York plays usually had the East River to fall back on or into—whatever! We were all convinced this play was a "pot-boiler"—that is, the author had just stayed up late some night with his coffee pot going, and "ground" out the melodrama, under a deadline.

Its twelve scenes best tell the mad-paced timing of this "Original Sensational Drama of Metropolitan Life," by Howard P. Taylor:

Act I

        Scene 1 — Drawing Room of Mrs. Dennison's Home,
                Madison Avenue
                New York City   *The Missing Banker*
        Scene 2 — Little Church Around the Corner At Night
        Scene 3 — An Open Lot Near East River.
                                Just in The Nick of Time

    Act II

        Scene 1 — Private Office of Dennison and Holt
        Scene 2 — Street in New York
        Scene 3 — Elevated Railroad.   *Bound to the Track*

Act III
    Scene 1 – Mother Skevotski's Dancing Dive
    Scene 2 – Street in New York
    Scene 3 – Pier at East River.   *The Rescue*
Act IV
    Scene 1 – Home Again
    Scene 2 – Street in New York
    Scene 3 – The Fire.   *Saved From the Flames*

In this madding melodrama, Georgie Cooper played six different roles:

Polly Morton, a rollicking young heiress
Maggie Maguire, an Irish washerwoman
Samantha Perkins, a down East Yankee
Lavena, a green German girl
Dinky Dan, a newsboy
Mrs. Haggerty No. 2

The very talented Miss Cooper was our "rough soubrette" and, as such, had to be versatile and equal to any situation. From

Georgie Cooper 1901   Central Theatre
Credit: Barrett-Miller Collection

her theatrical parents, Fred A. Cooper and Georgie Wood-thrope, she had learned her lessons well. Being a "quick-change-artist" was a very important must for any soubrette, and Georgie Cooper met the qualifications superbly. Often, as in this play, there was no time to run down to the dressing room for changes, so Miss Cooper would make them in the wings, where a chair and a table with the costumes and wigs were within easy reach. And yet, an aura of propriety was maintained at all times. Under her costume, she always wore a modest basic dress, or tights, or trunks to cover her; over this, went each change. Since this was before the days of zippers, a device known as "strip pins" (common pins on a string) was pinned along the garment's closing. By pulling up on the string, the pins were released and the garment quickly unfastened, thereby facilitating the fast changes required.

The unwritten law backstage now came into play. No actress had to worry about being watched during costume changes. Seasoned stagehands would never cast a glance at her, and strangers were not allowed backstage in those days. The occasional one who did stray there received a most hostile reception, and was summarily ushered out. It was like the commotion that explodes when a stranger ventures into a henhouse at night.

Our Miss Cooper, who later married the noted actor-manager, Landers Stevens, was a lovely young woman with just enough tomboyishness to enter wholeheartedly into wild dramas such as THE PULSE OF NEW YORK. She loved them, and this one had all the challenges and excitement we both relished. As the scene synopsis shows, there were: missing people; four rescues from perilous situations, one for each act; trains, water, fire, and the usual bustle attendant to such goings-on. But, in typical melodrama fashion, the dilemmas were resolved "just in the nick of time," before the final curtain; and all lived happily ever after. The gallery gods would have heard several rappings on the balcony rail, by the alert policeman; and when the "melo" ended, they would have done with stomping and roaring—until the next one came along. It was mad, but heavenly.

Agnes Ranken 1901   Central Theatre
Credit: Barrett-Miller Collection

Change from the more mad-paced American melodramas, came with innocuous English plays such as the "Romantic Drama," THE LAND OF THE LIVING, in which I played Daisy, Gerald (George Webster) and Kate Arkwright's (Agnes Ranken) little daughter. My fondest recollections of this one are not of the play itself, but of those with whom I worked—the charming and beautiful young actress, Agnes Ranken, who played my mother; the ebullient Georgie Cooper who played Gerald's cousin; and my dear friend Margaret Marshall, our character woman, as my Nurse Babbles.

It was Miss Marshall's son, Harry, who came into much prominence as a scenic artist. He was virtually unknown when he worked at the Central, but he had a most appreciative admirer in me. I was fascinated by his work. He had a special talent for producing three-dimensional scenes by using optimum highlights and shadows. So profound was the impression he made on me that, later, in my ventures into oil painting, I was guided by what I had learned from him. From Harry, I developed a fairly good sense of composition. His expertness at executing the proper balances required for stage settings, set a forceful example for me.

Harry was also unexcelled at creating set trees. Generally, there were two types of set trees, both supported by stage braces that bolted them to the stage floor: the small or average size set tree that stood by itself, with the aid of the brace instead of being fastened to or painted on a wing; and the tall tree, attached to a pull-rope and dropped from the flies, then propped by the stage brace. This size tree was readily raised back up into the flies, once the stage brace had been removed at the command, "strike."

Watching Harry create one of these set trees was an unforgettable lesson in stagecraft. After drawing and painting the tree on canvas, he stiffened the trunk, general outline of the crown, and main branches, by gluing them to wood. The remaining parts of the tree—the stems and leaves—he cut around, very carefully, discarding the blank canvas. Because the cut-out stems and leaves were now left limp, without support, he spread a coarse netting across the back of the tree's crown, tacking the mesh to the wood frame. To this taut netting, Harry glued the stems and leaves. The netting was invisible to the audience and allowed light to shine through the open areas, creating a very natural looking tree. Harry had a very delicate touch with this and scenery painting, so it was always such a joy to watch their unfolding.

As his reputation spread, Harry Marshall attracted the attention of greats like: Oliver Morosco and James Neill of the Burbank Theater in Los Angeles; Henry Miller, for whom he did some of his finest work during two summer seasons at the Columbia Theatre; and Selby C. Oppenheimer of our California Theatre. In time, Harry headed the staff of scenic artists for all the Neill-Morosco productions.

All this came to pass later. When I knew him, he was still a struggling young artist, subject to the embarrassments we all experienced at the start. One such occasion comes to mind:

Oddly enough, chamber-pots were often used for mixing paints, so they were a common utensil in the flies. At one of the performances, Harry was up in the flies on a scaffolding, sitting on a chamber pot, painting a drop. The chamber pot gave him that extra height needed to reach the top. As ill luck would have it, the border masking the flies had not been dropped down far enough. So, there he was, painting away, oblivious of his embarrassing predicament until the hysterical laughter of the audience startled him to awareness. Very quickly, the masking border was lowered and his mortification ended.

Another admirer of Marshall's was a talented young stage-struck teenager, Harry Kelly, who wanted to become a scenic artist. Young Harry was one of the rare exceptions to the rule barring all outsiders backstage. He had penetrated the mystique guarding the "inner sanctum," by virtue of his friendship with his mentor, Harry Marshall. Harry Kelly and I became very good friends and, in time, he built me a small theater, for which he painted some beautiful sets on cardboard. Because Kelly was the only other really young person (he was about fifteen years old) backstage, we gravitated to each other for companionship. He seemed to be a very fond admirer of mine, for he sent me many a bouquet of baby roses and box of candy. I was, therefore, not prepared for a most distressing episode involving him. On one of his occasional visits to our home at St. Ann's, he drew me a lovely Moorish set with delicate cut-out arches, for my little theater. The set was colored a beautiful rosepink and white, and I adored it. But there was something about it he did not like. Saying, "Oh, I can do better than that," he took the set and crumpled it into a hopeless heap. At the time, he was sitting on a carpet footstool. I was so incensed over the outrage, that I pushed him and sent him sprawling onto the floor. He was somewhat chagrined, but laughed off his embarrassment, as the mama rebuked me for my inexcusable outburst.

A respite from the usual hectic melodrama at the Central was a little dilly entitled THE MORMAN WIFE, a "romantic comedy drama" subtitled, "A Story of Life in Utah." This one had a slight change of sameness. Its setting was Salt Lake City, Utah instead of London or New York. We were spared the wild escapes and escapades germaine to the frantic East River settings. Falling into the briny, buoyant Great Salt Lake would, I suppose, scarcely have made dramatic rescues credible. Instead, the play employed the familiar melodrama formula in which the main characters appear in dismal surroundings, threatened by dismal forces. By the time the final curtain is lowered, however, the same characters have struggled out of a maze of unbelievable predicaments; and we see them in a contrasting setting: a lovely home where all is turning out just fine, thank you. In THE MORMAN WIFE, the chief tool was comedic, but it achieved the same result.

Another break in pace at the Central was a soft little play, DOWN YONDER, in which I played Viny, Mary Saterlee's (Oza Waldrop) child. It was a comedy drama in four acts, by Lee Arthur, the author of WE UNS OF TENNESSEE, and was presented by special arrangement with David Belasco. Being laid in Southern Georgia, the tempo of DOWN YONDER was refreshingly slower than any of the Central's melodramas in which I had played. In a soft play such as this one, there were no water tank, no fire scene, no one tied to the tracks, no horses, and no wild or hysterical scenes. Instead of heroic or madcap exploits, the play dealt with human feelings—an almost traitorous departure from the accepted melodrama's format. The characters were more realistic; and there were warm exchanges of emotions, for this play had plot and feeling.

Charles Francis Bryant c. 1901   Alcazar and Central Theatres
Credit: Barrett-Miller Collection

DOWN YONDER was the type of play best directed by a man like Charles Francis Bryant, borrowed from the Alcazar Theatre. An accomplished, sensitive director, he had a special talent for drawing the finest from his actors. He was truly a "pro" with the finesse of interpretaton a play such as this one demanded.

Most of DOWN YONDER took place on a Christmas Eve, making for much goodwill and joy among adults and children. The four black children, January, February, March, and April were Cumfrey's (Marie Howe) and Brutus Jones's. The third act took place in Cumfrey's cabin where a lovely, child's cradle was one of the important props. It is this cradle that bestirs the fondest memories of DOWN YONDER. Since I had never had a cradle of my own, this one held a special attraction for me. It was a magnificent piece of furniture in sturdy wood, with gracefully turned rungs supporting the rails. When the act was over, the cradle was removed backstage where my black playmates and I took turns being rocked in it. We looked forward to this very happy and fitting reward after our concentration on stage.

No one playing melodrama at the Central escaped an occasional vicissitude. In my own inventory, there was a share of vexsome moments. Some were a lark, but now and then there would be one so unexpected and perplexing, it defied solution.

Marie Howe, Character Actress   Alcazar and Central Theatres c. 1901
Credit: Barrett-Miller Collection

While playing little Mary Morgan in TEN NIGHTS IN A BAR-ROOM, I had just such an experience.

In Act III, Scene 2, Mary Morgan lies delirious from the blow to the head, accidentally inflicted by Simon Slade, owner of the Sickle and Sheaf Tavern, when he threw a heavy drinking glass at her father, and missed. In her delirium she imagines she must, once again, go after her father and rescue him from the perils of Slades Tavern; and cries out, "Father, father! Oh, dear!"

Morgan assures her he is there and implores, "Lie down, my child. I have not gone and left you."

With this "assurance" would begin the most awkward, sensitive, embarrassing, and uncomfortable sequences I endured on stage as Baby Dody. The gentleman who played my father was a victim of the stomach condition, "waterbrash," which ultimately manifests itself in a superfluity of saliva. My subsequent lines speak for themselves:

"Oh, I know you now! It is my father. *Stoop* down to me (drip, drip!). I want to whisper something. . . ."

Morgan: "Well, what is it, my child?" (more drip!)

With all the seriousness of the dying, I must look up at him and say,

"I shall never get well, father; I am going to die." (More apropos, "I am going to drown, if you don't stop, dear father.")

But the discomfort continued as I bared my conviction of imminent death, for my father's ears alone, with the supplication he not tell dear Mama. I could not turn my poignant plea in *any* direction but at the agonized, drooling face of my contrite father—while the unabated precipitation continued to fall upon me.

Mercifully, there followed a dialogue between Joe Morgan and his wife, Fannie; but the respite was not all that desirable for me. I had to lie on my deathbed pretending, convincingly, that I was moribund, when in reality I was miserably uncomfortable and aware there was more to come. It is such trying situations that separate the dedicated actor from the dilettante.

In the next sequence, Morgan, in a fit of delirium tremens, imagines all manner of hideous snakes, "leaping, dancing, and shouting with joy to think the drunkard's hour has come." At the first performance, during this high-pitched moment, Morgan hides from the menacing demons by crouching behind little Mary's couch. According to stage instructions, he must blacken one eye with black grease paint so that as he rises into view again, the impression is clear that he has suffered the black eye as he struck the couch, going down. In his hurry to come up quickly to complete his frenzied dialogue, he overdid the blackening operation. From the audience there arose such thunderous, raucous laughter, I was stunned and perplexed—until he came into my own view, exhorting,

"Keep them off I say! Keep them off! You won't let them hurt me, will you," as he clings to me. Lying thusly, on my back, I soon understood the reason for the audience's outburst. He had come up with an enormous black eye that covered most of a side of his face. He reminded me of a spotted pup I had once known. So ludicrous did he look that, though I had to be "dead serious" as he pleaded, "Pray for me, my child," (drool, spray!) I came very near losing all restraint and joining the convulsed audience. As luck would have it, he finally falls to the floor. Mary sits up in bed, with her hands raised in prayer (how appropriate!). Soft music. Tableau.

Between acts, I complained bitterly to the mama, "He *spits* all over me. Please, mama, tell him not to spit on me." And the gentle little Southern mama would try, softly, to explain to me how the hapless man was to be pitied for his serious affliction; and that I must be brave and never embarrass him, nor waiver from my characterization.

Fortified briefly with her "pep-talk," I would await the next onslaught when in Act IV, Scene 3, I am, once again, asking for more of same by calling,

"Father! . . . I'm so glad you're awake. I was afraid you were never going to wake up again."

Of course, father leans over me (dripity-drip) and asks eagerly,

"What can I do for you, my child?"

And we were off on the most devastatingly moist dialogue

of all. When Mary tells him he has always been good to her, his guilt leads him to demurers in which he sprays me with,

"Don't, Mary! Don't say anything about that—say that I've been very bad." ("How true, how true," I would have liked to counter.) But the seemingly interminable exchanges continued, as the remorseful father hovered over the deathbed, promising little Mary,

"God helping me, dear child, I will never go out at night again for a bad purpose. . . . I'll never go into a bar again!" (splash)

My bath nears an end now, as I gasp,

"Your Mary has lived long enough (truer words were never spoken), the angels have heard little Mary's prayers. . . . Goodbye, father; I shan't have to ask you to be good to mother now." Kisses father. (Ah yes, I remember it well.) "Goodbye, mother." Kisses her. Sings. Dies.

And so my suffering ended—and none too soon, I might add. It was now time for my own real mama to once again quiet my ruffled feathers, wash me off, and change me into dry clothes.

Between MASTER AND MAN and THE LAND OF THE LIVING, there was an hiatus from the Central when I appeared in the title role of LITTLE LORD FAUNTLEROY, at Oliver Morosco's Burbank Theatre in Los Angeles, California. This was the first time in my career that the special billing "Baby Dody And Company" appeared on the playbill and in all the promotions.

There had been much conjecture among Mr. Morosco, Mr. Fred A. Cooper the producer-director for LITTLE LORD FAUNTLEROY, and the mama over my capability to learn the inordinately lengthy part of the title role—the longest, at that time, written for a child. Until then, the problem had been solved by having the role shared by two children. Earlier, a much older child than I had played it alone; but Mr. Morosco and his staff had their qualms that an eight-year-old, as I was then, could memorize so much material and withstand the strain of such a long performance a full week.

Their doubts were understandable. Though they were not aware of it, it was a fact that while I was learning the rudiments of reading from the General Arthur Cigar sign and from the kindly dedicated Mr. and Mrs. White, at the St. Ann's Building, I was not exactly the most literate child for my age. My forte was, as mentioned before, my incredible feat of memory. Having heard a passage once or twice, I could then repeat it flawlessly. On this basis alone, were Mr. Morosco's doubts laid to rest. Mr. Cooper (Georgie and Ollie's father) knew, very well, my special talent and, therefore, entertained nothing but confidence. The mama had no doubt she could coach me for the part. As for me, I wondered why there should be any question at all. So, I was given the role of Little Lord Fauntleroy—becoming the youngest child ever to do it alone. The fact that the part was a taxing one for a very young child never crossed my mind, because memorizing had always been such a lark.

Convinced by both Mr. Cooper and the mama that I was equal to the demands the role entailed, Mr. Morosco booked me for LITTLE LORD FAUNTLEROY. With contractual details solved, Mr. Cooper, the mama, and I set off for rehearsals in Los Angeles. Promotions for the show appeared in all the Los Angeles papers.

The Los Angeles Express credited me with being "quite as clever as either of her famous predecessors"; and, "She has won enthusiastic comment everywhere."

The Los Angeles Times spoke of LITTLE LORD FAUNT-LEROY as, "one of the most appealing studies of child character in the English drama. The cast will be headed by Baby Dody; she has been greeted as a child phenomenon."

The Los Angeles Herald offered that, . . . "the title role is in the hands of a child artist who has captured audiences everywhere. Her name is Baby Dody, and though a mere infant in years, she is said to possess a considerable fund of experience in stage work."

Fortunately, I was not aware of the Burbank's great expectations. The mama sheltered me from fawning press releases; and since I could not read them anyway, I was immune to possible deleterious effects on my psyche.

A more down to earth consideration was where to live during our stay in Los Angeles, and that was met, most conveniently, by Mr. Alexander Miller's Rooming House, across the street from the Burbank Theatre. The house was a charming, white cottage with a picket fence around it. We had one of their "front corner rooms." It was very comfortable and cheery, and overlooked Main Street. Another window faced a lovely, colorful garden that surrounded the house.

Most of our time, however, was spent at the theater on rehearsals and preparations for the costumes. The costumes

Baby Dody as Cedric Errol in N.Y. "Little Lord Fauntleroy"   Burbank Theatre Los Angeles 1902
Credit: Barrett-Miller Collection

intrigued me most. For the first act, where the setting was New York, I wore a white blouse with ruffled cuffs, and a large, ruffled collar that draped over the shoulders. An "artist's tie" in black set off the shirt. Pants were the ordinary knee-britches of the times; mine, however, were in white and were accentuated by a fringed sash around the waist. Long red stockings and sturdy brown oxfords all but completed the costume. A wide-brimmed, off-the-face straw hat set the final note for this period before Cedric Errol and his mother, "Dearest," set off for England and fancier raiments.

In the next two acts, my costumes were much more elaborate and beautiful. The one I wore most constantly was the well known "Fauntleroy" suit. Mine included a black velvet tunic, with a satin sash fringed at each end and tied at the side; deep-pointed, white Vandyke collar and cuffs of rich lace; black velvet knee-britches with a row of decorative buttons down each side; black silk stockings and shiny, black slippers; and the large-brimmed, off-the-face, velvet, black hat with one large plume draped jauntily over the edge of the brim. It was the style of hat most popularly worn by young lads of English nobility of that era. Though the play's setting was 1885 England, the Little Lord Fauntleroy suit seemed to set the fashion in many countries through the early Twentieth Century, also. I felt quite dressed up in these silks and velvets and laces, but to many a young man, the costume must have been an abomination.

Since my doting grandfather, the Earl of Dorincourt, indulged little Lord Fauntleroy with all manner of clothes, toys, and a pony, my costumes also included a fancy riding habit that went with the latter. The habit consisted of a red velvet jacket and matching, narrow-banded cap; a white vest, buttoned down the front; a white shirt with a high collar that was stiffly starched and very uncomfortable; white riding britches of a heavy corded material; soft, black boots that reached high above the knee; and a very ornate riding crop to complete the costume befitting a young scion of nobility.

Earlier, little Lord Fauntleroy had been just plain Cedric Errol, living with his widowed mother, "Dearest," in New York.

Baby Dody as Cedric Errol "Little Lord Fauntleroy"
Burbank Theatre, Los Angeles 1902
Credit: Barrett-Miller Collection

Cedric's father had displeased his own father, the Earl of Dorincourt, by marrying an American woman; and had been promptly disinherited. When, later, the Earl's two older sons, Bevis and Maurice die, little Cedric becomes Lord Fauntleroy, by default. The irascible, dour, old gouty Earl, still refusing to accept "that American woman," assigns her to Court Lodge, a lovely house on his estate; but young Lord Fauntleroy comes to live with him at Dorincourt Castle.

Having decided not to like the boy, the old Earl is quite agreeably surprised to find his grandson is not an American "savage." On the contrary, young Fauntleroy was a very sweet, loving child who reflected his mother's gentleness, kindness, and grace. He was an unusual little boy who loved everyone. Though only a young child, he had a talent for always saying the right thing. He was so trusting of all, that he never perceived the true nature of his dour old grandfather. Fauntleroy was not aware that in a planned effort to wean the boy away from his adored Dearest, the grandfather had plied him and his needy friends with all manner of gifts—of course, to no avail.

The boy's faith in and affection for the old recluse, is most disarming. Before long, the tyrannical old Earl has gone through a metamorphosis that changes him from one hated by all his relatives, tenantry, and associates, to a quite acceptable human being.

When the title of little Lord Fauntleroy is challenged by what turns out to be an impostor, the event so unnerved the Earl that it caused him to re-evaluate his own relationship with Fauntleroy's mother. In the end, the intractable old Earl invites Dearest to come live with him and Fauntleroy at Dorincourt Castle. This completes the child's happiness, and they live happily ever after.

As much time as could be spared from rehearsals and costume fittings, I spent at the C.J.R. Carson Curio Shop, next door to the Burbank Theater. Mr. Carson's little girl became my playmate. She kept me well entertained with her "conducted tours," pointing out the scores of Indian crafted articles— arrowheads, spearheads, moccasins, colorfully beaded vests, belts, headbands, and an assortment of silver and turquoise jewelry—that adorned her father's shop. For some reason, the mama allowed me to play with her. Perhaps it was because her father was doorkeeper at the Burbank, and her presence at the theater, therefore, a natural sequence. She was a quaint little girl, an only child. Later, I was reminded of her in Dickens' Little Nell of THE OLD CURIOSITY SHOP.

In spite of a hectic week of rehearsals, costume fittings, and set designing, the play was "put together" and opened on Sunday, March 16, 1902, to very good reviews for Baby Dody and less than flattering ones for most of the remainder of the cast.

The Los Angeles Record's appraisal included: "Baby Dody who carries the star part of Cedric Errol, who becomes Little Lord Fauntleroy, possesses talent of a rare order in one so young." But the critic regretted that, "The dramatists put into the mouth of this infant prodigy a stilted language (I'm glad I wasn't aware it was stilted.), wholly unreal in one so young." He summarizes, "There was lack of talent and preparation on all but Baby Dody."

Baby Dody "Little Lord Fauntleroy" Dorincourt Castle, England
Burbank Theatre, Los Angeles, 1902
Credit: Barrett-Miller Collection

The Los Angeles Express assessment was mixed, but on the whole, favorable:

> *"Supernatural precocity" are two words that describe fairly accurately a mite of a child with long blonde curls and whose shrill voice recites hundreds of lines in LITTLE LORD FAUNTLEROY. This play was presented at the Burbank last night to a slim and undemonstrative audience.* (Happily, things picked up considerably, with larger and more appreciative audiences each succeeding performance.)
>
> *A capital Lord Fauntleroy is Baby Dody. Though a child of tender years, she carries the part well . . . despite long and irrelevant speeches. It seems a shame to burden a child's memory with so many hundreds of lines. If the ability to master 80 or 90 "sides" of smart aristocratic speeches, together with a proportionate amount of "business" constitutes "genius," then Baby Dody, despite her diminutive size towers among the giants in the profession.* (Had the gentleman taken the trouble to interview me, I would gladly have allayed his concern, for I truly enjoyed every word, line, and gesture in what, to me, was the most delightful play in which I starred as Baby Dody.)
>
> *The remainder of the cast, is made up of eight or ten persons, who evidently have missed their calling in life, or who purposely indulge in wax-figure histrionics so as not to overshadow the little star.* (The last observation was a bit out of line, for these were seasoned professionals with whom I was proud to play.)

Another so-called "drama expert" who might have profited by doing his homework better, betrayed his accuracy by referring to me as "little lad" and "he," in what was an otherwise very complimentary review in the Los Angeles Herald. The headline proclaimed:

> *BABY DODY WINS HONORS*
> *Little Lad At The Burbank Makes A*
> *Pleasing Little Lord Fauntleroy*
> *"Baby Dody and Company" is the way the announce-*

The Burbank Theatre   Los Angeles, California 1899-1969
Credit: The Los Angeles Public Library

*ments in the program read, and they come near telling the
truth, for Baby Dody as Fauntleroy is by far the best one of
the company. The little lad (sic)—**he** is scarcely more than a
baby—made nearly all the hits of the evening. He is a good
little actor and remembers his lines much better than some of
the older members of the company. The little fellow not only
speaks his lines well but he acts with a naturalness that is
not customary with children on stage. He is the Cedric of the
book, the Cedric that Mrs. Burnett's imagination created,
the Little Lord Fauntleroy of velvet suits and big sashes, the
Little Lord Fauntleroy whose winning ways win his old
grandfather's heart.*

Could it be I played a little boy so convincingly, I really
fooled that critic? Perhaps.

Having discovered the foregoing reviews, after seventy-
two years, I must admit, unabashedly, that I am enjoying them
thoroughly.

When I played the Burbank, it was one of Los Angeles'
leading theaters. It was located on South Main Street, on the
edge of an expanding city that would, in time, surround it.
Leaving scars in its wake, the sprawling city sought ever more
territory and moved on during its relentless growth. Mr. Oliver
Morosco had purchased the theater "on a shoestring" and
opened it with BIRD OF PARADISE, in 1899. Other successful
ventures such as PEG O' MY HEART starring Laurette Taylor,
HELP WANTED, and ROSE OF THE RANCHO set the
course for a very bright era at the Burbank Theatre. He also
coauthored several pieces, among them THE JUDGE AND
THE JURY and SO LONG LETTY. The era of drama was
followed by vaudeville and burlesque until, finally, the Burbank
reached an ignominious end as a pornographic movie house.
About 1969, it closed its doors; and in March of 1974, suffered
the fate of many old theaters—a victim of the wrecking ball, to
convert it into a parking lot.

Of the four Moroscos of the theater world, Oliver was,
perhaps, the most flamboyant and successful. Born Oliver
Mitchell, he and his brother, Leslie, had been adopted by

Walter Morosco who, earlier, had changed his own name from "Bishop." The older Morosco had a natural son, Harry, completing the Morosco foursome.

Oliver Morosco's success with the Burbank Theatre in time led him to ownership of several other California theaters. His SO LONG LETTY, coauthored with Elmer Harris, a very successful vehicle starring Charlotte Greenwood, with music by Earl Carroll, was still appearing as late as July, 1917, at the Cort Theater in Oakland, California.

By 1926, however, Oliver Morosco's fortunes in New York theater, where he had been for several years, crumbled. He returned to California, a relatively obscure man until his death in 1946. I'm grateful I knew him when his star was on the ascendancy. He was a handsome, forceful business man who treated the mama and me with utmost courtesy and kindness during my engagement at his Burbank Theater.

Another brief interlude from the Central Theater occurred when I returned to the Alcazar for AN AMERICAN CITIZEN. This experience was akin to building great expectations when we are about to return to our hometown after some years have elapsed, and finding things are no longer quite as we remembered them. In spite of the laudatory reviews I received as Cruger's office boy, Mercury, the play, to my mind, was a very dull one. When, years later, I read DAVID COPPERFIELD and met Uriah Heap, I finally understod the main characters in AN AMERICAN CITIZEN. They were all "Uriah Heaps."

But perhaps the real cause for my disappointing "return home" was that with the death of my dear Mark Thall, conditions had changed in my absence. It was not quite so homey and intimate as it had been. With his passing, the Alcazar had lost a guiding genius, whose warmth and direction had affected us more deeply than we realized. We had not recognized his many virtues until after he was gone. The loftier atmosphere of an Alcazar was Mark Thall's true milieu, not the Central, even though he was one of its three owners.

With this, my last appearance at my "Moorish Gem," I had taken one more step away from my "clouds of glory," and a bit of the "vision's splendor" had begun to wane.

After this brief break, I returned to the Central Theater, where they were outdoing themselves in preparations for staging a very elaborate production of Tolstoi's RESURRECTION, dramatized by Charles W. Chase. The play, according to reports, was creating a tremendous sensation in New York at that time. For this one, opening April 13, 1903, the Central Theater departed from the true melodrama format for which it had earned the sobriquet, "The Bucket of Blood." Gone were the garishness, exaggeration, oversimplification of human living, and escape from reality, common to real melodrama. Instead, under the capable direction of George P. Webster, all the refinements, subtleties, complexities of plot, and nuances of realism that make up a Tolstoi story, were deftly executed. That Mr. Webster was equal to the task was another demonstration of his phenomenal versatility. One publication of the time, the San Francisco Dramatic Revue, commented appropriately:

> *This popular company* (Central Stock Company), *which has been revelling of late in broadest of farce comedy, is suprising itself and astonishing the public by a more than excellent production of RESURRECTION. The dramatization has been staged with great care and intelligence by Stage Director, George Webster.*

Though the cast included many inveterate actors of melodrama, they were to render the play with all the refined techniques of the legitimate play of the Alcazar, yet with the forcefulness such a play demanded. To be sure, hero and heroine have obstacles to hurdle before the happy resolution, even as in a domestic melodrama. The young hero, Russian Prince Demetri Nekhludoff, played by Landers Stevens, divides his estate among those who work his land, then joins the army. He falls on intemperate ways and "betrays" the beautiful, illegitimate peasant servant girl, Katisha Maslova, who works for the Prince's two maiden aunts. When Maslova, played by Eugenie Thais Lawton, appeals to him to "right the wrong he has done her," he gives her gold.

Miss Lawton's portrayal of the hapless girl stoned out of the village when her "sin" is known, received the highest praise from all the local critics. She was the Maslova who reached her nadir when, ten years later, she is wrongly convicted of murdering a merchant with whom she "consorted," and is sentenced to ten years in Siberia. Among the jury who issue the verdict is none other than Prince Demetri. Soon, remorse overwhelms him and he resolves to marry Maslova and accompany her to Siberia. When he visits her in prison, he finds that she is a "drunkard, and debased to the very lowest"; but he perseveres, and shares her dreary march to Siberia. In the end, a new life dawns for both Demetri and Maslova, of course—albeit, not the book's version! In the latter, they go their own ways.

Staging for RESURRECTION was on such a large scale that only a stage the size of the Central's could have done it justice. The smallness of an Alcazar's would have made an adequate production of Tolstoi's play impossible. The cast was a very large one that included the Central Theater Stock Company, augmented by numerous others, as well as countless "sups" to dress the stage.

It isn't often that one person in so large a cast can set the tone for an entire play, but Eugenie Thais Lawton, our leading lady, did it flawlessly. It was a cast that played together in melodramas, and it could have overbalanced her. But she brought with her a rare technique that was contagious. She received fifteen curtain calls for what was considered her "marvelously realistic performance of the drunken and debased Maslova."

Landers Stevens as the handsome and manly Prince Nekhludoff was highly praised for his "great intensity" and superb remorse scenes.

My dear friends, Margaret Marshall, Edwin Emery, Ernest Howell, and George Webster (playing two different roles: Bousovkin, and Kouleshoff the juror merchant) were all lauded by the press and audiences.

As Bousovkin, George Webster was my father in the prison scene in Act II. I played Anna, perhaps one of the most dramatic roles I have ever played—indeed, as dramatic a role as anyone could play. My father was in the stocks and was dying. Crying, with my arms about him, I was trying, nevertheless, to comfort him. A guard, dressed in typical Czarian period tunic, cape, and shiny boots, enters and I run to him, pleading with him to let my dying father out of the stocks so that the poor man can die in comfort and dignity. The guard brushes me off. I plead and scream and cry. Again, he tries to brush me off. In desperation I grab him around a boot and he walks across the stage, dragging me with him all the while. My father groans. I arise, run to him, and embrace him as he dies.

Mercifully, the curtain drops. All the pleading, crying, frustration, and emotion had such a telling impact, I would leave the stage in tears. I refused to talk to anyone until after I had been alone for quite some time in the dressing room, and been able to compose myself. I lived that part as surely as if I had been the unfortunate, aggrieved little Anna. Looking back, I'm convinced this part was catastrophic to the emotional structure of a small child, as I was then. For this devastating part, I received much praise and recognition, with the word "precocity" liberally used in the reviews.

And so it was that at the Central Theater I had not only completed the cycle of emotions, with RESURRECTION, I had worn "my first love's" two masks—the one, reflecting the hilarity, joy, and sometimes sheer pandemonium of melodrama; the other, the deepest of tragedy, grief, and sorrow. The lessons would stand me in good stead in the years ahead.

About Miss Eugenie Thais Lawton's career, a brief addendum: With the two weeks' successful run of RESURRECTION, it began to soar, for she was always in great demand. In time, she was leading lady to the great Shakespearean actor, Robert Mantell. I had the honor of playing in several plays with them—Jessica, in THE MERCHANT OF VENICE, and other lesser parts as page boys. And Mr. Shakespeare had a plethora of those, it seems.

In one of the Shakespearean plays, Miss Lawton, Mr. Mantell, and I were waiting in the wings, about to go on. He was dressed in a toga, ready to take leave of us when he turned to Miss Lawton, and in a melodious sotto voce said, "It's a beautiful day for the race."

Startled, Eugenie Thais Lawton looked inquiringly at him and asked, "*What* race?"

Simultaneously with his entrance cue, and in character, he strode on to the boards with, "Why the *human* race!"

From its opening December 22, 1900 with David Belasco's THE HEART OF MARYLAND, to its closing with DANGERS TO WORKING GIRLS, when it was virtually destroyed by the earthquake and fire of 1906, the Central Theatre was San Francisco's most popular house of melodrama.

On that fateful evening of April 17, ironically, it presented DANGERS TO WORKING GIRLS. The list of implied dangers was a litany of pitfalls and temptations that plagued the "poor lil' workin' darlin'"; but nary an intimation of the dangers about to descend on them when nature dealt its merciless blow.

The Central was hopelessly torn by the temblor, and gutted by the fire that followed. Yet, as early as June, 1906, the second Central opened as the Park Theatre, in a building adjoining the site of the original Central. The opening bill was M'LISS, by Bret Harte—a story of early California days in the Gold Country.

By July 20, the name Park Theatre had been struck, and once again San Francisco had its Central Theatre, with a slight

The Second Central Theatre 1906-1909 Market and Eighth
Credit: Society of California Pioneers

change of address: from "Market Street *near* Eighth" to "Market Street *and* Eighth."

Unfortunately, the second Central fared poorly for various reasons. Perhaps San Franciscans were too sobered by the tragedy that had recently befallen their city. I presume that preoccupation with restoring their city and their own lives was paramount now. Their values and their priorities were altered; but, most significantly, melodrama's appeal had reached its zenith and was now on the wane.

From the San Francisco Chronicle of July 5, 1909:

". . . The Central, which used to stand 'em up and pack 'em in before the fire with such works of art as THE QUEEN OF THE WHITE SLAVES, WHY GIRLS LEAVE HOME, and . . . BERTHA THE SEWING MACHINE GIRL, had to turn traitor at last."

"In 'turning traitor' (Famous Playhouses of San Francisco) the Central had become a house of opera and minstrelsy. Sometime during that year (1909), without further notice, it quietly closed and the building was razed."

While the demise of the second Central was sad, *my* memories of the first Central are glorious ones: from March 1901 when I played there in UNCLE TOM'S CABIN, followed, at intervals, by some dozen "melos," to my final appearance there on April, 1903 in RESURRECTION. I fondly relish those wonderful days when I was a part of the first Central's story—a story that reflected the madness, abandon, and fun of melodrama's heyday.

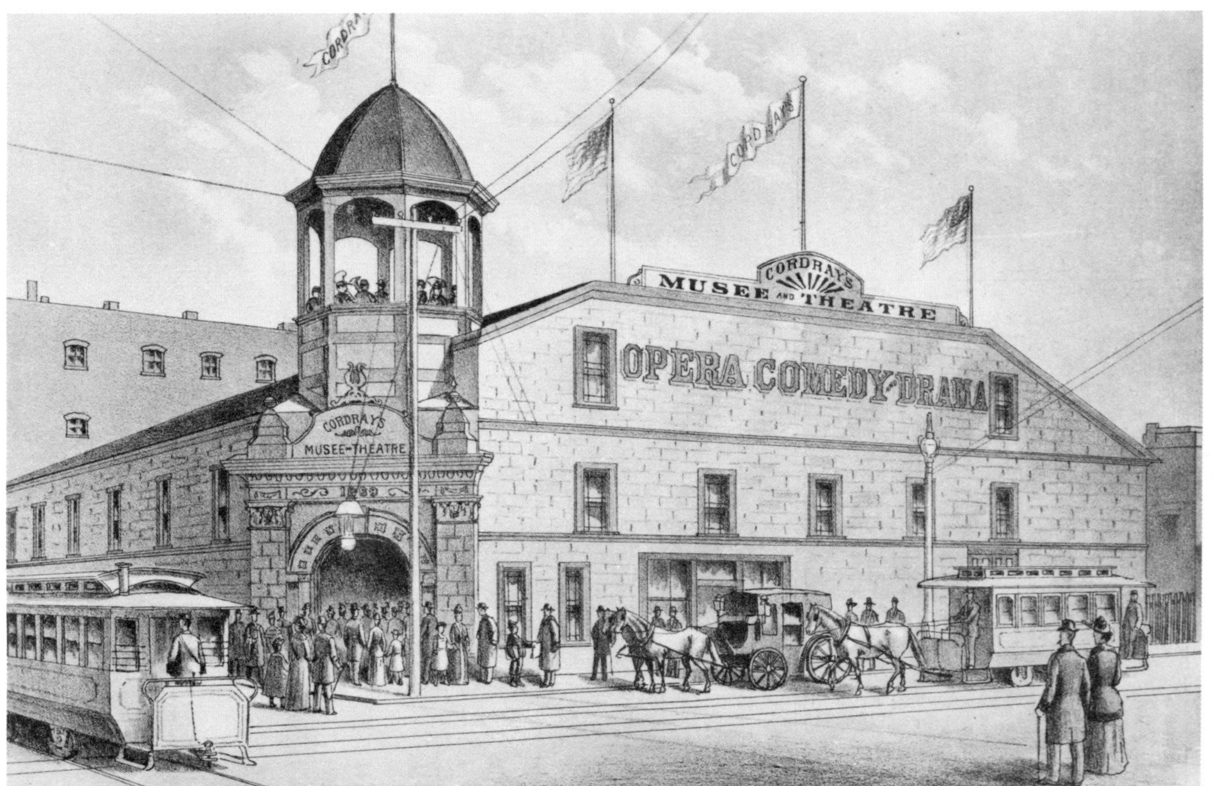

Cordray's Musee-Theatre   Portland, Oregon c. 1890 (Artist's Rendering –
"West Shore Magazine" 1890)
Credit: Oregon Historical Society

Chapter Six

Coast Defender Ventures East

1903—There would be reasons to look back on it as the year of change and adventure. Until then a true and loyal "Coast Defender" whose engagements were restricted to West Coast cities and towns, I was to have my first opportunity to venture beyond familiar California on the longest train trip theretofore. Figuratively, but even more significantly, I was to take the fork in the road that culminated, a few years later, in a very real encounter with "the shades of the prison house."

But, for the moment, there was great excitement afoot. The prestigious Edwin Mordant and Ola Humphrey Company had engaged me to play Little Elma in Theodore Kremer's latest hit, BURIED AT SEA. The company would tour Northern California, Oregon, Washington, Idaho, Utah, Wyoming, Colorado, Nebraska, Iowa, and Wisconsin.

Since we were to be away at least to the end of the year, and possibly longer (as, indeed, it turned out), my parents decided we would terminate our stay at our "aerie" at the St. Ann's Building. It was like burning our bridges behind us. The St. Ann's had been our real home for four years, the longest span of permanency, I would recall, during my childhood. It was while living at the St. Ann's that my career had blossomed. Wherever I played, San Francisco or on the road, there was always the assurance of returning to our "base of operations." And now, we were facing overwhelmingly exciting prospects, but with no grave thoughts about where we would live upon our return. The papa had only one misgiving: the mama's delicate health. But she was so dedicated to my career that her exuberance and determination were both convincing and reassuring.

Soon we were into rehearsals for BURIED AT SEA and, after two weeks, played at the MacDonough Theatre in Oakland, the week starting August 3. Kremer's new melodrama was an instant success; and with good reviews to add to the euphoria, we were on our way. Our only regret was leaving the papa in San Francisco. But it was comforting to know that he would stay with sister Bertha and her family, on Jones Street.

In Sacramento, we played at the Clunie Theatre where, according to the Sacramento Union, ". . . a very enthusiastic audience . . . applauded the new drama BURIED AT SEA to the echo, and ordered the curtain up at the close of every act. The scenic effects are very superior. One is a crown of scenic art, namely Trafalgar Square by night, with its historic lions at the base of the shaft." BURIED AT SEA was considered, according to the same critic, "a novelty not gravely improbable; assuredly winning the favor of the 'critics aloft' who revel with delight in applauding virtue and in whistling vice and crime down to punishment." The gallery gods were everywhere.

As we made our way northward by train, the stops were mostly one-night stands. For that reason, it was impossible to retain vivid impressions of towns, theaters, or the play itself, until we arrived for a week's run at Cordray's Theatre in Portland, Oregon. The newspaper accounts had it that the play had been, "highly spoken of by the press (from Morning Oregonian) wherever it appeared. Judging from the newspapers of the cities in which the company has played on its way to Portland, the play is one written for the masses, who greet it most enthusiastically." Having been well received in all the towns we had passed, the play, it was expected, would meet with popular appeal in Portland, also.

Cordray's Theatre, managed by John F. Cordray and W.M. Russell, had undergone some interior changes, with the additions of "new carpets, decorations and ornamentations . . . and an enlarged seating capacity" to prepare it for the opening of the dramatic season, three weeks before we arrived. The new season's presentations were THE PRISONER OF ZENDA, LEGION OF HONOR, and HILLS OF CALIFORNIA, by another Mordant-Humphrey unit. The latter vehicle starred Frank Bacon, my old friend of THE FIRST BORN. Prior to HILLS OF CALIFORNIA, Bacon had been with San Francisco's Alcazar Company for three years, but was now about to leave for New York where, as noted earlier, he scored great success in LIGHTNIN.

BURIED AT SEA was described as: "The Sensational Dramatic Novelty Plenty of Comedy Pathos Lots of Life Color and Action Special Scenery Strong Cast." It was a melodrama conceived by Theodore Kremer after having witnessed a burial at sea, in mid-ocean, while on a voyage to England. The event so impressed him that, upon his return to New York, he set about writing a play that would include such a "sensation scene," rendered with as much religiosity and authenticity as possible, yet with the "pathetic and somber elements relieved by well balanced comedy and funny situations."

The story's hero, Walter Allen, played by Orral Humphrey, was an inventor—young and talented, but poor and well liked, especially by the young New York belles. His latest invention was a printing press which would do headlines in "four colors and a foot high." A first rate villainess, Clementine Prescott (played by Evelyn Wynne), who loves the guileless and impoverished Walter, learns he is about to marry the lovely and rich Elma Goelet, played by Charlotte Burton. With the help of some unsavory characters, Clementine tries to steal the plans to Walter's printing press. But in spite of the countless travails that caper engenders, Walter and Elma get married and, in time, have a lovely child, Little Elma (which I played).

In Act III, the real action starts. We find the Allens and their coterie of loyal friends, which include an ingenue (Florence Chapman) and her admirer, Lord Archibald Spencer (Raymond D. Aldrich), on board the American Liner "U.S.S. Campania" headed for dear old England and the lord's ancestral home. The enemy, still after Walter, contrive to take the trip, too, in a last attempt to dispose of our hero and steal the plans. To that end, they feed him knockout drops; and reasonably sure he is dead, manage a very realistic and somber burial at sea for the hapless inventor. Of course, it would not have been a true melodrama had the evil forces come through the victors. So, upon hitting the cold water, Walter is revived. With divine help, much swimming, and a beer keg (thrown overboard, in jest, by the villain) to which our beloved inventor clings, he is eventually rescued by a whaling ship. Needless to say, the wicked villainess and her cohorts are apprehended and duly tendered their "comeuppances."

In the last act, Walter appears—a victim of amnesia, brought about by his ordeal at sea. He is now a demented, emaciated, white-haired peddler sitting on a box, selling toys. While strolling through the streets with my lovely mother, I disengage myself from her hand and run over to see the toys. Naturally, my father does not recognize me. I talk with him and tell him who I am. As our conversation progresses I, somehow, succeed in restoring his memory. In a very moving and dramatic scene, he finally recognizes me as his child and my mother, his wife—and none too soon, I might add—just in time to save mama from marrying the conniving villain. So, our little family is reunited and lives happily ever after, I presume.

Of Theodore Kremer, the prolific New York author of BURIED AT SEA, I shall remember fondly the week he traveled with our company. He had first come into prominence with the play, THE NIHILIST, followed by THE FATAL WEDDING. During his travels with us, he seemed quite impressed with me, though I must admit my part was not that impressive to me. I just had to be the little girl I was. However, he talked with the mama about my playing a leading child's part, the Little Mother, Jessica, in his very successful, THE FATAL WEDDING, scheduled for a tour of New York state in early 1904. The two "grown-ups" made all the plans, of course. I was not consulted.

While in Portland, I had occasional qualms over the mama's health; but like a trouper, she would quickly bounce back. Our run there proved to be the highlight of the entire tour. The company was received most cordially, the audiences filled the house every performance, and I was accorded a most rewarding accolade in the Morning Oregonian:

CLEVER CHILD ACTRESS AT CORDRAY'S
Among the good things to be found in BURIED AT
SEA . . . is the clever acting of little Baby Dody, who plays
the part of the hero and heroine's child. She speaks her lines

*in a manner that indicates that unlike other child actresses,
she understands the meaning of every word she utters and
her enunciation is as clear and distinct as that of any of the
older members of the company. As a rule, a child in melodramatic parts excites but little interest, but with Baby Dody
it is different. She shares the honors with the leading members of the Cast. The ladies and gentlemen who attend
Cordray's Theatre this week, are all in love with the pretty
little blond. She is only seven years old (I was near ten.)
and is one of the cleverest child actresses on stage.*

Again, finding such gems of praise, after some seventy
years, is a delightful reward. Of course, I was not aware of them,
then; but the dear mama must have been, for she seemed to take
unexplainable surges of energy and happiness from unknown
sources. No doubt, the reviews about my "splendid acting" were
as medicine for the poor ailing mama; and thus fortified, she
and I continued on our grueling tour. The remainder of the
itinerary of BURIED AT SEA, from Washington through
Nebraska, attests to what an exhausting ordeal it must have
been for the sick mama:

1903

Washington

Seattle	Sept. 20 – a week
Tacoma	Sept. 27, 28, 29, 30
Centralia	Oct. 1
Vancouver, Washington	Oct. 2

Idaho

Payette	Oct. 4
Mountain Home	Oct. 5

Utah

Brigham City	Oct. 6
Ogden	Oct. 7
Salt Lake City	Oct. 8, 9, 10
Provo	Oct. 12

Wyoming
>   Evanston . . . . Oct. 13
>   Rawlins . . . . Oct. 14
>   Laramie . . . . Oct. 15

Colorado
>   Boulder . . . . Oct. 16
>   Colorado Springs . . . . Oct. 17
>   Denver . . . . Oct. 18 — a week

Nebraska
>   North Platte . . . . Oct. 26
>   Kearney . . . . Oct. 27
>   Central City . . . . Oct. 28
>   Fremont . . . . Oct. 29

How we looked forward to the week's stop in Seattle and the much needed respite for the mama. She could hardly wait until we checked into the Hotel Continental (present site of the Seafirst Bank building) on Fourth Avenue, a block above the Third Avenue Theatre where our company was scheduled to play the week of Sunday, September 20, 1903 in BURIED AT SEA.

The Third Avenue Theatre, located on the northeast corner of Third Avenue and Madison Street, had once been the site of Seattle's first public school, the Central, 1870 to 1883. From 1889 to 1890, the location had become a warehouse for the clothing establishment of Toklas, Singerman and Company.

In September 1890, the warehouse was converted into a theater, the Madison Street Theatre. Shortly thereafter, it became John F. Cordray's, Cordray Theatre. This was the very same gentleman who, together with W.M. Russell would, in time, operate the Cordray's Theatre in Portland, where we had just played BURIED AT SEA. Seattle's Cordray's Theatre sat about eleven-hundred, and boasted of "opera chairs, elaborate boxes, and three-hundred-fifty incandescent lights." But it appears that the theater fared poorly, financially; for in 1894, the

Third Avenue Theatre   Seattle, Washington 1897-1907
(Formerly, Madison Street Theatre 1890-1897)
Credit: Courtesy The Seattle Times

Merchant's National Bank took it over and entrusted its management to Mr. "Pop" Russell. In 1897, Russell and Edwin L. Drew leased it and named it "The Third Avenue Theatre." As such, it was to become Seattle's most famous theater of melodrama until 1907 when it fell victim to the city's regrading project. Today, this historic corner is the site of the First National Bank of Seattle.

But theater had come to Seattle much earlier than with the Madison Street Theatre. In the early 1850's, the city's leading pioneer, Henry L. Yesler, had allowed the Cookhouse he had built for his millworkers, to be used as a place of entertainment. In those first days of Seattle's existence, this small building was, no doubt, the most likely edifice available. In 1859, Plummer's Hall became Seattle's first house of concerts and general entertainment. In 1861, Yesler built Yesler's Hall. It accommodated traveling theatrical companies until it was converted into an office building in 1870. He also built Yesler's Pavilion (1865), which served Seattle well, as a townhall and theater until it, too, was converted into an office building. In 1879, Squire's Opera House, an impressive structure for the times and considered Seattle's first real theater, opened to offer its patrons a variety of bills that included Shakespearean plays, as well as other popular plays of the times, still being played in my early days in the theater—FORGET-ME-NOT, THE TWO ORPHANS, and UNCLE TOM'S CABIN. Less notable theaters followed until, in 1884, Frye's Opera House, the most luxurious theater in the city's history till then, opened its beautiful portals to eager Seattle theatergoers, with FORGET-ME-NOT and TO OBLIGE BENSON. In 1888, the ultra-modern vaudeville house of John Cort, the New Standard Theatre, had its memorable opening night; but, like all the existing theaters in downtown Seattle, it too, was destroyed in the big fire that swept the city in 1889.

When the Madison Street Theatre opened after the fire (1890), it was to serve almost alone as Seattle's outlet for entertainment. The only other place available was Turner's Hall, used by the Frye Opera House for shows that had been engaged for the house, before the fire.

By the time I played at the Third Avenue Theatre in BURIED AT SEA, thirteen years later, other theaters had come into existence. Among these were: The Empire Park Theatre, The Seattle Theatre (managed by J.P. Howe, well known in San Francisco theater history), The Grand (John Cort, Manager), and The People's Park Theatres.

Although BURIED AT SEA was competing with the Seattle Theatre's EAST LYNNE with Inez Forman, and the Grand's ALEXANDER THE GREAT, with Louis James and Frederick Ward, records show we more than held our own. The popularity of Theodore Kremer's great hit was well known to the city of Seattle, for the play's reputation had been well touted. Reviews in the Seattle Daily Times indicated the Third Avenue Theatre was "having a good run of business with the melodrama BURIED AT SEA." The Seattle Post-Intelligencer carried more complimentary coverage:

"The enthusiasm which greeted the opening performance (of BURIED AT SEA) at the Third Avenue Theatre Sunday is manifested at every performance and curtain calls are the order after every act. The excellent production of BURIED AT SEA . . . has delighted everyone who has witnessed it."

Nothing could have boosted the mama's spirits more than the success we enjoyed at the Third Avenue Theatre. Her strength took an upsurge, enough so that she decided to take that special sidetrip the papa had requested. It was his wish we find Seattle's Yesler Way. With his detailed instructions and some local inquiries, we readily located Seattle's well-known street that seems to cut across the waist of this beautiful city. According to the papa, the street had been named after "old man Yesler who owned a sawmill and most of Seattle." To that simple summation, he could have added, "and is the history of the rise of the city of Seattle, Washington."

Henry L. Yesler (1810-1892) was born in Maryland; and in 1852 came to what is now known as Seattle (named after the Indian chief, Seattle), on the recommendation of a sea captain who had befriended him in San Francisco. The captain painted a rosy picture of the boundless opportunities in the untapped lumber resources of the area, and Yesler was convinced this was what he had been looking for, all his adult life. He was forty-three years old then. On the crook of Elliot Bay on Puget Sound, Henry Yesler found a few white settlers. These, readily accommodated him by relinquishing claims to their property and filing new ones, so that he might build his proposed mill on the most advantageous spot available. The access way to the mill soon became known as Mill Street, until 1888, when it was changed to Yesler Way to honor the patriarch of the city. Mr. Yesler, his lumber mill and its growth, spell the history of Seattle. In spite of adversities, such as seeing his mill burn down three times, and losing his two young children and then his wife in 1887, he was becoming, truly, "a man of property." Records show he had over three-hundred acres in the hub of the city, worth some two-hundred thousand dollars an acre.

It is this fact I wish the reader to bear in mind as I relate the following story about the papa and Mr. Yesler:

As a very young man, a few years after his Civil War naval duties during the Charleston Blockade, the papa came West and eventually went to Seattle, where he worked for Mr. Yesler. It was at a time when coins happened to be in shorter supply than property, so Mr. Yesler proposed to pay the papa with two lots on the hillside, in lieu of money. But being the carefree young man that he was then, the papa preferred coins in his pockets to lots on a hillside. The lots were situated in what is now the heart of the city of Seattle. The papa would have occasion to rue the day he made that foolhardy decision.

Mr. Yesler's financial fortunes fared better than the papa's, of course. Seattle's famous founder would, in turn, acquire holdings, real estate, and businesses that made him a wealthy man. Several times, he was county auditor and commissioner of King County; and twice, he was elected mayor of Seattle. He built himself a beautiful mansion in the middle of a whole block, between James and Jefferson Streets, and 3rd and 4th Avenues, where the County-City Building stands today. After Yesler's death, his mansion became the Seattle Public Library, until it burned down in 1901. No single man left his imprint on the history of Seattle as did Henry L. Yesler. His name continues in perpetuity, with such reminders as: Yesler Way, Yesler Atlantic

Project Area, Yesler Hotel, Yesler Neighborhood Center, to name but a few.

As any child would be, when the mama and I found Yesler Way, I was more impressed with the totem pole in what is known as "Pioneer Place" than with Mr. Yesler's great contributions to his city. It was explained to me that the totem pole had come from the Tlingit village of Tongass on Tongass Island in Alaska, and had been in Seattle since 1899. What no one cared to admit was that it had come to Seattle as a result of a caper by some of the city's business and professional men. It appears they came upon it in what seemed an abandoned village. The caper resulted in lawsuits brought by the aggrieved Indians the next month, and proved costly to eight of the Seattle men, who were fined five-hundred dollars each for damage claims—costly fines for the times. Had I known the real story then, it just might have jaded my appreciation of, and fascination for the lovely totem pole.

But the totem pole remained, and was very much an attraction until it was damaged by arson fire in October 1938. Seattleites were determined to replace it with a replica, and so a copy was made by the Tlingit Indians of British Columbia, at the Forest Service workshop in Saxman, near Ketchikan, under the direction of the native craftsman, Charles Brown. It was dedicated in 1940. Today, Seattle's most famous totem pole (she has some 17) still attracts natives and tourists—and perhaps it, like Mr. Yesler, will always be a part of this sparkling city.

Since Mr. Yesler had pioneered the state of Washington into one of the leading lumber states, the mama, always concerned with furthering my education, decided to take me on a tour of one of the paper mills nearby. The tour was a very impressive educational experience I never forgot. I watched the large conveyor belts, laden with wood fibers, move on through the many stages before becoming paper, as I knew it. The gentleman who led us through the plant pointed out to me that the texture of the screen on which the fibers lay as they traveled on the belt, determined the texture of the paper.

This "painless education" method, subtly employed by the mama, was to be repeated, over and over, as we traveled across the country. Whenever time permitted, especially on the longer stopovers, she introduced me to the industries for which the particular area was noted. Such outings were always "fun trips" to me, for the very young will forever stand in awe of new vistas revealed by the marvels of science. The exciting adventures to industries, parks, zoos, and mines not only were a healthy change from theatrical activities, they served as a most fertile source of knowledge. I daresay the travels and sidetrips proved of more lasting value than the formal schooling that started later. I can never forget, for instance, how enamoured I became of the hundreds of prairie dogs that scurried, then sat on their haunches, in defiance, or perhaps curiosity, as they watched our train go by. They seemed to register indignation that we dared to disturb their daily pursuits and intrude on their rightful domain. As I sat in the train, my favorite mode of travel, the world, with its animals and people, went past my window. Farms, meadows, hills, mountains, towns and cities were all natural sets in the passing drama. There could not have been a better medium of learning. I lacked only refined reading skills, and even those requisites would receive some attention in the months ahead. The theater, for the present, was my school; and the mama, my teacher.

The actor of my day learned by doing. There were very few schools of drama. We apprenticed "cold turkey," in a medium of trial and error, and we held acting schools in contempt. If we could not live up to expected standards, we fell by the wayside. By contrast, the modern-day actor, before receiving recognition, will usually have performed in high school and college dramatics, taken courses in drama in college, and have had some experience in stock. We did not. In my theater we were, as a matter of course, introduced to languages, literature, history, music, and art—all tools of our trade. From the theater I was to acquire a great love of the classics, mythology, and art, all of which have greatly enriched my life over the years. Because my educational experience was spontaneous and painless, it had virtues formal training sometimes lacks.

But in the medium in which I grew up, I would also be exposed to some of the caprices of human behavior—some pleasant, others disturbing. On one of the train rides for BURIED AT SEA, I was to learn about the insensitivity of some adults. Because, like most children traveling, I was at times restless, the mama allowed me to walk from one end of the car to the other. On one occasion, while strolling for exercise, I happened to approach Charlotte Burton, engaged in conversation with a gentleman friend. I paused slightly to exchange a friendly greeting, but with no intention of intruding on her conversation. The mama's strict discipline, I well knew, did not permit it. However, needlessly and in a manner that proved very humiliating, she brushed me off with, "Run along and sell your papers." The rebuff was so cutting, I never could bring myself to speak to her again, excepting on stage. How regrettable I should still remember an incident that does no credit to a beautiful, talented actress.

As in all roadshows, a drama that is played night after night soon becomes quite monotonous or routine. After a while, the director must call a rehearsal to show how far the actors have strayed from the script. Almost everyone unwittingly "ad libs" the dialogue to a point where a new scene has been created—one the author had never intended; then again, the players have been known to leave out a scene while compensating for someone's faulty memory. Reasons such as these dictated the director call his cast, from time to time, and guide the members back to the original intent and rendition of their roles. In BURIED AT SEA, we had our share of such corrective rehearsals during the long, arduous route of mostly one-night stands.

After Washington, the remainder of the tour through Idaho, Utah, Wyoming, Colorado, Nebraska, Iowa, and Wisconsin became a blur of railroad stations, hotels, performance after performance, hurrying, and worrying over the mama's health. When the tour finally ended at Janesville, Wisconsin in late November, we were greatly relieved at the prospect of the new commitments scheduled for Chicago, Illinois. They meant a long stopover and an opportunity for the ailing mama to get a much needed respite.

At last we arrived in Chicago, with its gray skies and its Loop and dingy buildings. It was December, and the beautiful white snow was now dirty slush, piled on each side of its streets. It all seemed so very depressing and gloomy. Perhaps this impression was, in no small measure, a natural one for a child whose mother's health was becoming more precarious. Her condition was absorbing a good deal of my concern at the time. I pondered what I could and should do about her—a responsibility of the gravest magnitude for a child of ten. But matters had not yet reached a crucial point; for, somehow, we carried on.

My engagement to play at Chicago's Cleveland's New Theatre, in EAST LYNNE, seemed to bolster the mama's morale. Her spirits rose to the occasion as I went into rehearsals for the part of Little William. Again, I was to play a dying-child part, so prevalent in melodrama of that period. By now I was a "seasoned dying child," for I had died with aplomb many times —as Little Eva in UNCLE TOM'S CABIN, as Chan Toy in THE FIRST BORN, and Little Mary Morgan in TEN NIGHTS IN A BAR ROOM. It was quite a fad for children to "die" on stage. Perhaps it was a convenient way to get rid of them, once their pathos value had been thoroughly exhausted.

The play EAST LYNNE, an adaptation by Brian Burton of the popular novel by Mrs. Henry Wood, was scheduled for December 13, 1903—the eighth week of Mr. W.S. Cleveland's new theater. It featured the Cleveland Theatre Company, and I was the visiting artist, engaged to play the child part, Little William. The story's setting is East Lynne, Lord Mount Severn's and Lady Isabel's estate, where the villain, Sir Francis Levison (Ralph E. Cummings), plays out his dastardly role. He convinces my mother, the weak, mistrusting Lady Isabel (Ida Glenn), that her husband, played by John Sutherland, is carrying on an affair with the beautiful Barbara Hare (Miss Ethel Elder). Utterly despondent, my mother abandons her husband and family. When, later, Little William becomes gravely ill, a governess is sought to care for him. Hearing the distressing news, the grieving, contrite Lady Isabel disguises herself as "Madame Vine," gray-haired, heavily veiled, and wearing dark glasses; and, is unknowingly hired by her husband to care for their dying child. (Very convenient!)

As Little William, at one point I ask, "Madame Vine, how long will it be before I die?"

Greatly distressed, the mother tries to hide her feelings as she temporizes, "What makes you think you will die, Little William?"

"Oh, it is nothing to die when our Savior loves us," he assures her.

Highly distraught, Lady Isabel takes off her disguises and says, "Oh, William, William, don't you know me; I am your mother."

The child reaches up to her, clasps her, saying "Mother!"; and dies in his mother's arms.

True to melodramatic form, Lady Isabel later dies in her husband's arms, thus paying the ultimate price for her weaknesses, for "the wages of sin is death." There could be no wavering from the established formula.

Advertised as, "The Safest Theatre In The Land, With Exits All Around The Building," Cleveland's New Theatre was located at Wabash Avenue and Hubbard Court, Chicago. The W.S. Cleveland Amusement Company was listed as "Proprietors" and the General Manager, W.S. Cleveland. The theater's published policy best tells the story of its early history:

> *In dedicating this new and splendid Theatre to the amusement loving people of Chicago, Mr. W.S. Cleveland, under whose General Management the house will be maintained, desires to outline in a comprehensive manner his intentions, present and future, for the entertainment of the Public.*
>
> *The Theatre is entirely an Independent one: the Management is not bound by any conditions whatever as to the attractions that may be presented from time to time.*
>
> *Mr. Cleveland has engaged a resident Company for the Theatre which will remain permanently, and be added to as occasion may require. This combination of actors is no ordinary "Stock Company." In its ranks will be found the names of players who have individually won positions of high rank in many Theatres and who*

are esteemed highly in nearly all of the principal cities of this country. This excellent organization alone would be an attraction for any theatre. But in addition it is Mr. Cleveland's intention as the season continues to especially engage stars of pronounced magnitude and to make productions of great plays in a fashion so elaborate and perfect that Cleveland's New Theatre will command a patronage of its own equal to that of any theatre in the land.

The Best of Everything will from time to time be in evidence.

As advertised since September 1st (1903), the management of Cleveland's Theatre will during the regular season make this a Popular Price Family Theatre.

> *Daily Matinees*
>
> *Gallery 5¢, Reserved Balcony, 10 and 15¢; Dress Circle, Orchestra and Orchestra Circle—Entire First Floor, 25¢*
> *NO HIGHER   All Seats Reserved.*
>
> *Nights and Holidays*
>
> *Gallery, Children 5¢, Adults 10¢; Balcony, Reserved, 15¢ and 25¢; Parquet and Dress Circle, 35¢; Orchestra and Orchestra Circle—The Very Best Seats—All 50 cents*
> *NO HIGHER   All Seats Reserved.*

While playing in EAST LYNNE, I had also been rehearsing my part of Little Beatrice in David Belasco's LA BELLE RUSSE, at the lovely, intimate Bush Temple Theatre. LA BELLE RUSSE had had its debut July 18, 1881 at the Baldwin Theatre in San Francisco, where the author, among other duties, was the theater's stage manager. Hoping to break into the "big time" with his play, Belasco had arranged to have two of the main male leads played by well-known actors from Wallack's Theatre of New York—Osmund Tearle, who played Captain Dudley Brand; and Gerald Eyre, as Sir Philip Calthorpe. Jeffreys Lewis played the title role, and the child part of Little Beatrice was entrusted to none other than Maude Adams who was, in time, to become one of America's famous actresses.

Although Belasco's LA BELLE RUSSE did make it to Wallack's Theatre two years later, it was by a circuitous route. It seems that Thomas Maguire, one of the Baldwin's owners mentioned in an earlier chapter, had a half-interest in his stage manager's play. When David Belasco tried to sell the play to

Bush Temple of Music 1905 (Housed Bush Temple Theatre) Chicago, Illinois
Credit: Courtesy Chicago Historical Society

Lester Wallack in New York, Maguire managed to quash the deal. Greatly upset by the turn of events, Belasco sold the rights to Frank L. Goodwin, Maguire's nephew, for a rather paltry sum. The latter, in turn, sold it to Wallack at a substantial profit.

When LA BELLE RUSSE opened May 1883 at Wallack's Theatre, the two main male leads were again played by Tearle and Eyre. In the cast appeared two names that would become quite well known in the theater world — John Gilbert as Monroe Quilton, attorney for Lady Calthorpe; and Rose Coghlan, in the title role. Little Beatrice was portrayed by Mable Stephenson.

The play was considered somewhat of a departure from the usually rigid melodramatic form. It was more true-to-life and so a forerunner of the more realistic dramas of the latter part of the Nineteenth Century. To be sure, the conniving, unscrupulous La Belle Russe who had ruined many a man's life, still pays a costly penalty in the end, though not with her life.

When the story opens, Philip Calthorpe had married the beautiful and virtuous Geraldine Haverly, twelve years earlier. Unfortunately, she was the daughter of a poor minister and no match for her husband, socially, so Lady Calthorpe disinherited her son. The young couple struggled unsuccessfully to make ends meet; and finally, Philip joined the overseas service, leaving his wife stranded. As the years pass and Lady Calthorpe's oldest son dies, her conscience drives her to try to make amends and find her remaining heir, Philip. When all efforts fail, she then prevails upon her lawyer, Monroe Quilton, to find the daughter-in-law she had spurned. In response to an ad in the paper, Geraldine the good one, is impersonated by her wicked, depraved twin sister, Beatrice. As "Geraldine," the latter manages to "remarry" Philip (yes, the contrite Philip comes to light about the same time "Geraldine" does!), to satisfy a whim of Lady Calthorpe's conscience. Philip's close friend in the "campaigns" is none other than Captain Dudley Brand, nee Robert St. Omer, who is out for revenge when he recognizes "Geraldine" as the infamous La Belle Russe. His only thought is to "drag her down into the hell she made for me."

Little Beatrice, the product of the sordid liaison between "Brand" and the "femme fatale," Beatrice or La Belle Russe, was, of course, a part beyond my comprehension. I was an innocent pawn in the sophisticated machinations of my parents and their problems. During most of the dialogue in which "Geraldine" and "Brand" exchange taunting threats and counter-threats, I am happily engaged picking flowers in Lady Calthorpe's beautiful garden, and out of earshot.

In the last act, when "Brand" is about to produce the real Geraldine and the real heir (a boy, born to Geraldine after Philip left), La Belle Russe realizes the jig is up. At this point, she confesses to Philip who she really is; and Philip tells her to leave the house, that he never wants to see her again. "Geraldine" tries to take me with her, but my father, "Brand," restrains her, telling her that, for the present, I will remain in his charge; and that only after she has proved herself truly reformed, will he allow her to see me. Emotionally overcome, my father takes me in his arms, kisses me affectionately, as he murmurs, "My Child! My Child!" When he releases me, I run to my mother who seizes me and "holds me to her heart," while "Brand" points to her and utters the parting:

Remember I will see you keep your oath (to reform). *Go!"*
Curtain

The beautiful Bush Temple Theatre in which I played in LA BELLE RUSSE was quite reminiscent of my beloved Alcazar of San Francisco, both in its plush interiors and its high standards. That it, too, strove to present first quality drama was evident from its notice to its patrons for the season 1903-1904.

> *We wish to give you a brief outline of what we have in store for you, during this our second season of the Player's Stock Company, at the Bush Theatre. We feel we have learned by experience during the past season, particularly during the latter portion, that you desire high-class productions and not those of the lighter, ordinary vein. . . .*
>
> *We have striven to get the best and most expensive people available, and intend to produce a high class of plays even though the royalties in many individual instances will reach nearly $1,000 a week.*
>
> *We feel grateful for your kindly encouragement and*

assistance in the past. . . . The following are the productions already arranged for:

WHEN WE WERE TWENTY-ONE, HAMPTON ROADS, MOTHS, GREAT DIAMOND ROBBERY, RICHELIEU, ALABAMA, YOUNG MRS. WINTHROP, PARISIAN ROMANCE, THE PROFESSOR'S LOVE STORY, FAUST, AMERICAN CITIZEN, AS IN A LOOKING GLASS, FORGET ME NOT, MACBETH, Hoyt's MIDNIGHT BELL, THE ENSIGN, RAG BABY, THE HONEYMOON, KING FOR A DAY, HELD BY THE ENEMY, MILK WHITE FLAG, MADAME SANS GENE, THE SENATOR, NIOBE, SECRET SERVICE, BARBARA FRITCHIE, HENRY V, AS YOU LIKE IT, and FRIENDS.

The popular Bush Temple Theatre was proud of its reservation system. It implied an inordinate amount of faith in the public's trust. Seats could be reserved for the season by simply leaving one's name at the box office, selecting the desired location, and indicating the matinee or evening performance at which the seats would be required each week. Seats so engaged would be held until *fifteen* minutes before the curtain rose. The Bush assured its patrons that, "No obligation is implied, but the seats so engaged must be called for before 2 o'clock for the matinees, or before 8 o'clock for the evening performances." Some of this faith in the public's good will could surely be ascribed to the tremendous popularity of live drama in America in this era before automobiles, movies, radio, and television came to play such significant roles in people's lives. The theater was the most popular medium of entertainment in those days; and I feel fortunate to have enjoyed its vibrant stimulation, both as a participant and a viewer.

Whether a player, a viewer, or an employee in the theater, each had parameters of behavior set down both in implied and posted rules and regulations of the house. Honor, decorum, and promptness were expected of the artist. The employee was under constant pressure and observation by the management. For instance, the Bush Temple printed on its programs:

"Ushers and attaches are positively forbidden to solicit fees or gratuities of any sort." Patrons were requested to "report to the manager any incivility or lack of courtesy on the part of any attache." So much for the employee.

Rules and regulations for patrons of theaters were varied, depending on the theater; but a composite list, gleaned from random printed programs, might include any or all of the following:

> *No intoxicating liquors sold or permitted about the building.*
>
> *Eating Peanuts is prohibited in the theatre.*
>
> *Boys are cautioned about making catcalls, whistling, and stamping feet.*
>
> *Profane or boisterous language is not tolerated.*
>
> *Intoxicated or improper characters not admitted.*
>
> *We regard all our patrons as ladies and gentlemen and expect all to conduct themselves as such, and anyone who cannot comply with the rules of the house must not be surprised if they are invited by the police officer of the house to vacate immediately.*
>
> *The audience is requested to REMAIN SEATED until the final fall of the curtain and not to annoy the people who desire to see the end of the play.*
>
> *Ladies are compelled to remove their hats by City Ordinance.*
>
> *There is a city ordinance against spitting on the floor of any public hall. It will be enforced in this theater.*
>
> *Mothers with crying babies will please retire to LADIES BOUDOIR without being requested to do so.*

In light of present-day casualness, perhaps some of the above rules and regulations seem ludicrous. But they voiced fundamental concepts of courtesy and concern for the other person, and might be considered well worth a second thought, even today.

Relationships among theaters themselves, were, at times, strained and competitive, albeit they had their finer moments, too. Theater houses might rally to help another in adversity, as pointed out earlier when the Baldwin Theatre in San Francisco burned down. Again, they might come to each other's defense, as during the period of the "syndicates" when many playhouses strove to fight a common threat. In this sense, like a family, they overlooked personal animosities, for the common good. But it would be inaccurate to convey the impression all was tranquil, with no "in-fighting," competition, or pirating.

Of special import during my engagement at the Bush Temple, was an occasion that typified the heated rivalries that sometimes arose between theaters over production rights. In this instance, the play was an adaptation of Tolstoi's IVAN THE TERRIBLE, scheduled as the next attraction at the Bush Temple Theatre. In bold print, the theater assured its public:

> *Don't let it worry you that the production of this most talked of all plays will not be presented downtown as anticipated, until next season, for it will be given its original production here in the BUSH TEMPLE THEATRE and by the PLAYERS' STOCK COMPANY within the next three weeks, threatened injunctions and efforts to prevent to the contrary notwithstanding. The elaborate production is already in the course of preparation. It will be **the dramatic sensation of the season**.*
>
> *. . . . The first presentation on any stage anywhere will be given at the Bush Temple Theatre, from a liberal translation of the manuscript* (written thirty years previously) *of Alexis Tolstoi. The translation was made some years ago by Gabriel Pollock, who was born in the Crimea. . . . Mr. Pollock, besides being a scholar, is an artist of distinction and all the elaborate scenery necessary for the production will be painted by him. Stanley Wood . . . has collaborated with Mr. Pollock in preparing the American version.*

Since the play IVAN THE TERRIBLE had been suppressed by the Russian authorities who had, time and again, confiscated copies of it in the Russian, the Bush Temple Theatre had a plum it was not about to relinquish. Its forceful notice was a warning to would-be competitors that the Bush

Iroquois Theatre, Promenade, Foyer of Iroquois Theatre, Chicago
Taken From The Iroquois Souvenir Program, Dedicating Performance
November 23, 1903.
Credit: Courtesy Chicago Historical Society

Temple had exclusive rights to this version and would be the first to present it—come hell or high water!

While playing at the Bush Temple, I was called for an interview at Chicago's Iroquois Theatre. The Iroquois, completed less than two months earlier, at the then impressive sum of $500,000, was considered one of Chicago's finest playhouses. It had opened on November 23 with the play MR. BLUEBEARD, starring the great Eddie Foy. The management wished to engage me for MR. BLUEBEARD, as one of the little fairies who, in the aerial ballet, slid down a wire from the balcony to the stage. When the mama heard this, she was outraged. She told the gentleman she could not possibly allow me to accept such an undignified part; that it was dangerous; and that Baby Dody was a *dramatic* actress, with emphasis on the "dramatic." She closed the interview, forthwith, leaving no doubt that the part, in short, was "not my line."

This timely decision of the mama's very soon proved to be a most fortunate one, for it saved me from the unspeakable horrors of the great Iroquois Theatre fire of December 30, 1903, a week later, in which six-hundred-and-two persons were killed.

Early accounts of the disaster were confused and replete with misinformation. Annabelle Whitford, the Queen of the Fairies, reported "mortally injured," actually was one of the first to reach a backstage exit to safety. She was offstage at the time, near the exit and, "at the cry of danger was enabled to reach the street with little difficulty." Still somewhat shaken with "nervous prostration," she left for New York the next day, as did the mama and I, incidentally.

In time, some of the facts relative to the cause of the fire, came to light. The fire had started during the second act of the matinee performance of MR. BLUEBEARD. Later testimony by the man who operated the calcium light that started the holocaust, furnished the most plausible information of all:

> *I was standing on the iron bridge at the right side of the stage from which the spot light is operated. The lamp seemed in good condition, but in the middle of the second*

*act, just as I changed a white light to a blue one, the arc
between the carbons sputtered and jumped. A spark struck
the frayed edge on the inside of the border of the curtain
drapery. A flame . . . shot up. I abandoned the light and
clapped my hand on the flame, but it spread in spite of my
efforts. I called to have the fire curtain lowered and notified
to have the house fireman help me. He came with a patent
fire extinguisher which had no effect on the flames.*

What was not known at the outset was that the tiny wire
used to guide one of the performers in the aerial ballet, was
"strung through the proscenium arch. When the call came to
lower the asbestos curtain, the tiny wire caught the descending
curtain and prevented it from dropping further. This wire is,
therefore, held to be the real cause of one of the greatest theater
horrors." It appears that the curtain came down only about
half-way, and the fire instantly sped under it to the auditorium.

Accusations were leveled by experts and non-experts,
alike. It was said the exit doors opened in instead of out. This
was both denied and "confirmed," depending on the person's
point of view. While Section 185 of Chicago's building ordinance provided that a building of the class of the Iroquois
Theatre should have a sprinkling system, there was none. In a
heated argument over this, between aldermen and building
inspectors, one of the latter maintained that, "The way the
theatre is built they can be left out. And, anyhow, the flames
spread so rapidly that no sprinkling system would have availed
anything." Another cause offered for the tremendous catastrophe was that the theater had no fire alarm system connected
with the city alarm system, thereby necessitating turning in the
alarm from a box more than one-half block from the theater,
thus losing precious minutes. Another fault held responsible
was that the Iroquois did not possess a ventilating shaft at the
rear end of the stage to conduct flames and smoke away from
the auditorium in such an emergency, as stipulated by law. This
point of view would persist in the months ahead. One authority,
C. Wegener, writing in a technical journal, maintained that
locating the main ventilating tube in the amphitheatre could

only result in a stage fire being sucked toward that focal point. He felt that under such conditions, neither asbestos nor iron curtains were the answer. It was this expert's opinion that, "the ventilating pipe should be located at the back of the stage. Three or more pipes should therefore be arranged at suitable places, being provided with reliable suction devices . . . at different heights, when the horizontal suction would instantaneously issue outside through the opening." Wegener felt that only then would such safeguards as fireproof curtains be of any use.

Other accusations were: that the exit doors at the north end of the building were "much too small"; that, "the iron doors were locked and the inner doors so close to the steel shutters that they could not be opened."

Accounts of the tragedy praised the famous Eddie Foy for working relentlessly to save the members of the cast as the fire spread rapidly through the scenery in the flies and on stage. Later, he was to observe, ruefully, that had the fireproof curtain worked properly, the fire would have been contained on stage and not spread so disastrously to the auditorium. He was fully aware that had the curtain not been impeded by the tiny wire, those on stage would have been the victims, instead of those in the amphitheater.

The greatest loss of life occurred in the balcony and gallery, where flame and smoke and crowded exits all contrived to trap the victims. The inevitable stampedes, combined with the loss of electric lighting, made an inescapable inferno of the Iroquois. In a matter of five minutes, hundreds were dead. Most of them were found on the marble stairways and against doors; but some were still in their seats, and others had plunged from the balconies to the main floor, in a last hope of escape. The Iroquois disaster would become an object lesson in studies on collective behavior, in psychology. Of the total 1729 seats, children were said to have occupied more than a thousand of them, for it was a matinee.

Immediately following the calamitous event, there were some ten arrests for negligence and manslaughter.

Hearings were held, and countless proposals to ensure

Iroquois Theatre The Day After The Fire Of December 31, 1903 (Taken by Charles R. Clark). Located: 24-28 W. Randolph Street, Chicago, Illinois.
Credit: Courtesy Chicago Historical Society

safety in all theaters were discussed. By order of Mayor Carter Harrison of Chicago, nineteen theaters and "museums" were ordered closed because they did not have asbestos curtains. Soon after, New York made a comprehensive check of its sixty-two theatres to ensure that all had proper fire curtains and that they also met other important safety measures.

From this horrendous catastrophe came some salutary results. I recall vividly the lesson of the inherent danger of theater doors that opened inwardly. After the Iroquois Theatre holocaust, laws were enacted prohibiting the inward opening exit and making mandatory a pressure bar across the door, rendering it possible to push it open, even though the door might be locked on the outside. To this day, whenever I leave a theater or public building by pressing against the bar on the exit door, I am reminded of that costly tragedy and the lessons that were learned from it. Further, stricter asbestos-curtain laws for all theaters were adopted throughout the United States. Other countries soon followed suit. From then on, Chicago theaters had to be provided with steel roll-curtains.

Sometimes I reflect on the quirk of fate that stood between me and my possible presence in the horrendous fire; and I wonder if the mama's decision was not only wisdom but, perhaps, a little prescience as well.

The morning after the Iroquois nightmare, we took the train for New York, leaving Chicago a little grimmer than we had found it. Even on the train trip to New York, the melancholy of the fire persisted in the gloomy talk about it. It preoccupied all of us and was the main topic of conversation in New York as well, when the weary, sick mama and I finally arrived there and were met by the Deans.

Etta Whaley Dean, the mama's close friend, was at that time living in what was then considered a very fahionable brownstone flat on Amsterdam Avenue, between 158th and 159th Streets, in New York. She and her husband, Peter, had invited us to stay with them while we were in the great city. They were solicitous about the mama's health, so it was a relief to be with friends who cared. Another member of the Dean household was an Irish maid, Nora, whom the Deans had imported from

Ireland—a very popular move among the wealthy then.

It was to the very lovely, understanding Nora I found myself turning, more and more, as the mama's condition worsened. Though Etta meant well, she came between the mama and me. Instead of being at the mama's side, doing for her, caring for her, as I had always done, I was now constantly told by Etta to go away and not bother my mother. It became a bewildering dilemma between what I felt was my personal obligation to my mother and my need to obey my elders.

Although the mama had never allowed me to play in the streets, Etta, a very forceful person, soon persuaded the weary mama to allow me to venture outdoors to play. I was supplied with a sled pulled by a short rope; and was told to take my vehicle outside and ride it. I was wearing my white coat, black velvet bonnet with the white ruching around the face, white leather leggings with black ornamental buttons almost to the knee, and white mittens, secured from loss by a ribbon pulled through the sleeves of my coat. I hasten to add, it was so unbearably cold that the last thing on earth this Coast Defender desired, at the time, was to remove the warm mittens.

What a novelty I must have appeared! I was not alone in the street very long before curious children began to gather about me. Dressed as beautifully as I was, I was an oddity that soon attracted an audience. This seemed quite natural to me, for I had been doing just that all my life. These were children of varying ages, some older, some younger than I. They circled about and wanted to know who I was and whence I had come. When I told them I was from San Francisco, they immediately wanted to know all about the Indians. I looked at them vaguely and returned, "What Indians?" They persisted there must be Indians. I hated to disappoint them, so I made up some convincing wild tales that seemed to satisfy them.

At that moment, a man approached us. Obviously impressed by my appearance, he stopped to talk to our expanding group. He dug into his pocket and came up with a handful of pennies which he proffered us. I held back, for I knew the mama did not approve of my talking to a stranger, let alone accepting money from one. But, he gave each of the children a

penny and turning to me said, "Here is a coin for you, too."
Now, in California I was used to five, ten, and twenty-dollar
gold coins. I knew the mama would not be seen picking up
penny change; but when the man offered me the coin, I put my
hand out and he put a penny in it. I looked at the lowly piece of
money and then up at him, and laughed. I thought it was all a
joke, so I threw the coin onto the snow. This angered the man,
and I must admit I don't blame him. He snarled something
about "the little brat," and went on his way.

"Don't you want your penny?" asked the incredulous children, as they clustered about me.

"What for?"

"Why, to buy candy with," they all chorused—strange, I
didn't know that! But I had visions of the lovely boxes and
baskets from San Francisco's Haas Candy Store on Market
Street. Why, a penny could not even buy the wrappings about
them, so I exclaimed, "Candy! With a *penny?*"

"Sure," they eagerly informed me. "We know a place where
you can get candy for a penny."

They promptly began the hunt in the snow for my penny,
and one of the boys soon found it. The oldest girl in the group
took it from him, saying, "Here, that belongs to her," and
handed me the chilled, wet coin. She took me by the hand, and
we all went racing to the little notion store where they, sure
enough, sold penny candy—what an incredible miracle, candy
for a penny. It was the first time I had ever seen penny candy.
But there, unbelievably, before my very eyes, were jars and jars
of every conceivable variety of confections, lined on rows upon
rows of shelves. One of the girls lifted me so that I might better
behold the wonders before me and make my choice. The tall,
clear-glass, candy jars held all manner, shapes, and colors of
candies—how could a novice such as I pick one from the infinite
options before me. Sensing my consternation, one of the girls
suggested I get a licorice whip. I trusted her judgement, this
paragon of wisdom and authority, and she purchased a shiny,
fragrant licorice whip. After the other children made their
purchases, we went off skipping, back to where we had first met.
On our way, I began to lick the licorice whip, quite oblivious to

how "drippy" these black marvels can be; so, it wasn't long before my beautiful white broadcloth coat was hopelessly smeared with black licorice. I shall never forget how the dear little sick mama suffered when, in a state of utter disarray and my face, mittens, and beautiful white coat bespattered with the gooey, black drips of licorice whip, I walked into Etta's immaculate house. I think it best, at this point, to draw a merciful curtain on the dear mama's dismay.

Looking back, I wonder why the mama permitted me to go out alone to play on the New York streets. She would never have considered such a thing in San Francisco, for there, she was constantly afraid I would be kidnapped. But I was not known in New York, so perhaps that accounted for her relaxing the rules of safety she had always imposed upon me. Then, too, her increasing debility rendered her helpless against Etta's coaxings.

While still at Etta's, waiting to go on tour with the company of THE FATAL WEDDING, I had an unforgettable reading experience. Until then, my exposure to reading, other than that by the kindly Mr. and Mrs. White at St. Ann's Building, involved train timetables, maps, brochures, and similar reading challenges of travel. I had often wondered, in awe, that someone could open a big, thick book and read it through. I suddenly and firmly resolved, that memorable day, that I would do just that. If others could do it, so could I. So quite at random, I selected a book from the Deans' vast library. I realize now, it was a sophisticated "drawing-room" story, replete with dialogue far above my comprehension. But, once having made my determination to read the book, I plunged in and laboriously conquered each page. I had not the slightest notion what I was reading. I only knew that, at last, I was fulfilling my resolve. I plodded doggedly, word by word. Many of the words were unknown to me, and perhaps it was just as well; however, when I finally completed the book, I only know that I had a sense of achievement I had never experienced before. Now, the reading of a book full through would never again pose the same challenge—a very important hurdle had been cleared.

Soon after the holidays, the wheels were in motion once

again; and I began the familiar pattern of rehearsals, this time for the Sullivan, Harris and Wood production of Kremer's THE FATAL WEDDING, scheduled to tour the state of New York. First, however, according to New York's child labor laws, I must have a special "minor's-work-permit." This requisite posed still another burden on the poor mama, whose health was becoming more precarious by the day. How she managed to summon the strength to attend to the legal formalities, will ever be a wonderment; but manage she did, in her usual, very efficient business way.

As Jessie, "The Little Mother," in Theodore Kremer's THE FATAL WEDDING, I was once again to play a leading child's part—one in which, happily, I did not die. The melodrama had many of the qualities of those in which I had appeared at the Central Theatre in San Francisco. There was a "sensation scene" in which I was rescued from a hut on the Palisades of the Hudson River in New Jersey. From the hut on the side of the sheer cliffs my rescuer and I had to get to another building, across a chasm, hand over hand on a rope. This never failed to arouse audience response. They would gasp as they grabbed their seats and urged me on. I thought of Georgie Cooper and our numerous escape scenes at the Central, and it seemed a shame I was not sharing these with her.

From an "alley rag-a-muffin" who was a little mother to many other tenement children, I would in time find myself in luxurious surroundings, with a lovely lady and kindly gentleman as my guardians. The situations of the typical melodrama's format must take their course, and THE FATAL WEDDING, though more refined than most, adhered to the rules. The virtuous but poverty-stricken "Little Mother," harassed and beleaguered at the start, in the end reaped her just rewards, as reap she must in a true melodrama.

The rigors of travel for this tour soon proved unbearable for the very sick mama. Between runs, we sought the comfort of Etta's home. There, the mama would rally slightly; but my worries over her alarming condition made my engagement in THE FATAL WEDDING a nightmare of confusing events. Etta had written the papa about my mother's deteriorating health.

He became very impatient for our return when he learned how sick she was. All circumstances dictated we terminate my engagement in THE FATAL WEDDING tour, forthwith, and go back to San Francisco. The urgency of the moment,for me, was to get her back to the papa, for she was truly failing. I quickly packed our trunks and suitcases, and Etta got us to the train, by taxi.

Traveling by train across the United States in those days, was not the most relaxing of conditions for one as ill as the dear mama was. I cared for her the entire trip, with a lump in my throat and fear in my very soul. When, at last, we arrived in San Francisco and I could entrust her to the dear papa's ministrations and protection, it was as though I had achieved the greatest assignment of my young life.

Chapter Seven
Scene Changes

Upon our return from New York, we lived with foster-sister Bertha and her husband, Jerome K. Sawyer, on Jones Street in San Francisco. With the mama so gravely ill, there was very little theater activity for me, and I found myself turning to Jerome, who became a very important person in my life. Jerome K. Sawyer was a nephew of Jerome K. Jerome, the English humorist and playwright who first attained fame with two humorous books, IDLE THOUGHTS OF AN IDLE FELLOW, and THREE MEN IN A BOAT; and plays such as: THE PASSING OF THE THIRD FLOOR BACK, BARBARA, MISS HOBBS, FANNY AND THE SERVANT PROBLEM, and THE GREAT GAMBLE.

Jerome, too, had been born in England, and he was a very interesting gentleman I greatly admired. There was no purpose to be served in turning to him with some of my problems, however; he was too diplomatic to interfere in family policies, especially where conflict arose between Bertha and me over mama's care. He seemed determined to avoid any involvement there.

Because he had been ill, Jerome was unemployed, and time hung heavily on his hands. During this period of his enforced inactivity, a Shriner's convention was scheduled for San Francisco; and the coming event inspired him to an action I thought quite noteworthy. Jerome approached me and asked, "Dody, do you have some watercolors and paper?" I replied that I did and gave him the art materials. In pencil, he sketched the various Shriner insignia and designs that could be used for promotional and welcoming banners, placards, and posters for store windows and building fronts. He then painted these in striking colors, and the results were truly lovely works of art. Jerome took off with the lot, in search of an outlet for his creations. He submitted his samples to various merchants and took orders from them to decorate their store fronts.

After receiving the orders, he went to a sign painter who agreed to do the first few orders on credit. The painter reproduced Jerome's designs on canvas, suitably stretched on frames, for store windows and doorways. I was very proud that I had become a part of this successful business venture when I made my simple, child art-materials available to Jerome. He parlayed this product of my meager art materials into a very profitable enterprise that rescued him from dire financial straits—all this by his ingenuity and self-confidence. To me, seeing him rise from an impecunious situation to one of being able to provide for his family, was a great object lesson in determination and perseverance.

Jerome, a tall man with titian hair and mustache, had fair skin, and light hazel eyes that caught and held one's attention as he puffed on his pipe. His tall frame was slender but muscular, and seemed appropriate to the firm, strong, decisive, controlled dynamo he was. Intellectually sharp and quick of mind, this dynamic and charismatic man would play a forceful part in our lives in the coming years. He could be called a soldier of fortune. He had participated in the Boer War and proudly wore a very large, beautiful silver medal given to him by Queen Victoria before her death, January 1901. As noteworthy as that may have been, I confess I was less impressed by the medal than by his resourcefulness and clearness of thought.

Living conditions at the Jones Street address were quite crowded. I had to sleep on a very uncomfortable couch with springs that kept me awake a good part of the night. Most importantly, the sick little mama needed a place of her own that was more spacious and quiet. The Sawyers, too, wanted another place that better suited their needs, so each family took separate units at 278 Turk Street.

There, the mama's condition seemed to improve for a short time—long enough for her to manage a last effort on my behalf. She saw me through an engagement as Francesco in Victorien Sardou's GISMONDA at the Grand Opera House on Mission Street, starting May 29, 1904. I had the singular honor of playing with the great Melbourne MacDowell who starred in the male lead, Almerio, and Ethel Fuller who played the title role.

What monumental effort it must have taken the mama to see me through yet another engagement, I can best appreciate now from the vantage point of retrospection. Her strength was ebbing inexorably to that day when she could no longer even try. For the moment, however, she again summoned her waning strength and determination in order to have me fitted for the beautiful costume I was to wear as Francesco.

While all the costumes were magnificent, naturally I remember mine best of all: a dark red velvet doublet, trimmed with gold braid; red tights to match; a small, red velvet and gold skull cap with a jaunty green feather; and dainty satin slippers. The creation of each article of the costume was carefully supervised by the mama, whose expertise in dressmaking I have already extolled. No detail escaped her scrutiny, for she had all

Baby Dody as Francesco in "Gismonda"
Credit: Barrett-Miller Collection

the instincts of the perfectionist. That her last preoccupation with a costume for me resulted in the most beautiful of all, was a fitting finale to her talent and to her commitment to both the theater and me.

Melbourne MacDowell, our very handsome leading man, was well known in the theater, and an especially great favorite with San Francisco theatergoers. So, when notices by Dave Weis, manager of the Columbia Theatre, Brooklyn, appeared in the San Francisco press that he was bringing Melbourne MacDowell for a West Coast tour in Sardou plays, the city was elated, indeed. It was disclosed that after playing at the Grand Opera House in "Frisco," the company would play all the large Western cities, then return to New York for a run, after which it would tour London and Australia. His supporting cast would be quite an impressive list that included: Robert Elliott, formerly leading man to the great Modjeska; James K. Hackett, formerly

Melbourne MacDowell c. 1904
Credit: Barrett-Miller Collection

of the Ben Hur Company and who would direct GISMONDA; Jack Webster, Ethel Fuller, Lillian Lorrell, Pauline Willard; and William Lytell of the old Cordray Stock Company in Portland.

The month-long repertoire of Sardou plays at the Grand Opera House, in which MacDowell played the male leads, included: LA TOSCA, CLEOPATRA, EMPRESS THEODORA, FEDORA, and GISMONDA. As Almerio in the latter, he was superb and highly acclaimed by all the critics. This was not surprising, for Melbourne MacDowell was every inch a man of the theater, an eminent thespian. It still shocks me to mention his name and discover that very few know of whom I speak. I hope this serves to, in some small measure, keep the name of Melbourne MacDowell alive. It is a humble offering to the memory of a fine gentleman and a great artist.

The Grand Opera House, a big, red-brick building, was located on Mission Street, between Third and Fourth Streets. Originally called Wade's Opera House, after its founder, Dr. Thomas Wade, the design was by architects S.A. Bugbee and Sons. San Francisco's newcomer was said to be the third largest in the United States at that time. It had a 110-foot frontage, 275-foot depth, and a seating capacity of 3,000. It's capacity would be expanded, later, to 4,000. The two-story building with the "Romanesque and Italian" front of iron grill-work, elaborate cornices, and a balcony "relieved by vases and small statuary" was yet another ill-conceived bit of architecture, in an earthquake-prone city.

Interior details of the Grand Opera House featured a skylighted 35 by 81-foot vestibule, in the center of which a magnificent crystal fountain sprayed eau de cologne, instead of ordinary water. The auditorium consisted of the orchestra or parquet, dress circle, balcony, family circle, and three galleries, the topmost, of course, for the gods. There were also twenty-two mezzanine boxes and twelve stage boxes. Its stage, 80 by 106 feet, was large for the times, though not a match for the vast one built, later, in the Central. Chairs, drapery, woodwork, and frescoes reflected the predominate color: pale blue. When it first opened, the Grand also maintained a 40 by 80-foot art gallery above its entry hall, with displays by local and European

Grand Opera House (Originally: Wade's) 1876-1906
Credit: The Archives For The Performing Arts, S.F.

Interior Grand Opera House (Mission, near Third)
Credit: The Archives For The Performing Arts, S.F.

artists. The art gallery had long since been eliminated when I played there, and the decor changed to reds and golds.

The story of the Grand Opera House begins in 1873 when Dr. Thomas Wade, a wealthy dentist, first conceived the notion of a theater to surpass all San Francisco theaters, especially the California Theatre on Bush Street. Beset by legal and financial woes, Dr. Wade's brainchild, although started in 1873, would not open until three years later, January 17, 1876. The opening bill was a German fairy tale, SNOWFLAKE, translated by Frederick Bert, the manager, who would come and go in the years ahead, as the Grand struggled to stay alive.

SNOWFLAKE starred Annie Pixley (an appropriate name, it seems), and was supported by: Winetta Montague, Mary Gray, Mattie Daniels, Cora Adriana, Signorina Christina, Mademoiselle Lupo, D.C. Anderson, Willie Sims, G. Galloway, and others. It was a whimsical play, "more remarkable for its scenery and the quality of its ballet dancing than for its dramatic interest." But, apparently, it was well received by its firstnighters, San Francisco's elite ladies and gentlemen who came to honor and "dedicate the latest marvel of Western architecture."

Only a few months after the Grand Opera House opened, Dr. Wade, its founder, had "somewhere along the line, been edged off the track." M.A. Kennedy took over the lease in March 1876, and appointed Charles Wheatleigh as manager. In September 1877, the Nevada Bank (Mackay, Fair, Flood, and O'Brien) foreclosed the mortgage on the theater and leased it to Jasper McDonald who was no more successful with the Grand's finances than his predecessors. Between 1877 and 1880, Thomas Maguire, Frederick Bert, Fred Lyster, M. Rogers, and Edward Evans all tried their luck at making the huge theater a paying enterprise, and all were defeated.

After a long blackout, the Grand Opera House was reopened October 1882 by Charles Andrews and L.R. Stockwell, with a pantomime and variety company, followed by "sensational and emotional drama."

In 1885, John Maguire (no relation to Tom) bought the Grand Opera House and placed John Riall as its manager.

By 1894, Walter Morosco appears on the scene of the

faltering Grand, with a background worthy of mention:

Born Walter Bishop in 1846, in Guilford, Connecticut, of Mayflower stock, Walter Morosco left home at the age of fifteen and joined a circus, as a rider and an acrobat. Wishing to adopt a stage name, he decided on "Walter Melville," but when he discovered there were too many acrobats with that surname, he dropped the "Melville" and replaced it with "Morosco." It appears circus life was to be more than a passing fancy of youth, for by 1880 he was managing the Dan Rice Circus. Two years later, he appeared with his son, Harry, in the Andrews and Stockwell Stock Company production of HUMPTY DUMPTY at the Grand Opera House. In 1884, he toured the West Coast and Hawaii with the Sherman Circus.

The following year he opened the Wigwam Theatre on the corner of Geary and Stockton Streets, former site of San Francisco's Spring Valley Waterworks. It is interesting to note that while initially he presented the entertainment medium he knew best, circus, it was a natural step that he should proceed to variety, the popular mode of entertainment in most theaters in the city. When vaudeville began to replace variety in the evolution of theater entertainment, Mr. Morosco's Wigwam followed suit. Of course, melodrama and drama, too, were part of the tapestry of Nineteenth Century theater throughout the country at that time.

Having adopted San Francisco by now, Morosco opened the Union Hall on Howard Street, in 1886, and it soon was known as "Morosco's Theatre." The theater boasted a first-rate stock company that played at popular prices. Catering to the "masses" as his counterpart, Mark Thall, did at the Alcazar, Walter Morosco achieved a very thriving business. After eight lucrative years, he sold the Union Hall.

Morosco then had the temerity, in 1894, to take a lease on the financially ill-fated Grand Opera House (owned by James L. Flood and John W. Mackay) where twelve years earlier he and his son Harry had played in HUMPTY DUMPTY. Since from its infancy the big Grand had not been noted for its financial returns, many doubted that Morosco could achieve the impossible by making it a paying business, but achieve it he did, with dispatch. The patriarch of the famous theatrical Moroscos (Walter, Harry, Oliver, and Leslie) gave a positive direction to the Grand Opera House, with well-known melodramas, rendered in the best possible tradition, and at popular prices:

Orchestra Floor, reserved . . . . 75¢, no higher
Dress Circle . . . . 50¢
Family Circle . . . . 25¢
Gallery . . . . 15¢
Seats in Boxes . . . . 75¢, $1 and $1.50
Branch ticket office . . . . Emporium
(San Francisco's new department store, then)

As the May 20, 1894 San Francisco Examiner so succinctly put it:

". . .society has taken to Morosco's. It wants melodrama— buzz-saws, millwheels, and spark-sputtering railroad trains, juggernauts; low-rumbling villainies, spine-shivering situations, ecstatic virtues, soul-thrilling heroism, etc." The vehicles employed had such captivating titles as: THE RED SPIDER, THE OPERATOR, THE WAGES OF SIN, SHADOW DETECTIVE, THE POWER OF GOLD, THE PACE THAT KILLS, A FLAG OF TRUCE (with "genuine Rand steam drills guided by skilled quarry men"), THE PHOENIX ("so realistic that the last two acts were enacted in a pall of smoke"), THE GREAT TRAIN ROBBERY, TEN NIGHTS IN A BAR ROOM, A BOWERY GIRL, etc.—over five thousand consecutive performances, when the Grand Opera House Stock Company presented its final show, HI HENRY MINSTRELS, December 31, 1898.

San Franciscans would long remember such favorites as: Landers Stevens (later our leading man in RESURRECTION, at the Central), John J. Pierson, W.H. Pasco, Julia Blanc, Will Brady, Harry Mainhall, Fred Fairbanks, Lettie Le Vyne, Fred Butler, Jessie Norton, Frank Lindeu, J.J. Dowling, and George Webster (later, of both the Alcazar and the Central).

So strong was the Morosco impact on the San Francisco theatergoers, that the prestigious name, *Morosco's* Grand Opera House, persisted long after Walter Morosco had relinquished all ties with it. San Francisco theater buffs had habit patterns they found hard or pointless to break.

After more than four years of presenting spectacular "melos," Mr. Morosco turned to grand opera (1899), as if to justify the name of the popular house. His choice of FAUST (starring the great Australian diva, Nellie Mitchell, or Melba) for the auspicious reopening, set the tone of the theater for as long as he was associated with it; and until its final performance, April 17, 1906, when Enrico Caruso sang in CARMEN on the eve of the great earthquake.

Melba (Nellie Mitchell)
Credit: Barrett-Miller Collection

On July 1, 1901, Mr. Morosco sold his lease on Morosco's Grand Opera House to Charles L. Ackerman, Morris Meyerfeld, and Harry Morosco, for a reputed $60,000. The deal was contingent, from the outset, on his son Harry having one-fourth interest in the projected new corporation, to be called The Grand Opera House Company.

With this transaction, Walter Morosco retired from the world of entertainment, to his large estate in the Fruitvale hills of East Oakland. There, he pursued his avocation of raising horses and Shetland ponies. Ironically, his retirement ended six months later, with his death December 25, 1901, at the age of fifty-five.

While GISMONDA had been a great success at the Grand Opera House, it had taken the last measure of the little mama's physical resources. She soon took to her bed, and her condition worsened. Since her parents, the Parkers, had died during the Civil War, the papa notified her only living relatives (on her mother's side), John and Will Fuller, in Florence, Arizona. It was to their large ranch she had gone on a visit after the death of her mother. The mama recounted her apprehension over the Indians her uncles employed, for she had never before lived with Indians about her. The Indians observed her critically as she went about her simple chores, by what they considered the most awkward manner; so, they soon dubbed her "that stupid white squaw." The truth of the matter was that the Virginia-born young woman had never had to do menial chores, such as making her own bed, and everything she tried to do was a new challenge. Her discomfort there soon led her to terminate the visit and head West, where, in time, she met and married the papa. Although she never returned to Florence again, she remained in touch with her bachelor uncles and received the Florence newspaper, regularly.

The uncles, John and Will Fuller, had settled in Florence in the late 1860's, after the Civil War. The town had sprung up about 1866, three years after President Lincoln signed the paper creating the Territory of Arizona. The area where the town arose had known four flags—the Spanish (during the Spanish explorations); the Mexican (after Mexico declared its independence from Spain in 1821); the United States's (after the Gadsden Purchase of 1854); and the Confederate flag during the Civil War, from February 14 till September 24, 1862. In 1866, however, American troops returned to the Territory of Arizona. With their return, and the measure of safety from outlaws and hostile Indians they afforded, many white settlers, the mama's uncles among them, migrated to the area of the Gila River around Florence. The waters of the Gila were diverted, by means of ditches, to irrigate the farmlands. History shows that the E.N. Fish Company of Tucson undertook the project in exchange for the farmers' products which were, in turn, sold to supply the army camps and forts.

During years of hard toil and diligent application, the Fuller brothers had created and developed a very prosperous ranch in which they raised cattle and fruit. They would make their impact on the history of Florence, and the Fuller School would be named in their honor.

Because now the mama's condition appeared to be terminal, the papa undertook the sad mission of alerting her uncles. Uncle Will soon came for a visit. I still had fresh memories of the dour Uncle John who had visited us some six years earlier and had upset the household, but my misgivings were quickly allayed when Uncle Will arrived. Concern over the mama's condition had cast a pall over our home, and Uncle Will's presence seemed to dispel it. He was a joy to the bedridden mama and the rest of the family. Uncle Will was dapper, white-haired, and mustachioed—the typical "by cracky" type whose humor and affability contrasted markedly with his brother John's more serious nature. But, of course, not even welcomed Uncle Will could stave the relentless course of events. He remained as long as he could and then left us with the inevitable.

After his visit, matters soon came to a climax. Toward the end, the mama's illness rendered her incapable of speech. She tried valiantly to communicate, but it was impossible. The night she was near death, I was sent upstairs to my room; while the rest of the family, the papa, Bertha, and Jerome gathered around the deathbed. In my room, despair soon forced me to bolt it and steal into the mama's room. The elders did not see me, for they had their backs to the door. I dashed between them and threw my arms about the dear mama. She died in my arms, and I was acutely aware that I held death close to my breast. The death scene in which I was now playing such a painful part was real, very real. The curtain had just fallen on the dearest person in my life. The "others" led me away. While they shared their grief, I was left quite alone with mine.

She was only forty-eight, and it seemed a cruel hoax that death had claimed her when I was only ten and needed her very desperately. My grief and bewilderment were compounded in the next few days by the comings and goings of well-intentioned friends and neighbors. Funeral arrangements were handled by Bunker and Lunt on Mission Street. From 25th and Valencia, we entrained to Mt. Olivet cemetery, in Colma, for the burial. While some moments were blurred by sorrow, I can never forget that I accompanied her to her final resting place, in utter desolation and disbelief.

How could I possibly have been prepared for such a devastating loss. No one but the mama had chartered and guided my life; and now, I was adrift in a sea of confusion. When less than two months after the mama's death an offer came for a part in JIM BLUDSO at the new Majestic Theatre on Market Street (opposite Larkin, near Ninth), the papa accepted on my behalf, though he was really not prepared or qualified to see me through such an engagement. It became apparent I was to go it alone between the time I was delivered to the theater and, picked up after each rehearsal and performance. But, it was a blessed relief for both of us. He discharged his obligation for the time involved; and I found myself back in the milieu I cherished most.

That I was considered for the part of Gabe (Little Breeches), Jim Bludso's boy, was in no small measure a decision of my friend Oliver Morosco who had been so kind to me when I played at his Burbank Theatre in LITTLE LORD FAUNTLEROY, two years earlier. The Majestic Theatre was one of the several California theaters over which he had controlling general management. He had prevailed on the papa to allow me to play the part in the popular JIM BLUDSO.

JIM BLUDSO was the third in a series of plays (MR. SENA-TOR and MR. POTTER OF TEXAS, the other two) Mr. Oliver Morosco was presenting at the Majestic the month of December 1904. He had brought his Scenic Artist, our mutual friend, Harry Marshall (earlier of the Central), to create and supervise the elaborate scenes in this spectacular melodrama that featured, "deeds of valor, comprising rescues from flood, fire, shipwreck, would-be murders and lynchings." Harry Marshall received the highest praise for his scenic effects in the fourth act. The play, by I.M. Morris, was based on the three very popular poems by John Milton Hay (1838–1905), United States Secretary of State: "Little Breeches", "Banty Jim," and "Jim Bludso," the latter giving the play its title. The story had an 1866 setting and featured, in its fourth act, a Mississippi River steamboat race between The Prairie Belle and the Movastar. Captain Scott, skipper of the Belle was played by John D. O'Hara who had played Roberts, the clerk, in the LA BELLE RUSSE production in which I had appeared at the Bush Temple Theatre in Chicago. It was always reassuring to see a familiar face, especially during those rather dismal days.

As engineer of the Prairie Belle, Jim Bludso, played by Howard Gould, had the responsibility of seeing that his men kept the furnaces well stoked to build up the necessary head of steam in the boilers. Everything that was burnable was used to win the race against their worthy opponent, the Movastar. But the Prairie Belle caught fire. I was the little stowaway down in the hold of the ship; and with the spread of the fire, my life was in danger. In this scene, I had to climb a rope, hand over hand, up to the deck. With a little assistance, such as loops in the rope and someone hoisting me, I managed to make it—into the flies, of course. And so ended the harrowing fourth act with the well noted "sensation scene"—the boatrace, fire, explosion, and shipwreck. The realism of the scenes in this act attested to Harry Marshall's great artistry. One reviewer felt it was, "a daring imitation of a real catastrophe and it is to be hoped that the week will pass without a mishap." One night, however, my pant leg caught fire from the pans of "red fire"placed all over the stage

Majestic Theatre (1904-1906) Interior Before 1906 Earthquake
Credit: The Archives For The Performing Arts, S.F.

to simulate the blazing situation in the hold. The curtain was promptly lowered and the fire on my smoldering pant leg quickly patted out. Luckily, I sustained no serious burns. This episode was the only "mishap" during the entire run of JIM BLUDSO at the Majestic. Considering the potential for "bigger and better" disasters inherent in a play of this type, I feel I was fortunate, indeed.

When I played there in JIM BLUDSO, the Majestic Theatre was quite new, yet it had had, up until then, a somewhat bizarre, short history. As early as the summer of 1903, publicity on the construction of two theaters by H.W. Bishop began to appear in the local press. One theater, in Oakland, the Ye Liberty Playhouse (famous for its revolving stage), was expected to open near Christmas. It would seat about 2000, have a comic opera stock company, and be managed by H.W. Bishop. The second, The Majestic, going up at Ninth and Market Streets in San Francisco, would open in March of 1904, with a four weeks' engagement of the great Mrs. Fiske. Management of the Majestic would be entrusted to Lewis Bishop. When it became obvious the builder, William Ede Company, could not meet that date,

Isabel Irving c. 1904
Credit: Barrett-Miller Collection

opening night was changed to April 18, and by that time Mrs. Fiske's own commitments precluded her appearance. Actually, the postponement proved of little help, for when the Majestic first opened April 18, 1904, with Isabel Irving in Winston Churchill's THE CRISIS,the theater was still incomplete, protestations in the press that this would not be the case, notwithstanding. The management's words:. . ."work has progressed on the house and the public will be surprised at the condition of the house. It will be all tinted by opening night, with the exception of the main entrance and the decorating in colors." The public was indeed surprised—but to find the Majestic in a woeful state of incompletion. Still, there was something promising in the alabaster whiteness prevailing. The usually ascerbic Ashton Stevens, in the San Francisco Examiner of April 19, noted, "I could see the rough structure of a round, compact, substantial little theatre that shall no doubt still be new when Market Street near Ninth, is regarded as a downtown location. (Incidentally, it did not take long for the city to move in that westerly direction.) It is builded (!) to last, and I don't know but the absence of gilding and gingerbread only served to point to the solidity of the thing."

Opening night festivities included what had been anticipated, one of Mayor Schmitz's witty and characteristic speeches, including the flowery line, "Majestic in name, let us hope it will ever stand for what is majestic in art." Isabel Irving christened the house by "breaking a bottle of champagne into a basket of California fruit and flowers, this idea being one of Manager Bishop's own." The instant fruit-and-flower-punch ceremony seemed to have made quite an impression on the indulgent audience which was still waiting at 9 p.m. for the curtain to go up, as photographers made a bid for "just one more" of the principals and of the curtain, "painted after one of Latimer's best redwoods."

Although prices for the gala opening performance of the Majestic were $1.50, $1, and 50¢, rather heady in those days, all the seats were sold, as well as "a goodly portion for the first week's engagement."

James K. Hackett c. 1900 Actor-Producer
Credit: Barrett-Miller Collection

The presentation, THE CRISIS, a James K. Hackett production, had a Southern setting, just before the outbreak of the Civil War. It highlighted the election of Lincoln, the outbreak of the war, and the effect it had on the relationships of the main characters, Northerners and Southerners. Miss Irving played "the winsome Virginia Carvel who was the object of a rivalry between Cavalier Colfax and Puritan Brice." There were the familiar Southern home with the wide verandas and broad lawns, and belles with hoop skirts and long, curled hair. Of course, all ends well, with rivalries resolved in the interest of true love.

Perhaps it might be pointed out that the author of THE CRISIS was not the well-known Winston Churchill of England, but the noted American writer (1871—1947). The play was a dramatization of his historical novel of the same name. Born in St. Louis, Missouri and educated at the United States Naval Academy, Annapolis, Maryland, Mr. Churchill achieved recognition for many historical novels. Besides THE CRISIS (1901), he also authored THE CELEBRITY (1898), RICHARD CARVEL (1899), THE CROSSING (1904), and CONISTON (1906), to mention a few.

When the CRISIS' two-weeks engagement ended, the Majestic was still far from completion, and bookings had to be revised. Originally, James K. Hackett had been scheduled to follow Miss Irving in an engagement of his own, but it was announced he would appear in the fall and that James Neill would appear at the Majestic when it was finally completed. As the months passed, Neill's presentation was also victimized by conflicting schedules, we presume, for we next learn that Lewis Bishop's magnificent new house would reopen on September 3, with THE HEARTS OF TENNESSEE, starring Howard Gould of the Oliver Morosco Company of the Burbank Theatre of Los Angeles. But the game of musical chairs continued until, finally, the Majestic did have its "formal opening" on Saturday evening, September 3, 1904—however, it was the F. Marion Crawford historical romance, IN THE PALACE OF THE KING. It was presented by the Majestic Stock Company, with the charming Grace Reals, formerly of the Dearborn Theatre in Chicago (and with whom I had played in LA BELLE RUSSE at the Bush Temple Theatre in Chicago), in the female lead. Among others in the Majestic's stock company were J.H. Gilmore, the leading man; Richard Thornton, Joseph Callaghan, Henry Stockbridge, and Eleanor Gordon.

When I played at the Majestic three months later in JIM BLUDSO, changes and additions to the Majestic Stock Company had taken place. New names like Frank MacVicars, Lloyd Ingraham, John D. O'Hara, Donald Campbell, Harry Mestayer, Al Luttinger, Adela Block, Elsie Esmond, and Margaret Maclyn appeared on the program.

Exactly two years to the day when it opened in make-shift fashion with THE CRISIS, the lovely Majestic was presenting a production of the comedy, WHO GOES THERE, starring Walter K. Perkins. On the fateful, early morning hours of April 18, 1906, however, the cataclysmic earthquake tore the theater asunder. Its rear wall tumbled onto the street, and its roof

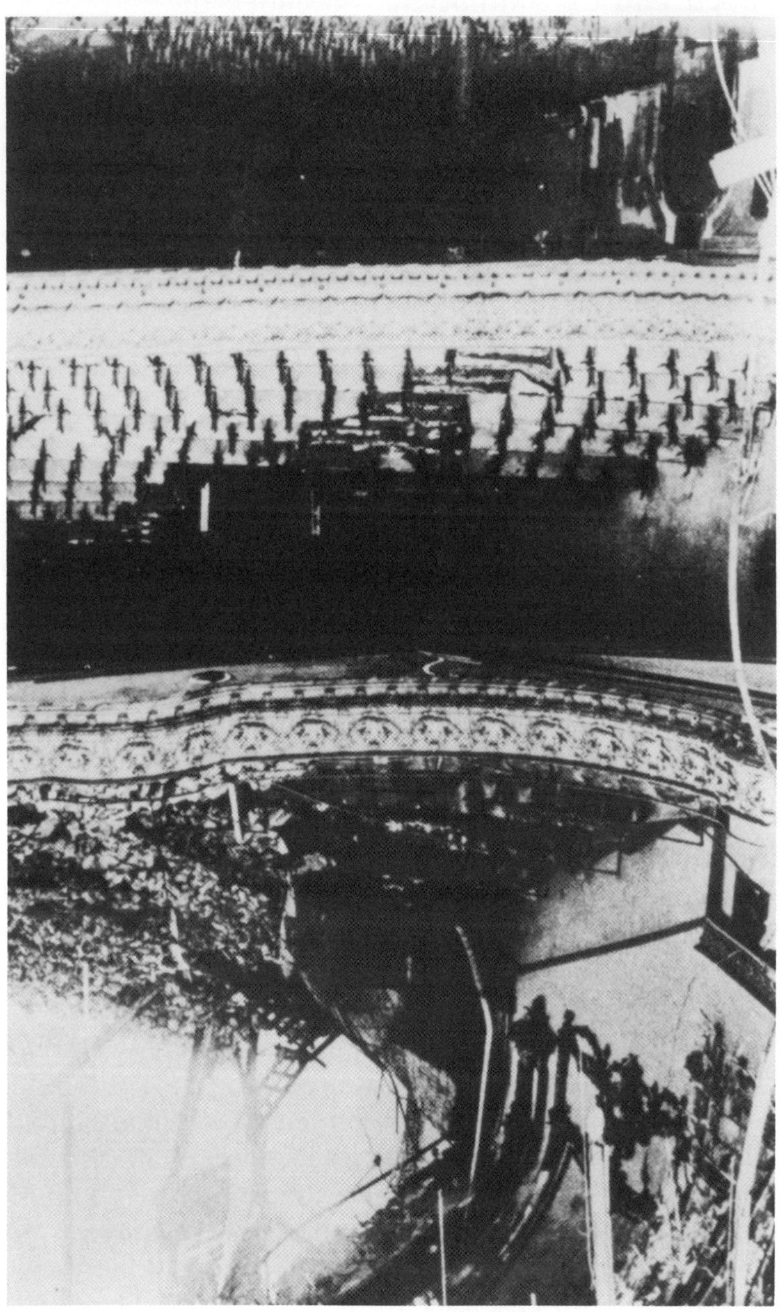

Majestic Theatre (1904-1906) Interior After 1906 Earthquake
Credit: The Archives For The Performing Arts, S.F.

dropped into the auditorium. So ended the short-lived and magnificent Majestic, "Frisco's Finest Theatre," according to my JIM BLUDSO program.

JIM BLUDSO had been a blessing in disguise; for otherwise, my first Christmas after the mama's death would have been even more unbearable. I was grateful I had spent Christmas Day playing matinee and evening performances. Life at home was grim and bleak, and the memories, still fresh and painful. Somehow, the doleful holidays came and went and we were into 1905. Changes had taken place overnight, it seemed. Why couldn't the family do things the way mama had? I found myself observing, "The mama would never have done it that way." Couldn't they remember! She had been gone but such a short while, yet it already seemed an eternity. I felt they were disloyal to her.

My sad reflections were interrupted a few months later when an offer came from the noted Chauncey Olcott to tour West Coast cities south of San Francisco, with his repertory show of Irish plays and folk stories. Once satisfied I would be well cared for by a woman who was accompanying her young son, a member of the company, the papa agreed to my going. The young boy and I were the same age. We played the child parts and supervised the child supernumeraries engaged in each town.

Since his start in New York in 1880 as a balladeer with the Emerson and Hooley's Minstrels, Mr. Olcott's fame had risen as he progressed into light opera. In 1886, at the Union Square Theatre, he sang in PEPITA, with Lillian Russell singing the title role. In 1890 he became leading tenor with the Duff Opera Company, and before long was appearing in London's Criterion Theatre. His popularity stemmed from the masterful way in which he rendered romantic and sentimental Irish comedy and Irish ballads. Among the latter, were his own composition, "My Wild Irish Rose" and two others he co-authored, "Mother Machree" (with R.J. Young and E.R. Ball) and "When Irish Eyes are Smiling" (with G. Graff Jr. and E.R. Ball). He played the romantic singing lead in such plays as: MAVOURNEEN, THE IRISH ARTIST, SWEET INNISCARRA, EDMUND BURKE,

Chauncey Olcott c. 1900 with dog Prince in "Sweet Inniscarra"
Credit: Barrett-Miller Collection

EILEEN ASTHORE, LIMERICK TOWN, and RAGGED
ROBIN.

To be among theater people, once again, was gratifying
enough, but to be with the cheerful and kindly Mr. Olcott was
more than I could have wished. I found myself in a far happier
and more comfortable environment than the one I had left
behind. The days of reckoning could be forestalled a bit longer.

Included in the tour, was a stop at lovely Santa Barbara,
California, a jewel nestled in the curvature of the Santa Barbara
Channel, against a backdrop of the colorful Santa Inez moun-
tains. It was here the Franciscan Fathers chose to build their
tenth mission,in 1786, the Santa Barbara Mission. The chain of
twenty-one California missions had started with the Mission San
Diego de Alcala in San Diego in 1769 and ended with Mission
San Francisco Solano, in Sonoma, in 1823. The beautiful city of
Santa Barbara is rich in Spanish traditions still guarded to this
day.

Although our arrival there with the Chauncy Olcott show
started on a rather disturbing note, for me, I hasten to add that
it ended most happily. The woman into whose care I was en-

trusted, thinking to economize and thus save expenses for herself, ordered a cot put in her room—for me. She and her boy and I were to sleep in the same room in a very ordinary hotel. Well! This did not fit my plans at all. I was self-supporting and I did not relish the thought of sharing a room with those two. I was quite aware that Mr. Olcott and others in the cast were staying at a very fancy hotel, so I walked out on my "sitter" and headed directly to where he was staying, the majestic Potter Hotel. I hastened up the hotel's broad stairway and presented myself at the front desk where I asked for Mr. Olcott. He was paged and soon appeared before me. No doubt, I had drawn him from his favorite libation at the magnificent bar. When he saw me, he smiled and asked solicitously upon seeing the scowl on my face, "What's the matter, Baby?" I told him of my indignation over having to share a room with "that woman and her boy," in what I considered a cheap hotel. He smiled indulgently over my pique, took me back to the front desk, ordered a room for me, and sent for my luggage. I was then ushered into a lovely, spacious room overlooking the ocean. The room was fit for a queen, and I felt like a grand duchess each time I descended the main staircase of the world-renown Potter Hotel. The fantasies in which I had indulged as a younger child, when I played the role of the elegant and beautiful "lady" descending the make-believe "grand staircase" of building blocks in the St. Ann's had, at last, come true. Baby Dody was herself again.

It was to Milo M. Potter, in a sense, that I owed my newly found re-emergence. The owner and administrator of the palatial Potter Hotel was a genius in hotel management and advertising. Before building the Potter, he had been the very successful owner-operator of the Van Nuys Hotel in Los Angeles. A group of Santa Barbara businessmen prevailed upon him to come to their city and build a hotel on the famous thirty-six acre tract that included a rise, the so-called, historic "Burton Mound." It did not take Mr. Potter long to recognize the potential of this ideal site. In January 1902, work was started on what would become one of the West Coast's most famous resort hotels. It would hold its own against its two competitors: Monterey's Del Monte and Coronado's Hotel del Coronado;

though, of the three, only the Hotel del Coronado remains today as a public caravansary.

From the word "go" to the architect, John S. Austin, no cost was spared to make the Potter Hotel the most elegant and comfortable resort possible. Mr. Potter dealt in superlatives that translated into a $1,500,000 five-storied hotel of unmatched accommodations and surroundings. The famed hostelry covered the area, roughly, between present-day Bath and Chapala Streets, and Montecito Street and Cabrillo Boulevard (then, Esplanade del Mar); and faced the beautiful blue Pacific Ocean.

Potter, a bold, innovative man, had Santa Barbara scanned for established trees he thought would enhance his hotel grounds. He converted what had been a wheat field into a veritable paradise of shade trees, shrubbery, flower beds, and gravel walks. I particularly remember that beautiful palm trees abounded on the hotel's spacious grounds and lined the main walk from the hotel to the beach. One of these palms, I have learned, was a twenty-five-year-old specimen with a spread of thirty feet and weighed ten tons when readied for moving from its original location, near State Street, to the middle of the right half of the Potter's front grounds. Another, of the same variety (Phoenix Canariensis), with a spread of thirty-five feet, was

Potter Hotel (1903-1921) Santa Barbara, California (Photo c. 1903)
Credit: Courtesy The Walker A. Tompkins Collection

moved from the corner of Yanonali and Anacapa Streets to adorn the counter-location, on the left. For the center of the grounds, in front of the hotel's two towers, a date palm, said to bear "from 200 to 300 pounds of fine large dates each year," was purchased from a Mrs. West at its location of many years, Montecito and Castillo Streets. I recall that the lovely gardens encompassed expansive flower beds of lilies, roses, bright geraniums, and many other colorful varieties; and that there were immaculately manicured lawns. There was also a zoo with monkeys, deer, and numerous species of birds. It took a crew of thirty men to maintain these grounds in all their glory.

The Potter Hotel itself epitomized elegance in living, with plush appointments and unmatched cuisine. In Goleta, adjoining Santa Barbara, Mr. Potter had his Potter ranch (formerly, the Kellogg Ranch) which supplied the hotel with squab, chicken, eggs, roasting pigs, and milk cows, as well as all manner of fresh vegetables. It was noted also that guests at the Potter "could cut their own artichokes, rhubarb, and other vegetables the year round." Most of the hotel's meat came from San Francisco. In winter, "a standing order of thirty-five loins and forty ribs of beef were shipped by boat each week." Prodigious amounts of frozen fish were kept for emergencies; but the fresh fish was generally readily available. The immaculate, big kitchen was supervised by a chef with fifteen cooks at his command. According to the hotel's steward, Richard D. Jones, "We used to do a lot of charcoal broiling. Each season we used a carload of 650 sacks for broiling in the kitchen." A spur track was built into the hotel grounds to facilitate, among others, the delivery of just such carload lot purchases.

The hotel had its own: electric, steam, ice, and cold storage plants; laundry, hot house, carpenter shop, fire department; a bakery for pies and pastries, another for bread; a vegetable room, a butcher shop, a post-office, and a famous two-storied stable located at Chapala and Montecito Streets, operated by the Carty Brothers.

The Santa Barbara Morning Press, December 24, 1904 provides an excellent record of the latter establishment. The stable's floor was paved to make it "the most serviceable floor for both horses and carriages." The Potter Hotel's stable had stall space for 160 horses, two harness rooms, and another that accommodated about a hundred saddles of "all sizes and styles." Rigs were kept on both floors and were raised or lowered by means of a "large carriage elevator." Grain and over 300 tons of hay were stored on the upper floor. Carty Brothers proudly announced in December 24, 1904 that the new Potter Hotel stable was "admirably equipped to meet all the demands of the hotel guests and its other patrons." To meet guest transportation needs, there were also two "buses," one of them an "omnibus for thirty people," drawn by four horses. Later, as the horse-drawn mode of travel gave way to the "horseless carriage," the Potter Hotel adapted to the needs brought about by the automobile.

The formal opening of the famous Potter Hotel, January 19, 1903, proved "one of the great social events in the life of Southern California." There were guests from all parts of the world. On that gala night, the men were in full tails, and the women, in fabulous gowns adorned with "fortunes in jewels." For the grand ball in the Palm Room, a full orchestra played to the "beautiful people" of that never-to-be-repeated era of pomp and circumstance.

Potter Hotel Lobby (Only known view extant.)
Credit: Courtesy The Walker A. Tompkins Collection

Nabobs from all over the world would be drawn to Mr. Potter's plush palace. Since the back of the hotel's grounds adjoined the Southern Pacific Railroad, with ample room for sidings, many of the nation's elite arrived in their private railroad cars, which were easily directed to their own sidings. Well-known names like Rockefeller, Carnegie, Swift, Armour, Cudahy, Vanderbilt, Gould, Spreckles, Schwab, Harriman, Studebaker, Fleischmann, and Peabody became familiar ones in the hotel's register; but the hotel also attracted names famous in the worlds of government, politics, the arts, and sports.

The Potter's rates in summer, when it usually accommodated only about 350 people, were "as low as three dollars a day" and up. Its winter, or "in season" rates, were "as low as four dollars" a day. Considering that the hotel operated on the American Plan, with three "squares" included, one can be forgiven for making invidious comparisons with present-day charges. During the winter, the Potter usually drew over 600 guests who flocked to the salubrious, warm climate of incredibly beautiful Santa Barbara. To serve these happy patrons, were 500 employees that included among them: 75-100 waitresses, 10 bellboys, 15 busboys, 40 dishwashers, and 15 cooks under the close scrutiny of the chef.

The magnificent bar at the Potter became world renowned for its innovative drinks and services. Drinks cost 15¢ for whiskey, 20¢ for cocktails, 15¢ for French cordials; and for Imported Champagnes, $2 a pint, $4 a quart. With the libations, went a spread that included: roast squab, roast beef and pork, fried frog legs, baked salmon in cream sauce, cold cuts, cheeses, relishes, bread, and hot biscuits. Patrons could make a meal from the proferred buffet and, no doubt, many did. Nothing was too good or too expensive for the guests of the majestic Potter Hotel.

As most good things come to an end, so did the fortunes of this famous and fabulous resort. Mr. Potter sold it to D.M. Linnard, who had managed the Maryland Hotel of Pasadena. According to Santa Barbara's noted historian, Walker A. Tompkins (SANTA BARBARA YESTERDAYS), the new owner changed the name of the Potter Hotel to The Belvedere.

Before long, the Belvedere was bought by the S.W. Straus Ambassador Hotel Chain (1919). As the Ambassador, it was destroyed by fire on April 13, 1921. Santa Barbara's ocean front, between Bath and Chapala Streets, would never be the same. The beautiful grounds of the once Potter Hotel would be subdivided and filled with motels; but Santa Barbara and its visitors had known true luxury, opulence, and gracious living they can never forget.

Having come to and partaken of the bounteous grandeur of the lovely Potter Hotel, at a time when my young life was in a very traumatic state, I appreciated its offerings far more than if conditions had been normal. Yet, I found myself wishing, over and over, that I could be sharing these impressive surroundings with the mama. She would have enjoyed this type of place; she always had. But the reality of my life at that time was that I was in a swiftly passing, joyous moment; that I had fallen in disfavor with my "nana," who was still residing with her son at the very

Chauncey Olcott and Children c. 1904
Credit: Barrett-Miller Collection

inferior hotel; and that, while the tour would soon end in San Diego, and I was confident I could hold my own until then, the truth was that after San Diego and Mr. Olcott's return East, I would have to return home to the drab, unhappy world I dreaded. For the time being, I enjoyed my fairyland surroundings at the Potter; and when the time came to bid Mr. Olcott "adieu" in San Diego, I reluctantly returned home.

The day of reckoning was, indeed, upon me now. The mama's death had not only been an unbearable grief, it was a shock that catapulted me into a different world. I suddenly became aware that she had shielded and sheltered me far too much. The foster sister, whose paper dolls I had upset when I was but a babe, had a genuine right to be jealous of me. She thought I was too dressed up, too pampered, and much too favored. That I was earning my way, was incidental and of no import to her. I'm sure she was under the impression our parents had always thought more of me, and that it was now in my best interest to take me to her level. So, under threat of it being cut off, my hair was braided. Gone were the beautiful curls on which the dear mama had spent so much loving care. Gone also were the stiffly starched white dresses. They were replaced with practical colored dresses. I felt like a character—a strange rag doll in multicolored clothes. In short, both the papa and the foster-sister were determined I was to be like all other children. Though it was a bit late to start, perhaps they did me a good turn, in the long run. I had to go through it, sooner or later. Unfortunately, it came while I was still in shock over the beloved mama's passing. The papa, I know, did not intend to be mean or cruel to me. I realize now, I must have posed quite a problem, for I was an odd child. I did not fit in, and I had to learn to do just that. Bertha was determined I would. Of course, it was inevitable: I could not be "Baby Dody" forever.

Since the metamorphosis was now taking place, it was also inescapable that I would be exposed to the usual temptations of childhood. Thus it came about that, for the first and only time in my life, I resorted to stealing. Down the street from us was a music store, whose owners had a little three-year-old girl. The little one often brought her box of toys out on the sidewalk, where she would while away the time with her treasures about her. Well, I was going to be like *other* children, was I. So, one day while playing with her, as I occasionally did, I spied a penny in her toy box. It was obvious to me the little girl had no sense of the penny's intrinsic worth. But, recalling the cold penny episode in New York and the candy I had bought with it, I was persuaded to the inevitable. I was not really desperate for money, for the papa gave me money from time to time. Still, that penny reminded me of New York and the exciting discovery with the children there, so I took the penny. That is all—but I have never forgotten the event and, to this day, I carry the guilt it engendered.

Like all other children, I had to attend a formal school now. For me, however, it first came when I was near twelve. I was enrolled in the Clement Grammar School on Geary Street. I still feel the pain of abject loneliness, cast as I was among multitudes of strange faces. I was very lost and very unhappy. These were not the lovely children I remembered, who brought flowers to Little Eva at the railroad stations. My schoolmates were rough and noisy, and I was apprehensive among them.

Further, it was very difficult to discipline myself to sit hours at a desk when thoughts of the mama were ever in my mind. It is small wonder I reached the nadir of despair. The teachers at Clement Grammar School did not know what to do with me. I had never been to a school; but, surely, I was old enough to be much further along than the first grade. Together they decided that since I could read, write, and do simple arithmetic, they would try me out in the third grade and see how I progressed. I romped away with third grade. I recall the class's preoccupation with drawing geography maps. How simple it was. I already knew about isthmuses, peninsulas, islands, and waterways, for I had long since been introduced to these geographic entities in my travels. Indeed, maps were the ubiquitous accompaniments of all our travels. Apparently, my achievements in reading, writing, and arithmetic more than met the requirements of the third grade because I was soon advanced to the fourth grade.

Conditions in the fourth grade were a decided change for the better. Our fourth-grade teacher was a delicate little woman by the name of Miss Bertha Dwazack. She had iron-gray hair; sharp, thin features; kindly eyes, with a modicum of soft lines around them; and a very sensitive nature. I recall how thankful I was that she believed in "learning by rote." She would show us a chart with the multiplication tables, point emphatically to them with a pointer, and have us recite the tables, over and over. Of course, with my kind of memory I could do it with my eyes shut—and all the while I thought of the mama.

The unhappiest moments persisted—when I had to leave the security of Miss Dwazack's classroom and go out to play in the school yard during recesses and lunch periods. I felt I was dressed for a pathetic part in a strange sort of play. There I was: in colored dresses and with my hair tightly braided. Was I playing a part? But there were no footlights. And for an audience, I had rude, boisterous and, sometimes, cruel children who sensed my defenselessness and did not hesitate to press their advantage. On one occasion, while playing tag, my drab, gray gingham dress of woven checks was severely torn by an exuberant playmate. The consequent exposure was an embarrassment, rendering me hopelesly humiliated. At this point, the sensitive little Miss Dwazack took me under her care and sewed the jagged, long rent. I shall never forget that it was the first display of motherly kindness shown me since the mama's death. She made it possible for me to walk home in dignity; and for this, Miss Dwazack will be enshrined in my memory forever.

Another manifestation of kindness during those trying days of adjustments, would come from one single peer—a boy. One day, he approached me on the playground and asked, "Why don't you play?" When I hesitated, he led me to a bench beside the fence, where we sat and had a long exchange of confidences. I poured forth a flow of pent-up frustrations and sorrows, and he listened with understanding beyond his years. When he told me that he lived with an aunt, I felt we were kindred spirits. We became good friends, and soon he was like a brother to me. At last, I had bridged my own generation gap. This one and only friend, Ronald Foley, always walked me home from school, and the papa fed him with the same attention he fed neighborhood cats and children.

Ronald Foley became my sounding board and my greatest comfort. He was very fond of listening to my theater experiences, so he became my loyal follower and audience-of-one. At last I had found someone who was kind and considerate, and who did not think my "dream-world" was of no significance. But my great joy was too short-lived. I saw him last, the day before the great earthquake. Since then, I have not seen him, nor have I learned his fate.

The Burning City, San Francisco, 10 A.M. April 18th 1906

1. Fairmount
2. Telegraph Hill
3. Hall of Justice
4. U.S. Customs House
5. California Street
6. Old St. Mary's Cathedral
7. Kohl Bldg.
8. Grace Church
9. Merchants Exchange
10. Calif. Safe Deposit & Trust Co.

11. Mills Bldg.
12. Occidental Hotel
13. California Hotel
14. Pine Street
15. Shot Tower
16. Union Trust Bldg.
17. Masonic Temple
18. Crocker Bldg.
19. Palace Hotel
20. Chronicle Bldg.

21. Monadnock Bldg.
22. Shreve Bldg.
23. Mutual Bank
24. Call Bldg.
25. History Bldg.
26. Temple Emanuel
27. Whittell Bldg.
28. S.V.W. Co. Bldg.
29. Butler Bldg.
30. Hotel Savoy

The Ruins of San Francisco, May 1906

31. Flood Bldg.	40. Hall Bros.
32. Academy Sciences	41. Post Office
33. Emporium	42. Mason & Sutter Sts.
34. James Flood Bldg.	43. U.S. Commandry
35. St. Francis Bldg.	44. City Hall
36. S.F. Gas & Elec. Co.	45. Union Ferry
37. Calif. Casket Co.	
38. Union Square Hall	
39. First Congregation Church	

Credit: The Anita M. Bradley Collection

Chapter Eight
The Prison Walls Close In

Tomes consuming reams have been written on the subject of the San Francisco earthquake and fire of 1906. It is not our intention to present a scholarly, scientific thesis on the geological or seismological aspects involved, but to offer one eye-witness' personal experiences through San Francisco's greatest nightmare. Anyone who lived through the city's great convulsion has his own vivid recollections. In many ways I shared similar or identical experiences, but there were also those that are mine alone.

After our return from school on Tuesday, April 17, 1906, Ronald Foley and I played for a short while. We said what turned out to be our last "goodbyes," and the papa returned from work. As usual, the papa was carrying the package of liver he picked up daily on his way home. The liver was for the neighborhood cats, whom he delighted in feeding each evening. This was a "hobby" of long standing, for he was unduly fond of cats. We had none of our own; instead, I had a precious little puppy I called Cleo.

As was his custom, the papa would step out in the back-yard, call, "Here kitty, kitty, kitty," and all the cats in the vicinity came running for the liver treats. He insisted all the cats were his, but I had my reservations about that. Nevertheless, it was true the cats came loping and leaping over fences, at his summons. The daily ritual of feeding the motely aggregation of neighborhood cats seemed very gratifying to the papa. In fact, he appeared to have a compulsion for feeding both animals and people. All my life I, too, have been a compulsive dispenser of food to both.

On the evening of April 17, however, the cats failed to appear, and the papa was quite distressd over the unique phenomenon. Later,we were to conjecture, many times, on whether cats are more prescient than human beings. Had they sought safety before the impending disaster?

Early the next morning, April 18, 1906, at about 5:13, my bed was tossed from one side of the room to the other, and I was summarily thrown to the floor. Our "L" shaped flat on O'Farrell Street, between Hyde and Leavenworth, where we moved after the mama's death, had a back bedroom that opened out to the backyard and in to the kitchen. This room, intended for servants' quarters, was my bedroom. During the great upheaval, the next-door neighbor's chimney fell; and bricks from it plunged through my window, shattering glass all about me. That I escaped being struck dead by them, was a bit of luck many were not so fortunate to share—among them, San Francisco's beloved Fire Chief Dennis Sullivan.

Instantly, I picked myself off the floor, grabbed my shoes and, with one bound, leaped over the blackboard customarily placed across my bedroom doorway to keep Cleo from venturing into my room during the night. In the kitchen, I gathered Cleo into my arms, when an avalanche of jars of jams, jellies, and pickles came tumbling from the pantry shelves as I flew by to my destination, the front hall. In the hallway, I dropped my shoes and puppy as the second, and stronger, spasm shook the house to its very foundations. From the hallway, I dashed into the front parlor, grabbed the mama's picture off the mantel, hugged the picture to me and said, "I'm ready, I'm ready," over and over, because I thought it was the end of the world.

At this precise moment, the papa sat up in bed and, looking at me through the opened, sliding doors of the "back-parlor" where he slept, exploded,

"Go back to bed, you damn fool. It's only an earthquake."

This truly brought me "down to earth." Since it was apparent I would get no solace or comfort from him, I turned and ran out the front door to our small front yard. The buildings were still shaking, and the cobbles on the street were undulating like ocean waves. The eerie "woo-woo-woo" of the swinging electric wires overhead added to the terrifying gothic drama of nature about me. Dressed in their night clothes, people spilled out of their houses; chimneys tumbled or crumbled; and pandemo-

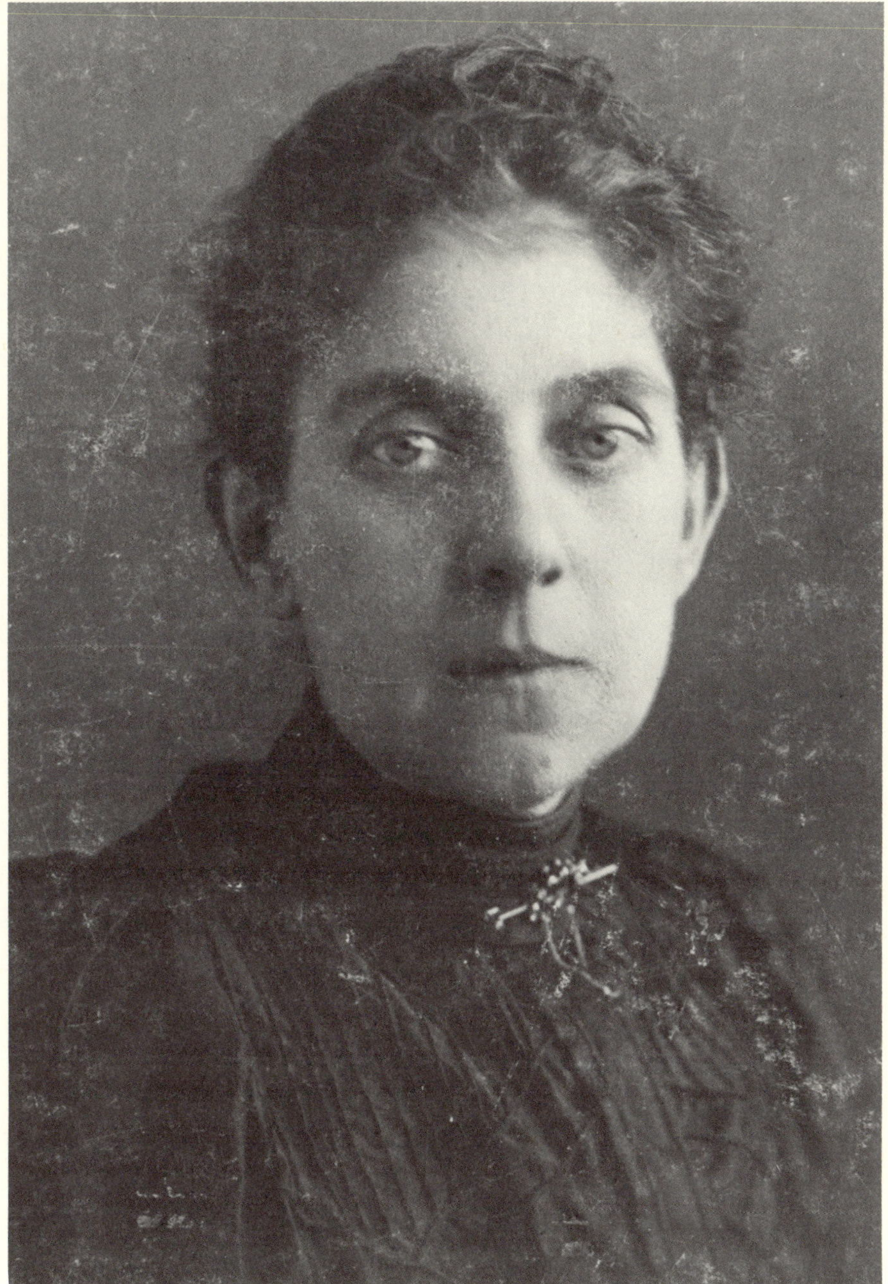

"The Mama" Ella Parker Scholz 1857-1904
Credit: Barrett-Miller Collection

nium prevailed everywhere I looked. By now, the papa, properly impressed with the gravity of the affair, had gotten into some presentable clothing. Dashing to where I stood in fascinated terror, the papa unceremoniously hauled me by the scruff of the neck, back into the house and to safety from falling debris.

Very soon, there were rumors of fire spreading through the lower Mission, downtown, and bayside areas of San Francisco. A quick glimpse of the red glow and smoke there, set the papa on a course of action. He immediately started planning for the obvious eventualities. His first move was to retrieve cans and food not damaged by the tumble off the pantry shelves. Those were the days of the ice-box, when only the most perishable of foods were to be found in it. Canned goods were not very plentiful, and packaged foods were a rarity. Staples like flour, sugar, and salt were purchased in cloth bags; and the others, dispensed from barrels into paper bags. The urgency of the moment dictated we round up what food and clothing we could. The papa sent me in search of a large bag in which to put things. When all I could find was a mattress cover, he told me to fill it with food, shoes, and clothing. This I did, but I also added an alarm clock to my "grab bag." Why I grabbed such a ridiculous item that I hated then and still do, shall remain one of those unfathomable acts everyone performed that fateful morning.

After we had gathered the most urgent articles for our future needs, the papa set about preparing the family steamer trunk for them. He began removing the contents of the trunk, throwing them out, helter-skelter, until he was satisfied there was room for the essentials. As luck would have it, he stopped short of the layer at the bottom of the trunk. This layer proved, later, to be copies of some of my theater programs, pictures, and theater memorabilia that have proved invaluable aids in writing these memoirs. The programs and pictures of me in various productions in pre-earthquake San Francisco theaters, were duplicates; and, alas, the collection is not complete. But I am grateful for the printed testimonials of some of my theater activities as a child actress in those halcyon days when San Franciscans looked to the theater for their greatest escape.

While our hectic preparations for a hasty retreat from the spreading fire were in full swing, big sister Bertha with her husband, Jerome, and their two children, two-year-old Herbert and three-week-old Gertrude, arrived at our house. It was a great relief to know they had all survived, but it soon dawned on us that our logistics had multiplied. Most pressing of all, was the urgent need for water. As did the entire city, we discovered the quake had abruptly severed our source of water, and that not a single receptacle of water was available to us. After cogitating on our predicament, Jerome and the papa remembered there might be one meager supply still available to us—the water in the so-called "water-back" pipes in our stove. To the uninitiated, these were a set of coils that ran directly into the stove and through the firebox, and furnished hot water whenever a fire burned in the stove. As the water heated, it rose into a very small water tank. This then, was the only water left, and it was limited, at that; nevertheless, it constituted a bonanza for which we were most grateful. We tapped it into bottles, jars, and any suitable container we could find. We would guard it zealously in the days ahead, for the three-week-old infant, Gertrude, compounded our water needs further.

No sooner had the Sawyers arrived, than Bertha went into heightened hysterics with each aftershock. While the rest of us labored, she carried on her laments. Then the soldiers came to our door to inform us we would have to leave, for very soon our house, along with other's, would be put to dynamite in an attempt to stop the fire's progress. Blocks and blocks of houses were to be leveled in this manner, in an effort to compensate for what a waterless town could not do. It was their fervent hope the fire could thus be controlled; but, in the end, it ran its course and engulfed at will.

There was no alternative now but to leave. Bertha carried on more than ever; and seeing her sustained crying, I gave way, for the first and only time, to the blessed relief tears can sometimes bring. The stoic papa became very angry and threatened to inflict all manner of punishment on both of us; so I knew I had better stop my bawling and live up to his trust in me when he would pat my head, whenever I was afraid, and say, "That's my brave little girl." To emphasize the fact it was time to keep our heads about us and enter into useful activity, the papa gave me a nickel and sent me to the corner grocery store to buy a loaf of bread. Alas, inflation and profiteering had already reared their ugly heads, for when I gave the grocer the usual five cents for the bread, he informed me I owed him twenty cents more. Bewildered, I returned home without completing my mission, much to the papa's disgust. His speech could be salty at times, and this was one of those times. Two days later, bread was selling for seventy-five cents a loaf.

Seeing Jerome planning the best course of action for us and watching his composure, were an inspiration to me. "That's the way we should act," I told myself; and from then on, I was a pillar of strength. Determinedly, I did not look back as we left our home to burn. We started out (minus the loaf of bread). A subdued Bertha carried the infant. Jerome was loaded down with all the paraphernalia necessary for his family of four. The papa was dragging our steamer trunk by a rope he had placed through the handles. I brought up the rear, pulling little red-headed Herbert in his "go-cart," or stroller. To the handles of the go-cart was fastened my personal "mattress-cover bag" with my shoes, clothes, food and (sic) alarm-clock. The bag was so heavy that I had to watch it carefully lest it tip the cart backward, with poor Herbert in it. I was fond of this little red-haired image of his father, and I think the boy liked me, too. In any event, our fates were tied to each other, and thus they remained to the culmination of our flight.

On went our pitiful caravan, leaving so many of our precious lares and penates to the whims of dynamite and fire. I thought of my theatrical trunk I had left behind. It was a Taylor trunk, a thing of great status in the theater in those days. Every professional artist had a specially built Taylor trunk, for his convenience during the hard travels of theater life. An innovation over the ubiquitous camel-top trunk, the theater trunk's till was strong enough to be used as an ironing board. In my Taylor, I had left my many lovely costumes, dresses, laces, and the mama's lovely jewelry. I recalled how the mama had always guarded her jewelry, even through rough times. She had always

Typical Park Scene April 18, 1906 — A Repository For Trunks
Credit: Courtesy Anita M. Bradley Collection

said they would be mine someday, but now they were all left at the house that was waiting to be consumed—the pearl earrings, the pearl ring, the diamond ring, and the lovely crescent-and-star brooch studded with nine diamonds. The mama had prized the latter so much that she had a special safety clasp made for it. A painful reminder, the only salvaged picture of her—the one I had hastily snatched off the mantel—showed the beautiful brooch, pinned at the base of her dress collar. And now, the material and sentimental objects had all been sacrificed in the interest of the essentials of survival.

Our assessment of the situation quickly revealed that we had only one good direction to go. To the east, there was a wall of fire between us and the waterfront, where the ferryboats were taking refugees to Marin County and the East Bay. The waterfront, with the aid of the fire boats, was being kept fairly well protected for the evacuation of those who could reach there. To the north, there were some of San Francisco's steepest hills to conquer; and to the south, devastation and encroaching fire made it impossible to venture in that direction. Our family had, really, only one choice—west to Golden Gate Park, with its broad lawns and safety from the fire.

The trek would be one of the longest and most arduous walks I have ever taken. Holding on to the go-cart and pushing it along, as I held my precious puppy Cleo, I tried to comfort and reassure dear little Herbert. At times I would lag behind, while the rest of our train moved on. It was during such intervals that I grew up. It occurred to me that, quite possibly, if it had not been for their interest in little Herbert, the family might never have looked back to see if I were coming. Though such insights were at first a great blow, a great shock, they had the compelling value of teaching me that from then on I was on my own. At that precise moment, I had passed through "the clouds of glory" that had been about me as a child, when I "beheld the light and whence it flows," to "the shades of the prison house" now beginning to close in on me. *I had suddenly grown up.* I had passed one of life's landmarks, and I knew it—no more the carefree make-believe world in which I had found all the comfort and security a child needs, in its "clouds of glory."

Clearly, since I had walked "over the threshold" at age twelve, it was now time to take courage, put my chin out, square my shoulders, and face the world of reality. While to some the cross-over from childhood to adulthood is imperceptible, mine stands out well delineated in time and place. Even the world of make-believe of the theater I had so loved, was now being assessed in light of my new perceptions. San Francisco's theaters were being decimated,one by one, as they crumbled in the wake of the fire behind me. There was a cruel finality to knowing that nearly all my beloved theaters were going up in smoke. The theater people I knew were, even then, being scattered, some never to be heard from again. Even my cherished but short-lived friendship with my playmate, Ronald Foley, would never be the same, should we ever chance to meet in the future.

As a new person, entering a new life, I was to be an individual looking out for me. "Baby Dody" had vanished. And it all occurred during that long journey from our house, over San Francisco's hills to Golden Gate Park. Though with this realization I felt very much alone, I did not whimper. Thoughts of the mama crossed my mind, and I was almost relieved she was not there to endure what we were facing. She had always been terrified of earthquakes. I wondered how she could have withstood our ordeal. So now, I stood quite alone. I leaned on no one, not even on Jerome whom I admired very much, and who had always set such a fine example of bravery, forthrightness, and ingenuity.

When we reached the crest of the hills, we turned around to look at our beloved city, burning. A pall of smoke shrouded her, and tongues of fire gyrated in a menacing dance over the "fairest of all." One wondered what the lovely lady had done to merit such a fate. Her South of Market districts, on her southeastern flank, were feeding the ravenous conflagration; and Market Street and its environs seemed resigned to their fates. All in the wake of the fire was leveled or charred, and bleak and pitiful. As if it were really necessary, again I was brought up short to the harsh acceptance that life was real.

There was no going back now. With resignation, we turned away from the depressing sight and hastened on. The streets were crowded with heavily weighted refugees, in search of loved ones and of a place to go. They carried, dragged, or pushed: beds on casters, trunks, boxes, bags, and all manner of bizarre articles, such as bird cages with no birds in them. We were all marching to the same drummer—the will to survive.

As we trudged toward Golden Gate Park, my brother-in-law Jerome met two friends with their wives. Both men worked at the well-known Techau Tavern on Mason Street, one as a cook, the other, a waiter. One of the wives was quite ill, so when we came by an abandoned buggy, Jerome appropriated it; and into it he put: the sick woman, Bertha and three-week-old Gertrude, and the heavy bundle he had been carrying. Jerome and the sick woman's husband took turns pulling the buggy. It was not an uncommon sight to see men instead of horses, in the shafts, pulling the buggies that tragic day. Before long, we had the good fortune of finding a horse tethered in a vacant lot. Jerome "commandeered" the animal. Out of one of our precious blankets, which he cut up, the resourceful Jerome made a makeshift harness, put the horse in the shafts, and let him pull

San Francisco Burning   April 18, 1906
Credit: California Historical Society, San Francisco

the buggy. Jerome then relieved the weary papa of the heavy trunk he was dragging, and we continued our exhausting walk to Golden Gate Park.

Although the horse had lightened our load, we were very tired when we finally arrived at the park. We sat down on the lawn in front of the first building within the park proper, MacLaren's Lodge. There were hundreds of people already there, milling around in utter confusion. Before long, the park would shelter over two-hundred-thousand people. No one seemed to know what to do, now that he had arrived at his destination. Conditions were hopeless. There was no water; there was no food. Those of us who had our loved ones with us were fortunate, indeed. Some had been separated from their families, and their agony was unbearable. They were distraught, and they wept uncontrollably.

In the midst of this chaos and while our family rested, I wandered off by myself. I happened to take a path that led up a hillock behind MacLaren's Lodge. There, I came upon an octagonal-shaped "summer house" of redwood logs. A large log served as its center pole. The roof sloped down, umbrella-fashion, and rested on posts marking its perimeters. Between the eight posts, smaller logs formed the backs of seats facing both inside and outside the building. The entire house was constructed of redwood logs with bark still clinging to them. Inside, around the center pole, was built an octagonal table, with four curved, movable benches. Each curved bench, supported by redwood brackets, spanned two sections of the eight-sided table. The floor was constructed of redwood slabs; but, with sand-filled interstices, created a fairly smooth flooring. On top of the house was a cupola of three diminishing tiers, made of smaller logs—these, too, with the bark still on them.

Having made my fabulous discovery, I could scarcely contain myself as I ran pell-mell down the hill to where the family was still resting on the lawn, debating alternative moves. Bursting at the seams with the news of my great discovery, I interrupted excitedly, "Come Jerome, I want to show you something I have found." I was sure the other adults would have brushed me aside and sent me on my way. With Jerome, how-

MacLaren Lodge   Golden Gate Park, San Francisco
Credit: California Historical Society, San Francisco

ever, I knew I had instant rapport. He never missed a bet. Very kindly, he turned to me and said, "Alright, I'll go with you." He followed me up the path; and when he saw the garden house and inspected it, he concurred it was the answer to our lodging problem. We returned to our group below, where Jerome informed them of our timely discovery; and very quickly, we moved into the summer house.

How to go about procuring much needed food supplies became the prime consideration, now that we had found shelter. All of us looked to Jerome for direction; and, in his usual resourceful way, he came up with the answer. He prevailed upon one of his friends from Techau Tavern to relinquish his white coat. Next, Bertha carried out her assigned task: From two strips of red cloth, taken from a red wool skirt, she formed a cross and stitched it on a sleeve of the white coat. It soon became evident to us that Jerome intended using this "badge of authority" as an entry to grocery stores. Everyone knew that only Red Cross workers and other authorized personnel with a Red Cross insignia were allowed beyond the lines of soldiers. Looters would be summarily dealt with under the provisions of the Mayor's Proclamation:

> *The Federal Troops, the members of the regular Police Force, and all Special Police Officers have been authorized to KILL any and all persons found engaged in looting or in the commission of any other crime.*
>
> *I have directed all the Gas and Electric Lighting Companies not to turn on Gas or Electricity until I order them to do so; you may therefore expect the city to remain in darkness until daylight of every night until order is restored.*
>
> *I warn all citizens of the danger of fire from damaged or destroyed chimneys, broken or leaking gas pipes or fixtures, or any like cause.*
>
> *E.E. SCHMITZ, Mayor*
> *Dated, April 18, 1906*

Seeing that his charges were now in relative comfort, considering the trying times, Jerome told us to wait there until his return; and then he set out on his perilous search for food. He took the horse and buggy, and looking very officious in his white coat with the red cross on its sleeve, drove down through "the lines." That he did so, safely, did not surprise us too much, for the tall Jerome of the impressive, martial bearing had the air of authority and command, common to military leaders. This had stood him well in the Boer War. Although San Francisco was now under the mantle of the Mayor's Proclamation, Jerome's makeshift uniform had protected him from the fate of the looter. One wonders how well his confidence and resourcefulness would have served him had he been asked to present credentials. But in the chaos immediately following the earthquake and fire, his "uniform," apparently, was enough. The daring Jerome made three trips through "the lines" and, each time, returned with the buggy full of much needed provisions. He had selected a store in the path of the fire, one he knew could not escape; and from it, he took hams, canned fruits and vegetables, canned milk, and any staple that would keep. A great help in alleviating our immediate liquid needs, were the quantities of root beer and sarsaparilla he brought us. These, we supplemented with the juices from the fruit and vegetable cans. The needs of the mother and infant were, of course, paramount.

After each food expedition, Jerome climbed on the roof of the summer house, removed some logs from the cupola, sequestered the food there, and replaced the logs. He was fearful someone might take the food away from us, so serious was the need for food at that time.

On another venture into town, Jerome found a trash can with a hinged lid, a wrought-iron scroll such as was used in front of fireplaces, and some metal pegs. After scouring the trash can with sand, he dug a hole for a fire pit; placed the iron scroll over it, as a grill; and secured the "grill" by running the pegs through it into the ground. On top of the scroll he placed the trash can on its side, struck a fire, using Chinese "block matches," and "voilà," an ingenious stove and oven. By simply closing the hinged lid of the can, we created a perfect "oven" in which we baked many a loaf of bread, while the surface served as a stove. The empty food cans made good cooking utensils for our "stove," and the outside benches, excellent repositories for our kitchen and cooking utensils.

A passing word on Chinese block-matches: They were made of soft-wood blocks, scored or cut barely down to the bottom, to create long matches that could be picked off one at a time. The tips of the blocks were dipped in a sulphuric medium that gave part of the stems their yellow color. The surface of the tips were then coated with red phosphorus. Since these colorful yellow and red matches were not safety matches, they were hazardous and had to be handled with caution. They were manufactured in China and exported to our San Francisco Chinatown.

Our "appropriated" horse and buggy served us well for the short time we could avail ourselves of its services. One day, however, Jerome drove the horse and buggy out of the park to the surrounding fields, disengaged the horse and left him there to graze. That was the last we saw of both horse and buggy. Perhaps it was only fair. We had put both to good use, and it was someone else's turn to use this priceless, scarce convenience. We hoped the horse had found a new master who appreciated him as we had. It is most likely he had been taken by the army and pressed into service.

Now we settled down to the business of living in our new "home." The four men took turns walking guard at night. There was a fine, level walk all around the house, making the chore a fairly easy one. There was never an unpleasant incident all the time we remained there, so we felt quite secure. Being off the beaten path and on the crest of a knoll, as we were, added further to our safety. One approach led to the only entrance to the house; while a second path, at the opposite or rear of the house, led through a path flanked by shrubs and trees directly down to Fulton Street.

Sleeping areas were quickly devised, for the inside construction of the house lent itself well to them. We strung Army pup tents between the supporting poles and down to the top of each bench. Since the log constructed benches were eighteen inches wide, they were used as beds. To cushion the irregular, rounded surfaces of the logs, we used rags and clothes. For privacy for the women, a curtain of blankets was dropped from the cross beams, down in front of the pup tents, thereby screening every two sections of the octagonal. The height of the cross beams between the poles being seven feet, afforded more than adequate space to each section. My pup tent was the first one to the left of the entrance.

My first night in Golden Gate Park was interrupted in the early dawn hours by terrible, blood-curdling shrieks. I was frozen in terror as I contemplated a fate worse than the one dealt us by nature's hand. Scared out of my wits and in a state of panic, I ran to my father, only to be informed that what I had heard were the natural sounds of the many peacocks that roamed freely throughout Golden Gate Park. In the nights ahead I would, in time, come to accept them with resignation and, finally, not even hear them at all.

While on an exploratory junket shortly after our arrival at Golden Gate Park, I discoverd where Troop G, 14th Cavalry, from Monterey, California had pitched camp. The soldiers had driven two stakes into the ground, strung a rope between them and tethered their horses to the line. Being the animal lover I am, I was immediately drawn to the lovely horses, and I quickly made friends with them. The young cavalrymen seemed quite preoccupied with our city's great disaster—the fire spreading in the distance, the swarms of refugees pouring into the park, and how they were coping with their many problems. The men were curious and anxious for any account of our own experiences, and they asked many questions of me. Among other things, I mentioned that my sister Bertha had a three-week-old baby girl. The young men took a very personal interest in my accounts, and two of them accompanied me back to the summer house to check our living conditions and our needs. They soon returned with numerous items: pup tents, army cots, blankets, a lantern, canvas to cover the sides of the house,to shelter us from the elements; cooking utensils to replace the cans we had been using; army cutlery to help us with our housekeeping; and other essentials, from their own issue. They were so fascinated with Herbert and tiny Gertrude that their generosity knew no bounds.

All considered, we fared well because of the magnanimity of many. In due time, various organizations set up relief stations for their own members. To them, they passed out food, clothing, medicine, and miscellaneous other needs. If one were fortunate enough to belong to one of these organizations, such as the Grand Army of the Republic (as the papa did), Foresters, Masonic Lodge, Eagles, Elks, or Woodmen of the World, he was immediately supplied with the bare essentials. When the city's general distributing centers were opened, however, the private ones closed.

At the general distributing centers, of course, long queues were inevitable, for there were hundreds of thousands whose only source of supplies was the relief station. It was a common practice for the adults to press the children into service as "place holders" in the long lines. When the "place holders" neared the head of the line, the adults took over. I did my share of standing in line until Jerome or the papa took charge. To insure that no one got more than his share, a system was devised at our stations in Golden Gate Park. Little blue cards with a list of articles were passed out to each family. As an item was dispensed, the relief worker punched a hole on the ticket, after the article indicated: a wash basin, a bucket, a lantern, a cooking utensil, a blanket, a pair of shoes; or some staple such as beans, flour, salt, sugar, baking powder, etc. The whole world had heard San Francisco's cries and had responded with great generosity—if not with money, then with much needed products or services.

Among the many articles issued was a handy "comfortbag." It was a little drawstring cloth bag with: a spool of white, another of black thread, a thimble, a pair of little scissors, a package of court plasters which were cut and used like the adhesive plasters of today, and numerous other medical and sewing aids. One of my priceless possessions from the little bag is a small, maplewood barrel about two inches high and of a comparable girth. The top of the barrel, with a hole near its outer edge, is easily revolved with a light twist. The barrel itself has nine cells which

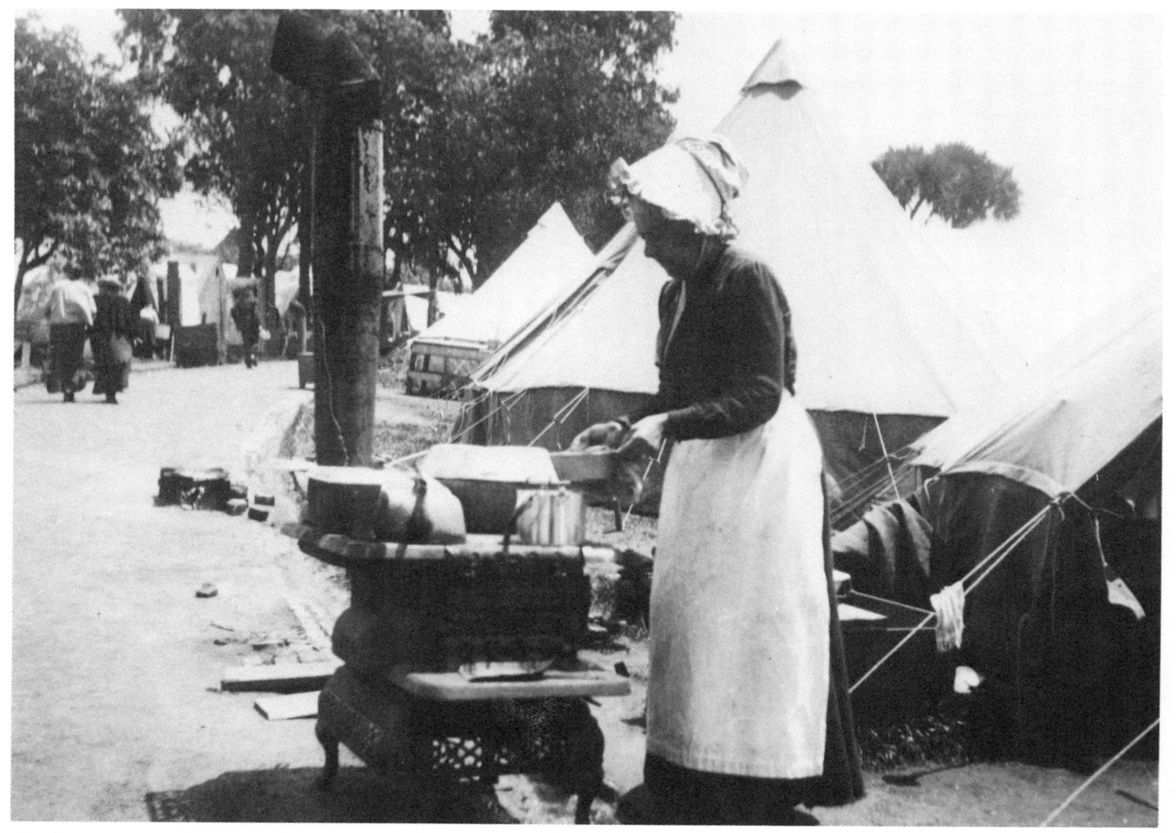

Refugee At Cookstove   Golden Gate Park, April 1906
Credit: California Historical Society, San Francisco

act as needle holders. Each cell holds a different size needle, ranging from one through nine. As one turns the top, the aforementioned hole moves over the cell whose needle size is indicated on the top edge of the barrel. A simple inversion of this clever little needle case onto one's palm, then, releases the needle. My lovely keepsake is beautifully finished in a high polish that has withstood these some seventy years since the earthquake. It bears: an inscription, "Accept My Best Wishes"; a Patent No. 2001; a trademark in the form of a modified arrow; and "Made in Germany."

After three days without water, our needs were supplied by tank wagons or ordinary street sprinklers. Since this water was transported from Marin County or the East Bay, in barges, then pumped into the tanks, we were allotted meager rations. Luckily, within less than a month's time, conditions improved immensely; and eventually, we could secure our water in buckets, from taps strategically placed throughout the park. For families like ours, who had infants, accessibility to a limitless source of water was an indescribably welcomed accommodation.

Sanitary conditions, at first, were of the crudest order— simple privies built throughout the campsites. When the army erected long barracks on the lawns in front of MacLaren's Lodge and on other sites to house the countless refugees, it placed latrines at the end of each row. We had our own "facilities," erected by the men of our group, on a spot away from our summer house, on the slope side toward Fulton Street. One of the city's gravest fears was that an epidemic might erupt, compounding her existing heavy burdens. But, somehow, we survived quite well. Perhaps our enforced outdoor way of living was healthier than we had imagined.

Further, being stranded in such lovely surroundings as our beautiful Golden Gate Park was not exactly the greatest hardship some San Franciscans endured at that time. There were many who envied the lot of the Golden Gate Park refugee. As for us, our living quarters were the best in the park, next to Mr. MacLaren's own. We thought of those whose homes were not destroyed by fire, but who could not or would not sleep in their homes for fear of another tremor. None were allowed to use their kitchen stoves, because of the possibility of damaged chimneys. Not until city inspectors approved the repairs, a time-consuming procedure, were they finally permitted to use their stoves. Until such time, San Franciscans resorted to building little makeshift kitchens on their curbs. Their sense of humor during adversity was manifested in all manner of clever and cogent little signs propped up against their impromptu "stoves"—one, I recall, read, "Dew-Drop Inn."

Many of the rich were, at least temporarily, reduced to the same level of the ordinary San Franciscan, for the earthquake had acted as an instant "equalizer." The following amusing poem by Charles K. Field captures the thought, with a charming degree of tact:

BARRIERS BURNED
A Rhyme of the San Francisco Breadline

It ain't such a terrible long time ago
  That Mrs. Van Bergen and me
Though livin' near by to each other, y'know
  Was strangers, for all ye could see
For she had a grand house, an' horses to drive,
  An' a wee rented cottage was mine,
But now we need rations to keep us alive
  An' we're standin' together in line.

An' Mrs. Van Bergen she greets me these days
  With a smile an' a nod of the head;
"Ah, Mrs. McGinnis, how are you?" she says,
  "An' do you like Government bread?"
She fetches a bag made of crockydile skin
  An' I've got a sack when we meet,
But the same kind of coffee an' crackers goes in,
  An' it's all of it cooked in the street.

Sure, Mrs. Van Bergen is takin' it fine,
  Ye'd think she was used to the food;
We're gettin' acquainted, a-standin' in line,
  An' it's doin' the both of us good.

Refugee Camp   Golden Gate Park, San Francisco, April 1906
Credit: California Historical Society, San Francisco

An' Mr. Van Bergen and Michael, my man,
(They're always been friendly, the men)
They're gettin' together and layin' a plan
For buildin' the city again!

Only once was our well-established and secure routine threatened. As the barracks were built, all stray campers throughout the park were mandatorily forced to live in them. At this point, when we were in peril of being included in the order, Jerome sought Mr. MacLaren and explained to him our dilemma. Mr. MacLaren accompanied Jerome back to the summer house and looked about it with a very critical eye. Satisfied that we were taking excellent care of the house and that we had not even used the thick bark off the redwood logs for firewood, he assured us he would intercede in our behalf. When pressed by the authorities about our tenancy in the summer house, Mr. MacLaren informed them, "We want this family to stay. They are protecting this building from possible vandalism. They are absolutely responsible people." With that endorsement by Mr. MacLaren, the threat of barrack life ceased, and we felt very secure once again. This happy arrangement continued all the months we were there.

Soon it became obvious that if Mr. MacLaren's precious Golden Gate Park was to be spared the fate of having its shrubs, trees, and lawns destroyed by exuberant and undisciplined children, schools would have to be created to contain the young, part of the day. A decision was reached to gather them together in tents and try to simulate the school discipline as nearly as possible, considering the unusual conditions. My clearest recollections of our "classroom" were that it was headed by a young woman who volunteered her services as "teacher" and who, I noted, would stand at the opening of the tent in flirtatious conversations with the soldiers, while we sang our lungs out. She had an abiding proclivity for patriotic songs. I had no idea there were so many. Whenever the little miscreants posed a problem, there was always "song therapy" to solve it— "Columbia The Gem of the Ocean," or "Tenting Tonight," or "America," or "the Star Spangled Banner." Hour after hour, the patriotic cherubs burst forth in renewed vigor, with their "teacher" pressing on. I don't recall learning the 3R's there—only patriotic songs.

As the months passed and conditions improved, four of our group, Jerome's two friends from Techau Tavern and their wives, like other San Franciscans, moved on to better quarters. Many San Francisco residents, whose homes were not hopelessly destroyed by the earthquake or fire, cleaned out their basements and rented them to refugees. Jerome and Bertha rented one such basement about three months after our arrival at Golden Gate Park. Another solution to housing the refugees was achieved by moving old street cars out to the sand dunes, where the "Avenues" are now so neatly laid out. The cars served as living quarters for many years, and a few still remain , well camouflaged with unusual exteriors but a reminder, nevertheless, of San Francisco's most agonizing period.

After Jerome and Bertha and their children left, the papa and I were quite alone. It was getting on to fall and winter now, so when the papa was able to get materials to build our own house on our property in San Mateo County, just south of San Francisco, we gathered what was left of our precious lares and penates and I was, it now seems, whisked away—but not without my dear little dog Cleo, whom I clutched ever so fondly, and who was to accompany me into my new life.

Behind me, I was leaving my "clouds of glory" and many recollectons—some happy, some quite sad, and some bittersweet. All the downtown theaters where I had spent many wonderful days in the mama's company were now gone—victims of the great cataclysmic upheaval. The list included:

The *California*, on Bush Street, where I had made my contribution to COLUMBIA THE HISTORICAL PAGEANT, for the benefit of the Childrens Hospital; and where I first met the affable musical director Eugene E. Schmitz, now mayor of San Francisco, trying his best to cope with burdens well beyond his ken, and surprising all with his determination and leadership. His legal problems would come later. It was also at the California that I had played with the great Nance O'Neill in THE JEWESS.

The *New Tivoli Opera House* (the third of the four Tivolis), Eddy and Mason Streets, the former site of the Olympia Music Hall. The second Tivoli, a half block away, where at age four I had played (March 1898) in the benefit program for the Maine Memorial Fund, had been condemned as a firetrap three years earlier. The New Tivoli Opera House and the Olympia Music Hall would always be inextricably woven together in my memory.

The *Mechanics' Pavilion*, on the north side of Market Street (site of our present-day Civic Auditorium), where I had received my undeserved medal for the Irish Jig in Kelleher and O'Connor's presentation at the Irish Fair of September 1898. It was the very spacious "barn" that had served the city well as a house for fairs, sports, and spectaculars; and finally, as an emergency hospital immediately following the temblor, albeit too briefly.

The *Columbia Theatre*, on Powell Street, next door to the St. Ann's Building (gone, too), where, in November 1899, I had participated in a song-and-dance routine in the annual Elks Benefit Entertainment. It was there I had first met Harry Connors, later of the Connors' Mammoth Pavilion Roadshow of UNCLE TOM'S CABIN and my "Little Eva" days; and Dutch Walton, "The Dutch Comedian With The Concertina"—later of Glen Park, the Chutes Theatre, and the Cineograph Parlors. It was at the Columbia I had had the great honor of playing with the incomparable Madame Modjeska.

The *Olympia Music Hall*, on Eddy and Mason Streets, the "Box House," with its variety, its afterpieces, and its sometimes dubious reputation; and of the great team of "The Fashion Plates," Violet and Kelly, in whose act (1899) I was included, singing from the balcony box nearest the stage. The Olympia Music Hall had closed three years earlier and become the New Tivoli Opera House; and so, my loyalty and affection had been shared by both.

The *Cineograph Parlors* of "Pop" Furst, on Market Street, the first true moving picture house in San Francisco, other claims notwithstanding—where, in 1898, I had sung and cake-walked, learned about "Black Art," and met the juggler, Bob

Lee.

My beloved *Alcazar*, on O'Farrell, the grandest of them all, the "Moorish Gem" of Fred Belasco and Mark Thall, where, in 1900, I had my first chance at "legitimate" theater, in SAPHO, FROU FROU, NELL GWYNNE, THE FIRST BORN, and AN AMERICAN CITIZEN. It was there the kindly Mark Thall had opened his house and his heart to such a little girl. It was the beautiful theater of columns and arches and opulence; and of the greats like White Whittlesey, Florence Roberts, the Stockwells, Herbert Farjean, Marie Howe, George Osbourne, Walter Belasco, Francis J. Powers, Georgie Cooper, Ollie Cooper, Clarence Arper, and many, many more.

The *Orpheum*, on O'Farrell, across from the Alcazar, where I had "played" the very tedious part of the little girl in THE LITTLEST GIRL, with Robert Hilliard; the Orpheum where, as in other theaters of the time, beer had flowed freely until 1904; and the theater that was considered the "mother house of entertainment to cities throughout the United States and overseas."

The *Central*, on Market Street, the great house of melodrama, where I had played in UNCLE TOM'S CABIN, LIGHTS O' LONDON, SILVER KING, LOST IN NEW YORK, TEN NIGHTS IN A BARROOM, and RESURRECTION, to list but a handful. The barnsize Central of the enormous stage and the infamous water tank; of unpredictable and surprising misadventures, sometimes involving horses or man, or both; of raucous gallery gods, and frenzied dramas resolved "just in the nick of time," before the final curtain drop. The Central that had earned the sobriquet, "The Bucket of Blood," and had thrived on pathos and hissing and booing. The Central of George Webster, Georgie Cooper, Harry Marshall the great scenic artist, Landers Stevens, and Eugenie Thais Lawton.

The Grand Opera House, on Mission Street—the big, red brick building where the mama had drawn her last measure of strength to see me through GISMONDA; the Grand Opera House of the talented, impressively handsome Melbourne MacDowell; the theater I would always think of as *Morosco's* Grand Opera House, in deference to Walter Morosco who had

San Francisco Burning   April 18, 1906
Credit: California Historical Society, San Francisco

brought it into prominence when he assumed its destiny.

The *Majestic*, on Market and Ninth Streets, that had opened two years to the day of the earthquake and fire; the Majestic of JIM BLUDSO, in which I had played Little Breeches and had my pants legs catch fire. The Majestic with such a checkered and frustrating history of projected starts and cancellations because of its belated completion. The Majestic that had been such a blessing to me after the mama's death. The Majestic of Oliver Morosco, my friend from the Burbank Theatre of Los Angeles, and his talented scenic artist, Harry Marshall.

These downtown San Francisco theaters in which I had played in my childhood, were now, like my childhood, a closed chapter. Some would be rebuilt on the same sites. Others would find new locations. Still others, would never have a renascence.

Worthy of note, however, is the fact that the Chutes, on the north side of Golden Gate Park, escaped the fate of the downtown theaters and in May 1906 became, temporarily, the second Orpheum Theatre (until January 1907).

Like the city, I had lived through an era that would never return; and like the city, I would rebuild my life. Ineluctably, both of us would enter a new phase—such are the promising forces of life. San Francisco and I had once reached our nadir. I had passed my "clouds of glory" onto a new child, but my beautiful San Francisco continued, tenderly veiled in its clouds of ephemeral fogs. And though the door was sealed on a nostalgic era, hope and promise in the future opened a new and vibrant one. On this up-note, I offer:

A RETROSPECT

> An iridescent bubble does not last
> A butterfly is gone when summer's past
> Their dream-stuff here on earth has made its mark
> Who once has heard, will always hear the lark.
>
> He who journeys farther from the east
> And trods the hills and valleys on his way

Is blessed, indeed, if he can glimpse the joy
Of morning in the light of waning day.

Fear not the closing of the "prison house"
But capture through its lattice, one thin shred
Of mystic light from which thou surely came,
And drape it in its glory 'round thy head.

Life lives again for him who sees
The beauties of his youth in memories.

Dora Barrett

Epilogue
The Start Of A Long Journey

Explanation: The preceding text was written in the first-person
Dora (Baby Dody) Barrett.

Perforce, the ensuing is first-person Rose C. Miller; for,
regrettably, the "final chapter" took place, in a sense, before
Dody was able to "read my book full through/Before the closing
cover's turned" (Foreword, Page iv).

Time was relentless and uncompromising. Delays in sub-
mittal responses over a period of two years were frustrating and
disappointing. In the meantime, Dora Barrett's health was
gradually deteriorating; and a feeling of urgency overtook us.
When, in November 1978, the doctor's diagnosis and prognosis
were, "cancer—six months," I undertook concerted efforts to
produce a private printing of Baby Dody's story; but even this
course has been frought with delays; and time, once again,
asserted itself.

When, in 1976, MY FIRST LOVE WEARS TWO MASKS
was completed, Dora Barrett was satisfied that the story had
been told precisely as she wished, from start to finish. She then
began exhorting, "Now it is done, Rose, and no matter what
happens, you must carry on." This then, is my tribute to a very
dear friend. It seems only appropriate now that, before "the
closing cover's turned," I append my finis to the story of Baby
Dody:

While it is never pleasant to write of a dear friend in the
past tense, much remains to be told in order to complete my
encomium to this multi-faceted, dynamic, restless, and per-
spicacious lady who once trod the boards of San Francisco's
theaters, as well as many others throughout California and the
rest of the United States.

Dora Scholz Barrett (28 December 1893—27 December

Dora Parker In The 1920's   Pantages Circuit
Credit: Barrett-Miller Collection

1978) continued an active career in the theater world for many years after her "Baby Dody" days ended. Her brilliant and creative mind found expression not only in her theater, but in her art, her poetry, and her prose.

For all her genius, she was one of the most unpretentious, "down-to-earth" individuals I have ever known. She championed and helped those down on their luck, even though her own means were modest, indeed. She was a catalyst that drew people from divergent paths to her door; and, somehow, we all became good friends, albeit with opposing opinions on politics, religion, or social philosophy. Dody was an "activist" on political and social issues long before the word found its niche in modern parlance.

Dora Barrett's quest for knowledge was insatiable, as witness the types of books that graced her bookshelves. In response to my admiration for her choice of books on such a wide range of intellectual subjects, she would reply, "I never had time to waste on frothy and frivolous reading. You will not find them among my treasures." Her bookshelves were crammed to overflowing with reference books on poetry, art, philosphy, religion, archaeology, mythology, and the theater. She had a deep affection for the encyclopedia and the dictionary; and, indeed, never disposed of her dictionaries because she never accepted the concept that they became "out-dated."

All this is not to say that Dora Barrett was all seriousness; on the contrary, she could be contagiously and outrageously amusing and hilarious. She delved into humor with all the abandon of an uninhibited comedienne. At times, she and I anticipated, then jumped each other's punch lines, much to our mutual merriment. Our rapport was never better than when we outwitted one another.

As the years passed and her blindness increased, I read to her, more and more—especially, excerpted articles from newspapers and periodicals, to keep her au courant. Besides these, she developed a great fondness for the cartoon character Marmaduke, the dog who thinks he is human and affects all his foibles. Because Dody was a great lover of animals and had a loving dog, Mac, Marmaduke brought her much pleasure

Dora Parker In The 1920's Pantages Circuit
Credit: Barrett-Miller Collection

almost to the end of her life. After Mac died, Marmaduke filled a void in her life, vicariously.

Another great favorite that brought much enjoyment to her, was the Irma Bombeck column. Bombeck's down-to-earth humor always drew chuckles from Dody, for humor was a talent the former little trouper thoroughly appreciated, In fact, as soon as I arrived for a visit, Dody's first question was, "Have you some Marmadukes and Bombecks today?" How could I ever forget to clip them!

She often apologized that her failing eyesight made it impossible to help with the book; so, as time passed, I left "book work" at home, and spent the time just reading and talking to her. Loneliness, the scourge of the elderly, constantly plagued her.

With a view to precluding lonely moments, Dody organized her time well. By means of her telephone with the magnified dial, she kept in constant touch with her many friends, wheedling and coaxing them into stopping by for a visit. Indeed, it seemed, at times, that her's was a revolving door—with one friend or set of friends replacing another. This was her fighting device against the scourge of loneliness.

Before I met her, Dody had led a very full and active life; then, failing vision forced her to forego driving her automobile. For some time, she was loath to part with it, for the move would seal the realization of her diminished mobility. But, of course, it was inevitable: one day I noticed her beloved old car was gone. She never whimpered about it, for she was too realistic. Once she made a decision, the deed was done and she went on to other matters. She seemed satisfied to just reflect wistfully on her "driving " years and regale us with many humorous episodes of her "driving career."

After her "beautiful Baby Dody" years, she became the "Beautiful Ingenue" and the "Dainty Soubrette," Dora Parker (the surname taken from her mother's family); and she played into the 1930's in a variety of dramatic and comedy roles, touring California, Oregon, and Washington in plays like: LOST PARADISE, RAFFLES, and CAMILLE, all starring the great favorite, William Desmond.

Subsequently, among dozens of other engagements, she appeared in: THE BROKERS, THE WOLF, TRILBY, LENA RIVERS, THE CUBAN SPY, BREWSTER'S MILLIONS, TENNESSEE'S PARTNER, JESSE JAMES, MY FRIENDS, and THE OUTCAST AND THE GIRL.

In 1915, Dora Parker ventured into the brand-new medium: motion pictures. She appeared in several films, most noteworthy of which was the great D.W. Griffith epic of the Civil War and Reconstruction periods, THE BIRTH OF A NATION. But Hollywood, she very quickly determined, was not to her liking. The lure of the "boards," with live people out in the audience, was, to her, nonpareil. Dody had known only the stage medium since her initiation into the theater world, at age three. She needed the live-audience response to sustain and draw the best from her "first love." Her ardent rapport with her audience had always been the sine qua non of her acting since childhood. She loved her work, and she loved her audiences. And, as for stage fright, she would say, "I never could understand actors having stage fright. How could they perform their best if they were scared to death!" And so she would dismiss the subject, with a flourish of her tiny arched hands.

It was not surprising , then, that acting before a camera proved frustrating and unfulfilling to the petite trouper. Further, she was convinced that Hollywood was not the sort of place where she could get ahead on simply her merits; and she was not prepared to meet implied "extra-curricular" expectations.

After this disappointing sojourn in Hollywood, Dora Parker formed a dance troupe that started out with seven members, then settled down to The La Rosa Trio. The trio became quite famous, doing Spanish and Flamenco dances, and touring the Pantages Circuit throughout the United States.

Ruefully, she one day admitted, her incursions into movies and vaudeville had been a mistake. They had cost her her "Baby Dody" connection and ruined her stage career.

Typically, Dody set her regrets in their proper perspective—behind her—and went on to a career in journalism. She spent some years with the Saramento Union, writing "human interest" stories. She also, somehow, found time to become Sacramento's Recreation Director.

When the crash of 1929 came, her own fortunes were dealt a blow. Salvaging what she could, she made a retreat to the San Francisco Bay Area and settled in a very modest home in the hills of El Cerrito. This would be her beloved "little house on the hillside," where she spent the rest of her life.

But Dody's retreat did not mean she was content to "vegetate and ruminate." She enrolled in classes at the University of California, Berkeley; wrote poetry and prose; and joined theatrical groups.

Dora Parker's love affair with the theater would be a continuing one throughout her life. In 1929, as a member of the Berkeley Playhouse Association, she played in Luigi Chiarelli's THE MASK AND THE FACE and Moliere's THE DOCTOR IN SPITE OF HIMSELF, in roles she repeated at the Wheeler Hall Auditorium on the University of California campus in 1931.

During San Francisco's Golden Gate International Exposition on Treasure Island, 1939-1940, Dody's artistry found expression in demonstrating various crafts. Her versatility seemed to know no bounds.

When World War II came, Dody ventured into an entirely new and different vocation. She became a journeyman shipfitter at California's Richmond Shipyard, translating blueprints into finished sections of the hulls, and overseeing a gang of ship workers. She was also cleared for classified work in ship degaussing—the method used to neutralize the electromagnetism of a ship to prevent explosive magnetic mines from being attracted to its steel hull. The difficult work of handling pieces of metal proved punishing to her tiny hands, and was quite exhausting, as well—but when did fatigue ever deter her from an undertaking in which she believed! She was making her contribution to the fight against Fascism.

Her patriotism during those war years also led Dody to an occupation more suitable to her talents: Director of Activities for the soldiers of California's Camp Roberts.

Following this assignment, she returned to the Bay Area to

The La Rosa Trio In The 1920's   Pantages Circuit
Credit: Barrett-Miller Collection

operate U.S.O's Hospitality House in Berkeley.

But perhaps the greatest and most challenging "role" came when, at age sixty, Dody took on the responsibility of raising two grandchildren. Playing the dual role of mother and grandmother was achieved with the same enthusiasm and efficiency she put into all her endeavors. She created a home for her little loved ones, with love and understanding. Her reward came with the love and devotion they returned her, especially during her final illness.

In her grandaughter Alice Wilbur, Dody realized her fondest academic aspirations. Alice proved an excellent, conscientious student who pursued her studies doggedly, and received a Bachelor of Science degree in Psychology, and a teaching credential in Psychology, Sociology, and English, from the University of Utah.

As Alice's graduation drew near, Dody's anticipation of the event preoccupied her thoughts and dictated all her activities. Joyously, she made plans for the plane trip to Salt Lake City, Utah; then watched, proudly, as Alice received her degree, with honors. Dody's profound pride and admiration in Alice's accomplishments were matched by Alice's reverence, admiration, and respect for her grandmother.

A firm relationship of mutual respect evolved between grandmother and grandaughter, over the years. Though always cooperative and subservient as a child, Alice's values would, in time, differ from her grandmother's—a not uncommon verity as children grow into adulthood and independence. Still, Alice would need to reassure her grandmother that this independence did not preclude close family ties and mutual interdependence between them.

Alice likened their relationship to that of the tree and the wind. While the tree stood alone, it, nevertheless, had depended on the caresses and buffeting of the wind to strengthen its roots and limbs until it finally stood tall and firm; but the tree's needs for growth and fulfillment would always be fortified by the symbiotic relationship it shared with the wind.

This lovely simile was one Dody could understand and appreciate well, for grandmother and grandaughter had always shared a very special love and respect for the nuances of nature. On this basis, albeit reluctantly at times, Dody resigned herself to Alice's independence.

Dody had always been overly protective of her granddaughter, setting definite parameters that served as guidelines during Alice's growing years. For Dody, the reasons were obvious: Alice was a girl.

In addition, Dody strongly stressed the imperative, "Learn factual information," but not as an end in itself. Rather, she averred that more important than the acquisition of information, was the *pursuit* itself—i.e. knowing *how* and *where* to look for facts. This focus had been a compelling drive in her own life; so, she provided her grandchildren with the sources wherein they could find knowledge—books, books, and more books, on all worthwhile, stimulating subjects. Her library was a testimonial to the importance of that imperative, for its diversity of subjects, already alluded to , was open-ended.

Dody was endowed with an extraordinary ability to mentally collate and coordinate seemingly disparate facts into meaningful order—an insight only one possessing her acuity could master.

While deeply appreciative of her grandmother's special talents, Alice acknowledged the wisdom of pursuing her own goals in her own way. If she were to become the strong individual her grandmother could respect, Alice had to "branch out," free of the restraints cast by the shadows of her grandmother's brilliance, yet always "borrowing from the wind," even as the tree must do. Only in this freedom could Alice's love, respect, and gratitude for her grandmother flourish; and only in this freedom did Alice come to realize her grandmother's unfulfilled aspirations.

During Dody's final illness, Alice experienced her deepest feelings for her grandmother. With tenderness, understanding, and determination, Alice set about creating the conditions of home care necessary to make it possible for Dody to stay in her beloved "little house on the hillside," till her "long journey" started. Alice's devotion is summed up quite beautifully: "The final month of grandmother's life was a gift to me."

Along with raising the grandchildren, Dora Barrett still found time to become El Cerrito's first Park Director. Earlier, she had organized the city's first Camp Fire Girls troop. To both she brought her knowledge and skills in various arts and crafts, and left profound impressions on her charges. Her joie de vivre was contagious.

For all her diminutiveness (four-foot-ten-inches), or perhaps as a counter, she was a tower of strength and determination. The lessons of courage and self-reliance "Baby Dody" learned during her long trek to Golden Gate Park, in the wake of the 1906 Earthquake and Fire, stood her in good stead all her life. Hardships, she had many, but resolve conquered them all. Obviously, it had mattered little that she was small of stature. She had played with some of the greats of her day, and she had

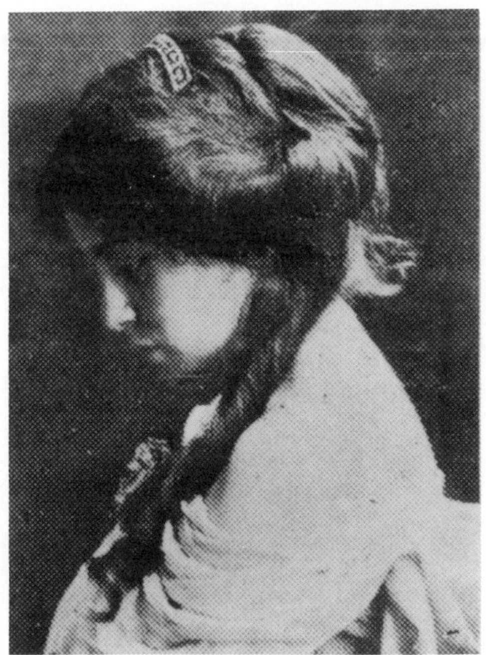

Dora Parker the "Dainty Soubrette" in Bret Harte's "Tennessee's Partner" 1910
Credit: Barrett-Miller Collection

reaped accolades of her own for her special talents. Culled excerpts from reviews of her countless appearances after her "Baby" days, in plays too numerous to list, produced the following sampling:

"Miss Parker is in the leading role as Tennessee Kent (TENNESSEE'S PARTNER, by Bret Harte) and she plays the part in a manner that makes the play seem real and makes her a favorite with the audience from the minute she enters upon the scene. . . . She has proved the best in the company . . . strong in the comedy scenes. What she lacks in stature she makes up by her good acting."

Madera Daily Tribune

"Dora Parker as Hilda in THE WOLF was a delight to the eye and her acting was better than the audience has seen in many more pretentious performances."

Porterville

"Dora Parker moves her audience to laughter or tears at will." (THE PRICE OF FRIENDSHIP)

Bakersfield

"Dora Parker is the cutest pocket edition of a woman I have ever seen." (THE FIGHTING HOPE)

Mother Lode Magnet

"Dora Parker who assumed the title role (LENA RIVERS), won her way into the hearts of the audience from the first, by her naturalness and ease of her acting, and the freshness and youthful vigor which were so evident in her interpretation of the character."

Sacramento Star

"Dora Parker was distinctly one of the stars of the play (THE OUTCAST AND THE GIRL) and her laurels were her just due. Her cleverness and charming appearance and manners made her a pleasing addition to the company."

Fresno

Of her La Rosa Trio performances:

". . . .she is fascinating. Every movement is one of beauty and the eyes of the spectator follow her whirling form as she evolutes in the intricate steps of the Spanish dance."

Bakersfield

". . . .A petite and coquettish little dancer. . . .performed a spirited fandango, clicking her castanets for all the world like a belle of old Madrid. The delighted crowd encored the girl until she could dance no more."

Los Angeles Morning Tribune

Final entries in her list of talents include song lyrics, poetry, and art. Among the first, she wrote words to two songs published in 1921 by the Melody Shop Publishing Company of Sacramento, California:

That Wonderful Sweetheart Of Mine by Winnie J. Cutter and *Lucky* by Jack Mitchell and Winnie J. Cutter.

Dody left a portfolio of poetry, copies of which she presented to her relatives and close friends in 1975. The collection, which I prize dearly, reflects the wide range of emotions she experienced throughout her life: from sorrow to joy, from mundane observations to profound meditations.

My friend particularly enjoyed painting in oils. She had a very special touch and feeling for miniatures. Of all her canvases, I admired her miniatures most; but the miniatures reflected only a departure from the many canvases she left. One of the great voids in her life came when with encroaching blindness, Dody was forced to set aside her easel and, literally, hang her palette on her living room wall.

As a born activist, Dora Barrett espoused causes, with a fervor that catapulted her to action—verbal and or physical. In later years, she resorted to the telephone and to modest monetary contributions to help perpetuate her adopted causes.

Earlier, her love of animals had impelled Dody to become active as a founding member of Berkeley, California's Society For The Prevention Of Cruelty To Animals (SPCA). She continued making contributions to this and other chapters of this worthy organization throughout her life.

In 1961, when the third Alcazar Theater (built in 1912 at 260 O'Farrell Street, near the site of the first, the "Moorish Gem") was destined to be razed for a parking lot, Dora Barrett fought desperately to save it. Together with Randolph Hale, Freda Klussman (well known to San Francisco as "the lady who saved the cable cars") and William P. Sutherland (representative of numerous labor organizations affiliated with the Theatrical Federation of San Francisco), Dody pleaded for the continuance of the Alcazar, "Tear down all the landmarks in San Francisco for freeways and parking lots and who will come to use them?" Other fervent and persuasive pleadings by leading San Franciscans in the arts also were to no avail, for the business contract was valid and irrevocable. Early in January of 1962, the Alcazar Theater was crumbled to dust by the wrecking ball. But Dora Barrett, as usual, could never be accused of insouciance. If she believed in a cause, she fought loyally and hard—no matter that she sometimes had to go down swinging!

When in 1971 the San Francisco Bay became awash with oil as a result of a two-tanker collision, Dody's anguish over the helpless birds who were victimized, brought her anxious moments. She exhorted her grandson Ray to join the many people who were cleaning the hapless birds of the oil on their bodies. Dody kept to her radio and television during those trying days, listening to the running accounts, and then making telephone calls to solicit help and contributions to ease the plight of her threatened feathered friends. She grieved for every lost bird.

Dody's espousal of political causes was considered quite radical in her earlier days, but by current standards she could only be designated a left-of-center loyal Democrat who went down fighting for the McGovern-Shriver ticket. Loyal to the end, she prized her McGovern-Shriver banner so highly that it adorned her bedroom wall, to the end!

The McGovern-Shriver campaign was her last active one; but she would, in the political scandals that followed, be reinforced in her beliefs that the wrong man had won. In light of the events that unfolded, of course, it was a futile exercise in illogic to argue her point.

Dody remained a loyal Democrat and continued to endorse the party's candidates; but with the McGovern-Shriver debacle, she had expended her physical capabilities as an active participant in her party. The Ford-Carter campaign saw her a disillusioned observer, albeit she cast her last vote as a true Democrat.

Dody's ability to draw on reserves of energy was never so astounding as when, rising to the occasion, she would determine to go on an outing or a long trip with her grandson Ray Wilbur. Life in the theater had accustomed her to late hours. Indeed, she considered herself a "night person" and was at her best as night-fall approached. So, taking off on overnight drives with Ray, be it in his car, truck, or camper, was something she thoroughly enjoyed. Both were "cut of the same cloth," as it were. They enjoyed night travel, and seemed better stimulated to philosophical and religious discussions and exchanges in the nocturnal setting. Their last trip, less than a year before she died, took them in a trailer to the Pacific Northwest, for a week of concentrated travel that would have leveled most of her younger friends. Her determination always sustained her, as did the special rapport she enjoyed with Ray. This unusual relationship could never be matched by anyone, be it a relative or close friend. Perhaps more than anyone, Ray understood his "Grand Mere" and her philosophy of life and religion better than the rest of us; yet, he candidly admitted that the two agreed on nothing else.

Never a true iconoclast, nor an agnostic, Dody studied all religions, especially the Eastern religions, with their adherence to the karmic approach to life now and in successive lives. From all her readings, observations, and meditations, Dody culled the best for herself. She "saw God" in all the wonders of nature, but she could never accept worship in the conventional way: within the confines of an edifice. This, she felt, constrained her ultimate communication with her God.

Dody's all-encompassing approach to life and death as a continuum, she reasoned, would one day take her on "the start of a long and joyous journey." Her body was merely a receptacle for her soul; and, like the empty jar of perfume, lost its raison d' etre with the escape of its essence. She, therefore, did not want "mourners" when her journey started; for she felt that there certainly was nothing to mourn about the meaningless "shell" she would leave. For Dody, life, i.e. her soul, would go on to another plane.

In keeping with her profound beliefs in humility, she insisted on the most humble, functional funeral and burial possible. She now lies in a serene plot she chose on a gentle hillside, a fitting continuum of her corporeal existence in her "little house on the hillside."

To paraphrase what Wordsworth's "Ode On Immortality" had simply stated for her: her birth had been but a sleep and a forgetting; her life's star had elsewhere had its setting and had come from afar. This belief in Reincarnation would lead her to the conclusion that: "Trailing clouds of glory do we come/From God, who is our home. . . .("Ode On Immortality" by William Wordsworth).

My dear friend is now returning "home," for that joyous reunion with her God and, it is hoped, all her colleagues who trod the boards with her, so many years ago. Godspeed, Baby Dody!

BIBLIOGRAPHY

Bagley, Clarence C., *History of Seattle*. Vol. 2: Henry L. Yesler. Chicago: S.J. Clarke Publishing Company, 1916.

De Ford, Miriam Allen, *They Were San Franciscans*. Caldwell: Caxton Printers Ltd., 1941.

Gressinger, A.W., *A History of Florence, Arizona*. Tucson: Arizona Pioneers' Historical Society (Producers and Designers). Prepared for the dedication of the Pinal County Historical Society Museum in memory of A.W. Gressinger, 1970.

Harding, Alfred, *The Revolt of The Actors*. New York: William Morrow and Company, 1929. Westport: Greenwood Press, reprinted 1974.

Hart, Jerome A., *In Our Second Century*. San Francisco: The Pioneer Press, 1931.

Jackson, Mrs. F. Nevill, *A History of Handmade Lace*. London: L. Upcott Gill Publisher, 1900.

Krout, John A., *United States Since 1865*, New York: Barnes and Noble, Inc., 1955.

Ladd, James William, *A Survey of The Legitimate Theatre in Seattle Since 1856*. M.A. Thesis in Speech, The State College of Washington, 1935.

Lewis, Phillip C., *Trouping*. New York, Evanston, San Francisco, London: Harper and Row, 1973.

Manchel, Frank, *When Pictures Began To Move*. Englewood Cliffs: Prentice-Hall, 1969.

Sayre, J. Willis, *This City of Ours*. Seattle: Frayn Printing Company, 1936. Copyright: J.W. Sayre

Stevens, William Oliver and Westcott, Allan, *A History of Sea Power*. New York: Doubleday, Doran and Company, Inc., 1942.

Thomas, Lately, *A Debonair Scoundrel*. New York: Holt, Rinehart and Winston, 1962.

Tolstoy, Leo, *Resurrection*. New York: New American Library, Times Mirror, 1961.

Tompkins, Walker A., *Santa Barbara Yesterdays*. Historical vignettes, 1786–1960 (Milo M. Potter's Fabulous Hostelry; Fire Razed Potter Hotel). Santa Barbara: McNally and Loftin, 1962.

Van Gelder, Arthur Pine and Schlatter, Hugo, *A History of The Explosives Industry In America*. New York: Columbia University Press, 1927.

ANTHOLOGIES

America's Lost Plays, Vol. XVII. By Barrett Clark. Edited with an introductory essay by Robert Hamilton Hall.
LA BELLE RUSSE by David Belasco
THE HEART OF MARYLAND by David Belasco
Bloomington: Indiana University Press. Copyright 1940—
Princeton University Press. Reissued 1965 by arrangement with Princeton University Press.
Dramas From The American Theater 1762—1909. Introductory essay by Richard Moody.
UNCLE TOM'S CABIN by George L. Aiken
Boston: Houghton-Mifflin, 1969.
Great Illustrated Classics. Introduction by Langston Hughes.
UNCLE TOM'S CABIN by Harriet Beecher Stowe
New York: Dodd, Mead & Company, 1952. Printed by Cornwall Press, Cornwall, N.Y.
Hiss The Villain, by Michael Booth.
TEN NIGHTS IN A BAR-ROOM by William W. Pratt
New York: Benjamin Blom, Inc., 1964
London, England: Eyre & Spottiswoode Publishers, Ltd.

COMPILATIONS

The American Stage of Today. Introduction by William Winter. New York: P.F. Collier and Son, 1909.
Magazine of Western History, Vol. 11, No. 6. New York: Magazine of Western History Publishing Company. Copyright 1889.
Pioneer Western Playbills, Number 3. Edited by Frank L. Fenton. The Grand Opening of The California Theater, San Francisco, January 18, 1869. Commentary by Oscar Lewis. San Francisco: Copyright 1951 by The Book Club of Cali-

fornia. All rights reserved; reproduced by permission. Oakland: Printers, Alfred and Lawton Kennedy at Westgate Press, 1951.

San Francisco Theater Research Monographs, Mimeographed. WPA Project by the San Francisco Federal Theatre (1938-1942). Famous Playhouses. Theater Buildings.

The Illustrated Directory of San Francisco Buildings, by E.S. Glover. San Francisco: E.S. Glover, Publisher, 1894.

NEWSPAPERS AND PERIODICALS

Argonaut, San Francisco.
Call, San Francisco.
Chronicle, San Francisco.
California Historical Society Quarterly #21, 1942.
Colliers — March 30, 1956 — San Francisco by Robert O'Brien.
Daily Times, Seattle.
Democrat, Fresno.
Dramatic Revue, San Francisco.
Examiner, San Francisco.
Express, Los Angeles.
Figaro, San Francisco.
Herald, Los Angeles.
Morning Oregonian, Portland.
Morning Press, Santa Barbara.
Music and Drama, San Francisco.
News-Press, Santa Barbara.
News, San Francisco.
Polytechnic Journal #5, Dinglers.
Post-Intelligencer, Seattle.
Post, San Francisco.
Record, Los Angeles.
South of Market Street Journal, San Francisco.
Times, Los Angeles.
Union, Sacramento.
Wasp, San Francisco.

COLLECTIONS

Agard, Vols. 1-7, Bancroft Library.
Ghirardelli, D. Lyle, Bancroft Library.
Graves, Roy, Bancroft Library.
Jordan, A.L., Stage Scrapbook #30, California Historical Society.
Lumbard, Juliet H., Stage Scrapbook #3, California Historical
Society.

PRIVATE COLLECTIONS

Barrett, Dora.
Vol. 1, Personal Theatre Programs.
Vol. 2, Theatre Clippings.
Books: Theatre; San Francisciana
Souvenir of San Francisco, C.P. Heininger, 1888.
The American Stage of Today, P.F. Collier and Son, 1909.
Thall, Charles M. (courtesy, son, Marston Thall).
Vol. 1, Playbills.
Vol. 2, General Scrapbook—San Francisciana.

MISCELLANEOUS

Baldwin Hotel Souvenir.
Bancroft Library, University of California:
San Francisco Theater Programs:
Alcazar, Baldwin, Bush Street, California, Central,
Columbia, Majestic, Morosco's Grand Opera House,
Olympia, Orpheum, Tivoli.
Oakland Theater Programs: The MacDonough Theatre.
California Historical Society Library: Majestic Theatre.
Oakland Museum Library: The MacDonough Theatre.
City Directories; City Maps. (1869-1907). San Francisco:
Crocker; Crocker-Langley. Oakland: Polk's; Husted. Los
Angeles. Santa Barbara. Seattle.
Nineteenth Century Almanac.
Song: "Break The News To Mother." New York: Charles K.
Harris, 1897. Copyright 1924 by Charles K. Harris Music
Publishing Co. Used by Permission of Publisher.

ARTICLES

Los Angeles Times—March 14, 1974:
"Theater Where Stars Were Born Sees Final Curtain"—
Al Martinez
Oakland Tribune—June 18, 1944, KNAVE column:
"San Francisco's Pop Furst"
Santa Barbara News Press—Broken Files, November 12,
1904—August 10, 1955:
"Shade Trees on Potter Grounds"
"Hotel Owners In Session Here"
"Carty Bros. Move To New Stables"
"Potter Filling With Guests"
"Fabulous Tales And Personalities of Old Potter Hotel
Days Recalled By Richard D. Jones, Former Steward"
—Homer George
"The Potter And Arlington"
"Opening Of Fabulous Potter Hotel 50 Years Ago Marked
One Of Santa Barbara's Biggest Affairs"
"Old Potter Hotel Offered Real Luxury"
Seattle Times—May 9, 1943:
"City's First Entertainment Was Staged In A Log Cook-
house" By State Senator Robert T. McDonald
San Francisco Archives For The Performing Arts, Russell Hart-
ley, Director: A SHORT HISTORY OF THE ORPHEUM
THEATRE, San Francisco 1876-1977—by Russell Hartley.

NOTES

pp. 5,6 *"Break The News To Mother"* Used by permission of
Charles K. Harris Music Publishing, Inc. New York 1897

pp. 18,19 From A.P. Van Gelder and H. Schlatter, *History Of
The Explosives Industry In America.* New York: Columbia University Press, 1927. pp. 729-730.

p. 82 Quoted lines 33 and 34 taken from *Quarterly Number
21-1942*, by permission of The California Historical
Society.

pp. 142, 143 Based on and taken from *The Revolt Of The Actors*
by Alfred Harding and used with the agreement of Green-

wood Press, Inc., the reprint publisher.

pp. 163-165   Based on: Introductory Essay by Richard Moody (pp. 352-358) *Dramas From The American Theater, 1772-1909* Houghton-Mifflin Company, 1969.

p. 256, Paragraphs 2 and 3; p. 258, lines 1,2,3   Based on *A Survey Of The Legitimate Theater In Seattle Since 1856* by J. William Ladd Washington State University, 1935.

p. 268, Paragraph 4, last line; p. 269, lines 11 and 14   From *America's Lost Plays* by Barrett Clark. LA BELLE RUSSE by David Belasco. Indiana University Press, 1965.

INDEX

A

B

C

D

G

H

I

J

M

N

O

P

T

1 **ALCAZAR THEATRE**
   a) 116 O'Farrell
     (1885-1906)
   b) Sutter and Steiner
     (March 18, 1907)
   c) 260 O'Farrell
     (Dec. 1907-Jan. 1962)

2 **CALIFORNIA THEATRE**
   444 Bush (1869-1906)
     (Rebuilt 1889)

3 **CENTRAL THEATRE**
   Market near Eighth (1900-1906)
   Market and Eighth (1906-1909)

4 **CHUTES THEATRE**
   (Opposite page) (1897-1902)

5 **CINEOGRAPH PARLORS**
   747 Market (1897-1906)

6 **COLUMBIA THEATRE**
   11 Powell (1895-1906)

7 **GLEN PARK THEATRE**
   Chenery and Diamond (1898-1906)

8 **GRAND OPERA HOUSE**
   Mission near Third (1876-1906)

9 **MAJESTIC THEATRE**
   1213 Market at Larkin (1904-1906)

10 **MECHANICS PAVILION**
   (Four sites, six pavilions)
   Sixth: Hayes, Grove, Polk, Larkin
   (1882-1906)

11 **OLYMPIA MUSIC HALL**
   S.W. Cor. Eddy and Mason (1897-1903)

12 **ORPHEUM THEATRE**
   119 O'Farrell (1886-1906)
   (First of five)

13 **TIVOLI OPERA HOUSE**
   28-32 Eddy (1879-1903)
   (Second of four)